Praise for

Blindsided by a Diaper

"The stories in this collection are thrillingly honest, laugh-out-loud funny, and heartbreakingly poignant. It's a must for couples who didn't see it coming and need to know they're not alone."

—Brett Paesel, author of *Mommies Who Drink: Sex, Drugs, and Other Distant Memories of an Ordinary Mom*

"Most books about parenthood misguidedly focus on children. This savvy collection recognizes what PARENTS need—camaraderie, wisdom, humor, and most of all, the knowledge that we are not alone in this crazy, chaotic new world."

—Leslie Morgan Steiner, editor of *Mommy Wars* and washingtonpost.com columnist for On Balance, the #1 mommy blog on the Web

"To sleep, or to sleep with you—that is the question we never thought we'd be asking. For a new generation of sleepless, sexless parents, *Blindsided by a Diaper* shines a light inside the American bedroom and genuinely illuminates the state of our unions." —Ian Kerner, Ph.D., sex therapist and author of *She Comes First*

"As someone who has scientifically researched this topic, I am struck by the power of these boldly honest and beautifully written personal essays. *Blindsided by a Diaper* lifts the veil of secrecy on marriage with children. No reader will ever again be able to wonder 'why didn't anyone tell me it would be like this?'"

—Jay Belsky, Ph.D., coauthor of *The Transition to Parenthood* and director of the Institute for the Study of Children, Families and Social Issues at Birkbeck University of London

"*Blindsided by a Diaper* captures the complicated odyssey of early parenthood in a unique, touching, and thought-provoking way. The contributors' brave and insightful commentaries shed much-needed light on this most complex of marital transitions and leave the reader feeling less bewildered and alone, more optimistic and hopeful. I will be enthusiastically recommending it to new and expectant parents."

—Brad Sachs, Ph.D., psychologist and author of *Things Just Haven't Been the Same: Making the Transition from Marriage to Parenthood* and *The Good Enough Child: How to Have an Imperfect Family and Be Perfectly Satisfied*

"The most honest, irreverent, and gloriously accurate depiction of life for couples in the midst of parenthood. It is such a relief to know we are not alone in the insanity or in the equally intoxicating love we have for our children. There is no greater paradox. This book will save marriages, comfort many, and make you laugh out loud."

—Laura Berman Fortgang, MCC, author of *Living Your Best Life* and *Now What?: 90 Days to a New Life Direction*, and a nationally known life coach and ordained minister

Over 30 Men and Women Reveal How Parenthood
Changes a Relationship

THREE RIVERS PRESS
NEW YORK

blindsided

BY A diaper

Edited by Dana Bedford Hilmer

Copyright © 2007 by Dana Bedford Hilmer

Published in the United States by Three Rivers Press, an imprint of the
Crown Publishing Group, a division of Random House, Inc., New York.

www.crownpublishing.com

Three Rivers Press and the Tugboat design are registered trademarks of
Random House, Inc.

Library of Congress Cataloging-in-Publication Data

Blindsided by a diaper: over 30 men and women reveal how parenthood
changes a relationship / edited by Dana Bedford Hilmer.—1st ed.

  1. Parenthood.   2. Parents—Psychology.   3. Life change events.
4. Parent and child.   5. Marriage.   I. Hilmer, Dana Bedford.

  HQ755.8.B615 2007

  306.874—dc22   2006102624

ISBN 978-0-307-35134-0

Printed in the United States of America

DESIGN BY ELINA D. NUDELMAN

10 9 8 7 6 5 4 3 2 1

First Edition

For
Dave, of course
and
Zach, Mikey, and Danny
I love you all the way up to Pluto and back

contents

PART ONE
the roles we play

contents

contents

contents

foreword

· Ann Pleshette Murphy ·

*T*he voices in this book are hoarse with exhaustion, loud with laughter, shrill with anger, and wild with love. They echo down familiar corridors—some dark, some warm, but all illuminated by high-wattage intelligence and unflinching candor. It's not easy to get couples to open up about their life together as parents. Oh, sure, they'll entertain you with a funny story about some Lucy and Desi moment during those first exhausting days when they knew absolutely nothing about babies, but it's the rare mom and even rarer dad who willingly shares the heartbreak along with the hilarity; who invites a total stranger into their bedroom or shines a big, bright light in their own eyes and says, "Look, this is what it's really like. This is how our relationship has changed." Whether these stories soothe or shock—and there are plenty of both in this book—the messages that emerge are poignant, funny, inspiring, and wise.

The thirty-two men and women who share their relationships with us in this book do so from all stages of their parental development, so their perspectives are diverse, their experiences varied. Listen carefully and you begin to pick out melodies that echo from one essay to the next. Or they may be songs that you've sung yourself, perhaps only in private—or that, as a woman, you thought were exclusively mothers' tunes. I felt that way reading Michael Finkel's essay "Welcome to the Babyhouse," about putting his life on hold for the sake of his daughter and experiencing that bittersweet cocktail of resentment and reward. I've always maintained that guilt is endemic to motherhood, that dads rarely wrestle with feeling derailed by fatherhood, because they tend to pick up where they left off before their baby arrived. But all of the fathers in this book write me wrong. They may not feel exactly as their wives do, they may seem a bit more breezy or browbeaten or bewildered, but their lives and their relationships have clearly been turned upside down by the children they adore.

As the title of this collection implies, parenthood knocks you sideways, catapults you into a world that may feel wildly out of control or wonderfully chaotic but rarely resembles the path you thought you were on. Together. For life. Suddenly the person you love most in the world seems to be orbiting in a different galaxy, or at least he's not the dad you thought he would be; she's not the patient, loving partner you pictured cradling your baby. In fact, you may look over and wonder, "Who the hell are you?" And the answer may be as simple and wise as Beth Levine's discovery that "Bill and I were not the same person after all." Whether parenthood provides a sense of shared purpose or puts you at decidedly cross-purposes, it forces even the most loving couple to reevaluate their roles and to negotiate an altogether new definition of "we." As several contributors discovered, the very things you adored in your mate, his spontaneity, her self-confidence, may make you want to run screaming from the room, let alone the relationship, once there are children in the house.

But don't imagine for a minute that there's no way to be prepared for the changes in your relationship postpartum. As these insightful, articulate writers reveal, the clues are everywhere. If you or the person you love manages anxiety by compulsively organizing life into lists or, when overwhelmed, tends to explode, shut down, or get drunk, then chances are those behaviors will surface *big-time* once you're parents. If your relationship was characterized by a kind of joined-at-the-hip, match-made-in-heaven bond, then accepting that your soul mate can't actually read your mind after all can come as quite a shock. But as each and every one of the contributors in this book will attest, if you take the time to pay attention to those clues, to say clearly and unapologetically what you do want (him: more sex) and what you don't want (her: more sex), to nurture your relationship, then you're going to open yourself up to the greatest gift parenthood provides: the opportunity to rediscover and love each other in ways you never imagined. For Sandi Kahn Shelton, that meant learning to date her husband again; for Rick Marin, it meant learning to be the "good husband"; for William Squier it meant embracing his wife's religion; and for Susan Cheever, it meant realizing too late that the best thing she could do for her son "was to stay married to his father."

If you are reading this as a new parent, come back to the book in a few years and the stories will read very differently; the words will be the same, of course, but your take on the world will be entirely new. How can it not be? Every single day of parenthood forces us to juggle the practical along with the ineffable, to strive for connectedness along with autonomy, to quarrel and question and, in the end, to let go. Along the way we hone muscles, develop skills, make mistakes, and learn, as these contributors confirm, that we are not alone.

foreword

Children change the prescription on the glasses we've worn comfortably for years. And as we struggle to accommodate this new and slightly dizzy vision of ourselves and of our lovers, we're bound to bump into one another sometimes, with painful results. But as Lisa Unger aptly puts it, "Parenthood is a kaleidoscope; the picture shifts with each turn of your wrist, with each change of light. What you see depends on how long you linger on any given moment." Like that kaleidoscope, this book allows you to glimpse parenthood and your relationship from dozens of shifting perspectives, to eavesdrop on conversations that feel at once highly individual and totally universal.

Try on your new glasses, and see for yourself.

introduction

· Dana Bedford Hilmer ·

*M*y husband and I have been together for more than half our lives. We met in college and for the last twenty-one years we've had lots of time together—to frolic, talk, romance, and listen, time to *just* be a couple and share an incredibly carefree, spontaneous life in the postcollege playground of New York City. It seems as though we've always been Dave-and-Dana, Dana-and-Dave.

Then we had a baby. And after that another, and—well, then another. In six years, we have created a brood of three beautiful little boys and every day we are astounded and grateful. But now the couple who enjoyed the nightly restaurant bop is lucky to finish a conversation or get out on the town alone half a dozen times a year. I realize how much life has changed, we have changed. And much of this change has caught us quite by surprise.

introduction

As it turns out, we're far from alone. Most couples find themselves surprised—*blindsided* even—by all the ways parenthood changes their relationships. Whether you've been together for one year or twenty-one, things do change. From falling in love with your partner all over again, to seeing a whole new (perhaps undesirable) side to him or her, the challenge of redefining yourself—and your relationship—in the roles you now inhabit, to the sobering realization that you must, despite all the new demands on your time, put each other on the always-long priority list—or else. These changes are at once profound, beautiful, irrevocable, and scary. They knock you off balance, forcing even the most secure couples to go back to the basics in figuring out how to define a new version of "we."

Many if not most couples find this to be a challenge. Ample evidence supports Nora Ephron's claim that "having a baby is like throwing a hand grenade into a marriage." Divorce rates give a couple only slightly better than a fifty-fifty chance of survival. According to a 2003 *Newsweek* article, "The year after the first child is born has always been a hazardous time for marriages. More divorces happen during those sleepless months than at any other time in marriage, except the first year." In fact, sixty-seven percent of parents complain that after kids, they have less sex, less fun, and more arguments than before. As the National Marriage Project at Rutgers University concludes, "Children seem to be a growing impediment for the happiness of marriages."

Daunting information to be sure, and a tad bit depressing. Especially, and ironically, because all this despair comes out of a couple's most optimistic desire to create a beautiful family life. Obviously no one is saying that there isn't a lot of wonderful joy that couples experience together as parents. But there is an awful lot of the other stuff, too—challenges and dismay and confusion. And when it comes to challenges that counter a rosy family image, parents too often keep quiet. The need to keep these difficult feelings private all too often gets in the way of open, honest dialogue. It seems to me that if couples can find ways to talk openly—with each other and with other couples—about the changes they're encountering, they'll be better equipped to navigate the challenges. If we can learn from, laugh with, and even cry over others' experiences, perhaps we can then begin to see ourselves more clearly, our partners more openly, and bring more compassion and understanding to our relationships.

Before I started this book project, it was only on rare occasions that even my closest friends would open up about their relationships with their partners. Sure, they'd talk about how tired they were, or complain about how their husbands weren't taking on more of the domestic workload. But the door rarely felt totally open to commiserate about the real things that fester and keep me up at night. Things like how much I miss my carefree "boyfriend" (and the carefree me for that matter), the man who has been my lover and my best friend for decades who is now often exhausted by responsibility. How my love for him is more profound now and scarily vulnerable . . . we have so much at stake. The feeling of guilt (and gratitude) I have because my husband is currently earning the grand majority of our income while I focus primarily on the kids. And how our equilibrium has changed as a result—our lives, our paychecks, and, I would argue, our decision-making powers. How we now seem to be living a good chunk of our time in parallel universes, often thinking and talking about things that aren't on the other's radar screen. And sadly, how there is now little time . . . to frolic, talk, romance, and listen. But, when I mention this book, it's as though I've hit a raw nerve and made a statement that has made it okay for my peers to also admit that their lives together have changed. And wonderful, open, and honest conversations have transpired—between my husband and me and with my friends.

introduction

It has become abundantly clear to me that parents and parents-to-be need a book that tells it like it is for couples in the trenches of parenthood. We need to hear the good, the dirt, and everything in between. The thirty-two talented men and women who have dared to write for this book have done just that. They have had the courage to boldly and publicly grapple with the kind of personal material most of us won't dare admit to ourselves, not to mention to others. They have invited you inside their bedrooms, their minds, and their lives as parents.

Like each day of parenthood, the essays in this book take you on a rollercoaster ride of love and frustration, tears and laughter, gain and loss. From Lisa Unger's conclusion that they were prepared for everything but the love, to Ariel Gore's realization that her only choice was to leave, the writers reveal the choices they have made; the joy and heartaches they have experienced; the challenges of trying to maintain a sexual and intimate life; and how their experiences together, as parents, may or may not be what they were expecting.

The pages you are about to read will have you and your partner looking in the mirror, kicking each other under the table with thank-goodness-it's-not-only-us relief, and will allow you to glimpse, as Susan Maushart did, where the bruises are. In every story a highly personal but more-often-than-not universal truth is revealed. The result is a collection of bravely honest, humorous, and thought-provoking essays that will provide comfort, sympathy, and wisdom for readers at any stage in their parenting journeys.

We're all blindsided, to some degree, by the addition of little people into our relationships. The question is whether or not we'll be able to regain our balance and embrace being a family, with all its lumps and bumps and imperfections. It is my hope that this book will get couples talking, and in so doing foster a better understanding of one another and raise the odds that more couples will stay together and favorably change that alarming fifty-fifty equation.

introduction

So far, it has for my husband and me. I think we understand each other better, laugh more, and take more time to marvel at how fortunate we are. And most important, we are now extremely aware of the importance of not taking each other for granted . . . of not, as Susan Cheever says, letting the other be "the dropped ball."

I'd like to now turn you over to the thirty-two men and women who have done what I alone could not: put this mind-boggling experience into words. May they enlighten, amuse, and inspire you as they have me.

–Dana Bedford Hilmer
November 2006

the roles we play

They peer haughtily at us from bookstore shelves as we approach to beg their counsel. They loom over us in mighty stacks on our bedside tables, those tomes, those merciless manuals instructing us—it must be said—on what all walks of life have been doing for all of history without any written instruction. And yet we buy them. The baby books. We submit to their sternness, obediently dog-ear their pages, and we do so because they all teach us (despite the fervent differences in their teachings) a single lesson: Outward behavior is based on inner development. Behind the growing pains and growing assortment of child-rearing challenges is the phenomenon of actual growth. Our babies are changing in ways that are invisible to the naked eye, and it's a relief to flip pages that reveal the evolution beneath their surfaces. It's only a shame that not one of these books details the unseen developmental progress of the newborn dad.

Because the truth, new mothers, is that you've got two babies in your home. Sure, it looks like one: a single crib, one stroller in the hall and onesies in the drawer and one gurgling and burping focus to your life. But nearby is another clumsy new being struggling to evolve. Just as your child is making bodily progress amid the naps and tantrums that wouldn't necessarily suggest it, your husband is braving his way through a maze of new emotions and a tumult of conflicting feelings that generally go undiscussed. The man is being a baby, too. And only by looking at him as a baby — by examining the stages of his physical, cognitive, and linguistic development during this critical time — will you truly be able to understand him.

Of course, to the casual observer, he's busy being a dad. There he is, straight and tall, on board and on duty: changing the diapers, warming the bottles, or simply muttering encouragement at three A.M. before rolling over and returning to his REM cycle. He appears a willing partner in the chaos of caretaking that is now your life. And undoubtedly he is. But behind his heavy-lidded eyes, beneath that mussed hair, there is a secret and klutzy developmental process under way. It is a process marked by changing husbandly behaviors and the physiological developmental milestones that cause them. Let's go through them — in the tradition of best-selling baby books throughout the world — chronologically.

Month Zero
The Growth of the Spine

In Month Zero, we meet the husband at the first stage of his evolution. This is newborn man: naked in the world, working to belong, belonging to work, and somewhat, often secretly, adrift. He appears to have it all. Married, employed, and energized, he has a glowing future ahead of him. The next step, obviously, is to embrace that future by starting a family. But he is not quite ready. He loves you, sure. And of course he wants children. He *sees* the potential of a great and crowded household—he just isn't quite ready to *seize* it. After all, there are just a few things he intends to tick off his list before you get pregnant: big things, small things, vague and disturbingly elusive things. There are accomplishments to be accomplished, a place to be set. And there the guy falters, stuck in his ways.

The physiological reason for this behavior is simple. At this stage, the spine of the young husband has not formed. His backbone has not yet solidified, and as a result, his actions are flailing and tentative, skittish in the face of looming fatherhood and its unfathomable responsibilities and labors. Procreation, in his mind, is for when one is done with self-creation. He is happy to form another being with you as soon as he is done forming himself. And he's not quite there. He has not made enough money, accumulated enough potency, achieved a position in life comfortable enough to take a deep breath and take on more. He lacks the backbone that eventually will enable him to shoulder greater burdens. The good news, however, is that the growth of that backbone begins now.

I remember the stage well. I had married Amanda eagerly, gratefully, with none of the pre-ring jitters or time-honored foot dragging generally associated with the American male. Therefore, three years later, I myself was surprised by the foot dragging that ensued. She was ready for children. I was ready—sure, heck—to start to think about someday having them as well. After all, I thought, we were both full-time writers in hectic New York City, and some degree of fiscal and logistical stability had to be achieved. Maybe when I wrote and sold my second book: *then* might be a more reasonable time to start supporting dependents. Or else the novel after that (yes, right, a third book: stability), particularly if it sold to other countries (ah, *international* stability), would provide the kind of solid foundation on which a sprawling family could be heaped. Meanwhile, Amanda was baffled. We had talked eagerly about having kids since we'd met, and for me to put on the brakes for only the most general and nervous of reasons seemed to her like unnecessary stalling. Which, naturally, it was. I was an invertebrate, languid and jellyish, unable to stand up—regardless of timing and funding—for what I wanted.

What I had no way of knowing back then was that spines grow when called for. Life does not wait for babies, or ever lavishly provide for babies: babies just appear, rarely at the precise moment that you feel most serenely well-equipped but always with the magical ability to make you think they couldn't have come at a better time. Life *bends*, it turns out; it doesn't break. Rather than being shattered by the arrival of a new person, a loving home is miraculously bolstered by it, as is the power and posture of the man in its middle. The crashing entrance of our daughter Savannah in May of 2000—full years before we would have enough money for Manhattan school tuition, a month before my second book was due to the publisher's, and a week before we had gotten around to packing Amanda's hospital overnight bag—was perfect. Before she got here, I didn't have the backbone to see that the improvised half life Amanda and I had cobbled together could support, indeed deserved, another person. It took the birth of Savannah to teach me to stand tall.

Month One
Physical Abilities

In Month One, the father is in the full throes of early development. His world has changed dramatically, flabbergastingly, and as a result his physical capabilities are changing as well. Month One is when the growing husband first stretches to accomplish physical feats that mere weeks ago would have been impossible. Cognitive development is still many weeks away. Object recognition, or the ability to see and value what's in front of him, remains a skill of the future, as is the linguistic ability to discuss what he thinks. This is not a time for intricate thoughts and emotions. Month One is a stage of life exclusively devoted to manual labors for the man.

I, for one, was startled by the physical demands of Month One. The Olympic skill of cradling a human being while rhythmically bending both knees and singing baritone, it turns out, was only the beginning. One-handed bottle warming. Three-hour hallway pacing. Assembling seventy-piece cribs according to cartoon instructions in Swedish. Peeing while wearing a Baby Bjorn. Amanda, to be sure, was performing impressive tricks of strength and endurance daily; the difference was that in my case, it was all I could do. Not included in the emotional connectedness of breast-feeding, not quite a member of the warm partnership of two people who had shared the same body for the past year, I had no choice but to support my fledgling family through physical labors on their periphery. Luckily, I found I wanted to. I suppose this was a primal call of nature, a deep Darwinian instinct to lift, haul, and repair. Yet it was more than that. There was the relief of actual accomplishment. There was the sense that I was learning the hands-on mechanics of caring for someone, and that—like my baby—I was doing something new and doing it better every day.

The problem was that the physical outlet proved difficult to shut off. In fact, my manly manual efforts soon replaced my husbandly efforts to relate to and listen to my wife. Amanda was grateful for the assembled cribs and warmed bottles, but when every one of her attempts to talk about her maternal concerns about Savannah prompted me to embark on a macho solo mission of walking the baby around the block sixty-five times, Amanda was—despite the help—disappointed. Sometimes, she eventually had to explain to me, she just wanted to talk. Not every late-night baby concern was a call for me to build, break, or fix something. Many, rather, were opportunities for us to work together. In fact, that just might be the fun of it. Trickier to master than my stiff-lipped willingness to lend a hand was the need, every so often, to leave my hands by my sides.

So the baby graduates beyond the pleasure of getting physical to the deeper and lifelong pleasure of partnership.

Month Six
The Dawn of Mobility

Month Six is an exciting stage in the development of the father. With the backbone intact and strong, and having mastered both manual tasks and their relinquishment, the man now becomes mobile. Gradually he learns to navigate the new landscape of his changed world: moving back and forth between mandatory activities, hustling off and hurrying back. Emboldened to leave the comfortable chaos of mother and child, he begins to wander once more—and to take baby steps toward the kind of independent masculine life he may have led, or aspired to, before. But these wobbly first steps often end in a crash. Such is the challenge, and the key developmental hurdle, of walking away.

Upon the arrival of our daughter, I got a steady job in an office—which provided both health insurance (the good news) and a reason that every day I had to leave home (the bad). This departure was excruciating at first; still, it was apparently how things were done, according to the hackneyed American tradition of the briefcase-wielding husband trudging off to work. I took some comfort in that old-fashioned blueprint for life, in that musty and corny tradition. I got used to it. But leaving the house for other reasons—for hobbies, for the hell of it, for get-togethers with goofball friends—was more confusing. I was mobile now, leaving home on a regular basis, but did that mean I could play basketball with the gang, as in the old days? And should I play one pickup game or four? I used to go fishing, which I now deemed categorically out of the question. But was it? Until when? I said no, as a matter of policy, to social invitations. But shouldn't I at some point see friends? Amanda was encouraging, but also confusing. She pushed me to keep my friendships alive, but plainly missed my help during the long evenings I wasn't there. I began not to believe her tired words of encouragement. I canceled all plans and was quietly disappointed that I had to. After all, the last thing I wanted to be, even briefly, was the kind of absent new father for whom a cold beer with a buddy took precedence over a warm diaper at home. But while Amanda appreciated the compromise, she also sensed that it was just that—a compromise—and the fact that I was silently yearning for greater freedom pissed her off.

I had learned to walk away from our baby girl and the full-time job of caring for her, but running back and forth between my old life and her new life proved harder still.

The truth, I gradually learned, is that you can do it all. Well, let me be clear: not *all* of it all, but rather a careful and timely selection of it all. What I came to understand after those staggering first six months of parenthood is that a guy doesn't have to quit every one of his previous habits and pursuits when he becomes a father. He simply must, like Noah selecting animals, choose the two he would like to survive. That's right: two. And keep in mind, work counts as one. For me, the second pursuit has rotated. Basketball fit the bill for a while, and now, perhaps temporarily, it's been replaced by softball. Poker, before the baby, was a growing obsession, as was painting, but they simply didn't make the cut. Two is the number, according to my years of painful research, when it comes to a husband's independent activities. And the discovery of this magic number came as a profound relief. I began to have fun outside the house, and to have the sort of balanced life—a life of friends *and* family, of unimportant extracurriculars *and* deep domestic satisfaction—that fills your days, fills your heart, and fills your wife with pleasure at your pleasure.

Learning to walk away was one thing. Choosing where to go was more difficult. Yet, then and now, the constant and the deepest comfort by far was and is the flooding pleasure of coming home.

Month Twelve
The Communication Breakthrough

With the arrival of Month Twelve, we at last see the ability of the growing father to communicate. His physical development has been impressive: He has become both mobile and cognitively capable of deciding where to go; and now, for the first time, he can talk about it, too. Actual conversations become possible between husband and wife: candid admissions and genuine exchanges in place of the harried dumbness of the past year. He forms sentences of his own volition. He asks questions that resonate and make sense. The man is leaving the babyish stage of mute apprenticeship and inarticulate effort and, for the first time, seeing and speaking of things with perspective. This marks the end of the babyhood of your husband—and, more important, the beginning of his talking about the growth process himself.

For a year, there seemed to be no room for that. There was no time for my theories and queries about our evolving relationship as parents, no call for holding forth on life's (at least our life's) larger questions. Amanda was way ahead of me on this front. For her, part of living through that frenetic first year of parenthood was talking about it all the while: expressing worry, hazarding predictions, evaluating past decisions—not necessarily with any grand wisdom, but with the instinct to bring it all up. I, meanwhile, treated her talk more or less like the garbled squawking of a baby monitor: worthy of attention, even action, but generally a one-way conversation that required no articulate response. We had a million serious pow-wows that first year of parenthood, and yet we never really talked.

I provided her with my effort and my affection without bothering to speak my mind. And then, with a year under our belts, I opened up.

I suppose, for me, the ability to speak freely came with the sheer relief that our daughter appeared to be here to stay. So much of her early life was spent vigilantly monitoring her, desperately nurturing her, that calm musings about anything larger seemed a luxury best put off. But then—suddenly, it seemed—Savannah was full-fledged and fine: an actual girl, standing and actually toddling forward, wearing actual clothes, and even putting out joyous soprano communications, a helpful signal that I might try a joyous word or two myself. We had done it, Amanda and I: we had raised a baby into a mini-person. And it was this swooning sense of triumph that emboldened me to raise other things—difficult subjects, daring questions, the volume of our laughter—that I had worriedly put aside for a year.

It was a year, I can say now, of astonishing creativity and record-breaking tiredness, of unprecedented teamwork with Amanda, of momentary distance from her and the miraculous pleasure of snapping back. It was a year, among other things, marked by the ceaseless reading of countless baby books—guides to those awkward first movements, those unexpected growth spurts—the construction of friendship, and the unfathomable satisfaction of growing up.

to sleep, perchance to scheme:

A Couple Survives (Barely) the Sleep Wars

· Adam Wasson ·

I came across prisoners who signed what they were ordered to sign, only to get what the interrogator promised them. He did not promise them their liberty; he did not promise them food to sate themselves. He promised them—if they signed—uninterrupted sleep!

—Menachem Begin,
White Nights: The Story of a Prisoner in Russia

Without enough sleep, we all become tall two-year-olds.

—Jo Jo Jensen, *Dirt Farmer Wisdom*

We had been warned. My wife, Lael, and I had repeatedly been cautioned by our experienced friends to expect severe, relationship-altering sleep loss after the birth of our daughter. The truth was, though, that we looked forward to the challenge. Like changing diapers and not having sex, sleep deprivation seemed to us a rite of passage of new parenthood, and we approached it with manic resoluteness. We were prepared. We were a team. We had read *What to Expect When You're Expecting* twice.

We tore through that first month on caffeine and adrenaline, proudly weathering the exhaustion that apparently felled lesser parents. I even began to enjoy advertising my sleeplessness. There's a kind of baby-fatigue chic that's popular with new dads: yawning, unshaved, pushing a stroller to Starbucks while sporting pajama bottoms and bed head. The effect is similar to wearing a Lance Armstrong wristband or listening to the latest Norah Jones album: it tells the world you're a sensitive, self-sacrificing new-age man with a confidence that disdains traditional vanity (this look can be enhanced by spiking your bed head an inch or two with mousse).

Other men eyed my puffy features with respect; women offered kind words or one of those "you're so sweet, let me help you" half smiles. It was a pleasant kind of attention, but therein lay the rub: no matter how tired I was, I didn't get any of the same sympathy from my wife that I got from relatives, friends, and complete strangers. My patented "sore back" twist with exhausted eye rub, so effective at eliciting attention at the mall, didn't even get me a second glance from a spouse who was just as exhausted as I.

And vice versa. Her plaintive yawns meant nothing to me, and even her "help me, please" scowls went largely unnoticed. As the weeks wore on and the novelty wore off, it began to dawn on both of us that these midnight, 3 A. M., and 5 A. M. wake ups weren't just some fashionable phase. We were exhausted, we would be exhausted tomorrow, and we would be exhausted next year. In fact, we were going to suffer some form of sleep deprivation every night for the foreseeable future. Fatigue chic ceased to seem as cool or hip or fun as it had been the first month. We had moved on to what you might call fatigue fatigue.

The books will tell you that babies begin to smile at exactly this point — six to eight weeks in — as a matter of survival. Exhausted parents have reached their limits of endurance, and exchanging smiles with their child reaffirms feelings of love and allows the nurturing process to continue. What the books don't tell you, however, is that this is also the time parents stop smiling at each other.

I remember the day that this became clear. It was around noon, and Lael and I had both been up for much of the night. She was feeding and making goo-goo eyes at our daughter, when suddenly she cast an accusatory look at me as I reclined on the couch. "As long as you're not working," she said, "could you watch her for twenty minutes while I take a shower?"

After offering my own peekaboo smile at the baby, I glared back at my wife and said, "I *am* working. I'm thinking. That's an important part of my work. And I still have two hours until it's my turn."

She said, "I'm tired, I'm covered in baby formula, and I haven't showered in two days."

"I'm tired, too," I said. "I haven't showered either, and I'm trying to think!"

She replied, "It's just a twenty-minute $*#@ing shower."

I said something like "It's just my career, my art, my single remaining escape from the friendless, sleepless purgatory my life has become."

She cried.

I sulked.

No one took a shower.

Of course, that was one of our more healthy, reasoned, daytime exchanges of opinion. Nighttime was when the true dysfunction set in. Our P.M. arguments were vicious, underhanded, and inevitably centered around the same three sleep-related topics: the baby monitor, sleep training (also known as "Ferberizing"), and the ever-prickly question of who would get up with the baby in the middle of the night.

The baby monitor is, in my opinion, one of the most devious sleep-deprivation systems ever devised by man. Its genius lies in the fact that, when turned to full volume, it actually picks up breathing noises. My wife seemed to find this feature comforting: If she couldn't physically watch her child every second, she could at least listen in. (Come to think of it, that monitor might actually prove useful once we get to those "we're going to study in my room with the door closed" teen years.) The problem we had was that the amplification required to hear the baby's sighlike breaths meant every cough, squawk, and kick resounded loudly enough to jolt us out of sleep and, upon one occasion, right onto the floor. Such rude awakenings could happen as often as three or four times a night. Combined with the times the baby actually did wake up and need attention, that meant that neither of us got more than two uninterrupted hours of sleep. Ever.

We had terrible arguments over these earsplitting wake ups (I wanted to turn the monitor down), yet they were not even the most nefarious aspect of that devil machine. The worst thing was the quiet. Even the most sensitive monitors cannot *always* pick up breathing noises. Sometimes the baby rolled away from the microphone or just breathed quietly, and we couldn't hear a thing. At this point Lael inevitably became concerned that the baby was not breathing. Nor was she shy about voicing this concern.

"Can you hear her breathing?"

"I'm not listening. I'm sleeping."

"I can't hear her breathing."

"You can't hear your mother breathing either."

"My mother's in San Francisco."

"Exactly. Yet you assume she's still breathing. So why not assume your child is, too?"

"Suppose she's not breathing. What if you could save her and you don't?"

I couldn't believe she had said that. It was conniving, manipulative, and surprisingly effective. I knew perfectly well that my daughter had shifted into a position where the microphone couldn't pick up her sounds, but now I couldn't erase the specter of a nonbreathing child from my half-unconscious brain. Irrational baby anxiety is contagious, especially at night. It wasn't long before I was the one slithering up to the crib on my belly to ensure that my sleeping, perfectly healthy child was, in fact, still breathing.

I argued, threatened, and cajoled, but my wife refused to give up the monitor. Accordingly, I began to hatch Wile E. Coyote–like plans to destroy it. I'd bump it off the nightstand with my foot; "accidentally" drop it down a flight of stairs; surreptitiously short-circuit it in a deluge of water. Unfortunately, none of these plans ever bore fruit. Like that eerily self-satisfied revenant of a road runner, baby monitors are apparently indestructible. I did manage to unplug and hide the monitor once, reasoning with my wife that the baby's room was only ten feet away and that when the child actually did wake up we would hear her easily. I calmly explained that people had gotten along for millennia without baby monitors in the bedroom. She responded that she would get along just fine without *me* in the bedroom, but she needed that monitor. So I returned the device and retreated to the couch, more convinced than ever that baby monitors are one of those "helpful" new technologies that make life much, much worse.

Sleep training, on the other hand, is a wholesome, low-tech, old-fashioned idea about which we also managed to have vicious disagreements. The premise of sleep training is simple. You put the baby to bed before she is asleep, and when she cries for attention you refrain from comforting her so she can learn to fall asleep, and stay asleep, on her own. In our case, though, my wife could not bear to hear the baby cry without immediately going in to console her.

Even when I explained that it was for our daughter's own good, Lael could not stop herself from entering that room.

How long would this continue, I wanted to know. Were we going to let her eat candy because she was crying? Buy her a car? Let her date some motorcycle-riding bass guitar player? The time for discipline was now! Our daughter's plaintive sobs weren't easy for me to hear, either, but I was willing to do what it took to get her, and us, more sleep. My wife was not.

What was so frightening about this sleep-training disagreement was that it illustrated a fundamental difference in the way we approached parenting. My wife was willing to sacrifice her physical and mental welfare (and mine as well) to make sure our child suffered no emotional discomfort—even if that discomfort was temporary and for the baby's own good. I, on the other hand, felt we needed to ensure our own well-being if we were going to be effective parents, and in this case part of that well-being was getting some sleep. I felt angry and betrayed when Lael abandoned the sleep-training plan, and my sense of indignation played a big role in our subsequent arguments over who would get up in the middle of the night.

Like war veterans and prison guards, experienced parents never forget those middle-of-the-night sounds. A rustling, a slight croak. A throat-clearing groan. Then that cringingly hopeful moment of silence before the all-out wail that forces desperate, sleep-deprived people into a direct confrontation with "the question." The question is familiar, even innocuous sounding, yet it has broken more young marriages than has any other question (with the possible exception of "Whose earring is this?").

Who's going to get up with the baby?

In our case, this question was rarely answered directly; rather, it was answered through an intricate, passive-aggressive battle of wills. I became quite adept at the nocturnal version of these exchanges and liked to think of myself as the master of the mumble. My wife would awaken and say something like "I'll get this one and you get the next one, okay?" and I would respond with something like "Mrrrph." This unintelligible murmur served two purposes. First, it planted a seed of plausible deniability when she asked me to get up the next time—maybe I really hadn't made an agreement, maybe I hadn't even been awake. And second, a well-executed mumble sounds a cautionary note. It says, "I'm not even capable of speech. Do you really want me handling our child in this handicapped state?"

No slouch herself in the passive-aggressive arts, my wife quickly learned that any deal she wanted to strike would have to be made during daytime. She particularly excelled at the art of negotiation through comparison.

"Jessica's husband gets up three mornings a week," she would say. "And I know for a fact that Eric Perez takes care of Antonio every single weekday morning."

Supposedly I was less helpful in the morning than every husband of every mom in Mommy and Me. My wife knew that playing on my competitive instincts was a good way to manipulate me. I didn't want to get up in the middle of the night, but neither did I want to be outfathered by some early-rising investment banker named Gerald.

I hadn't met enough new parents to compete at the comparison game, but I did have a few weapons of my own. Chief among these was an arsenal of shadowy, hard-to-refute excuses to avoid wake-up duty: back pain, flulike symptoms, and the ever-popular important next-day meeting were some of the most useful. Once, in a particularly desperate moment, I even faked a doctor's note alleging my medication made getting up on short notice impossible. That I never used the note is immaterial; the fact that I wrote it illustrates how desperate I had become.

In the aftermath of the sleep-training fiasco, though, I rarely needed to resort to such subterfuge. I had discovered my wife's weak point: She needed to be needed. All I had to say was, "The baby wants you. She doesn't want a bottle. She needs her mom." Our daughter aided me in this strategy once she started speaking. She would call "Mama" when she woke up in the morning, which made it very clear who was being requested. And Lael, as previously noted, could not refuse a request from her daughter.

Finally, after more than a year of sleep deprivation, the tide was turning my way. Lael seemed resigned to the fact that the baby wanted her more than me, and I was allowed to sleep in comparative peace (albeit often on the couch). I may have lost the battles over the baby monitor and sleep training; I might have been beaten by the fabled Gerald in a husband-of-the-year contest; but I was, at long last, winning the war for sleep.

Then an amazing thing happened. My wife had been away for a few days on business, and I'd dutifully arisen every time our daughter woke up (without need, I might add, of the baby monitor) and gone in to comfort her. I'd listened to her familiar cries of "I want Mama" and patiently rocked her back to sleep. When Lael returned home, it seemed initially that things would go back to normal. She volunteered to get up the next morning; I looked forward to sleeping in again. But when the baby woke up and Lael entered her room, she was greeted by the most astonishing words: "I want Daddy." This was an unprecedented event, like the Red Sox beating the Yankees in the playoffs: everyone was shocked, most of all the Red Sox themselves. As I lay in bed savoring the words — "I want Daddy" — an important truth dawned on me. I hadn't been winning the war for sleep; I'd been losing, without even realizing it, the trust and affection of my daughter. I'd been losing the struggle to be number-one parent! That was a competition I hadn't even realized existed, but once I did the sleep wars took on an entirely new meaning.

Lael and I had directed so much love and energy toward our child (and, consequently, away from each other) that we were starved for attention ourselves. Once the baby was able to give some concrete affection back, we both wanted it. Suddenly sleep seemed like nothing compared to my desire to be needed and trusted and loved by my child. Meanwhile Lael, though stunned to find me such an able competitor, was not about to give up her George Steinbrenner–like dominance at the top of the game. Soon we were both bounding out of bed at the slightest peep from our daughter, wanting to be the first one in there to do the comforting. Lael began staying up later to answer the midnight distress calls that had always been my purview; I trained myself to leap out of bed in the morning and move toward our daughter's room without a single wasted motion. We were like two frantic candidates running for a constituency of one. Sleep was no longer a goal but a liability, a hurdle to clear in this fervent though unspoken battle for our daughter's affection.

What had once been excuses now became seemingly kind offers—"No, you go ahead and sleep, honey, let me get this one"— and the outright hostility became more of a faux consideration. Perhaps the most interesting thing about our battle for our daughter's affection, though, was that it made us do things together. My wife and I had been so exhausted during that first year that we rarely did anything together: when one of us had the baby, the other would seize the opportunity to work, eat, shower, nap, or hang out with someone "on the outside." Now both of us were playing with the baby, feeding the baby, and bounding together out of bed when she awoke in the night. So there was a kind of mutual respect established through this unspoken competition. I might not have agreed with Lael's philosophy on sleep discipline, but I was grudgingly impressed by the ferocity with which she could descend the stairs in order to be the first face our daughter saw in the morning.

A couple of times we both thought we heard our daughter waking up, and rushed in from different parts of the house only to discover it had been a false alarm. There was something lovely about just standing there in the half light, two besotted adults staring down at the slumbering child who has caused such upheaval in their lives. We still weren't on entirely firm ground: The first year's sleep battles had been too brutal for that. But there had been a definite shift in tone. We weren't less tired, we just didn't care as much about being tired. Yes, exhaustion made us less effective at work. It made us worse lovers, worse drivers, and less interesting conversationalists. But it was also its own kind of bond. Our shared willingness to sacrifice for our child was a reminder of the qualities—like tenacity, compassion, and even competitiveness—that had drawn us together in the first place.

In the end, it was a statement by our daughter that put the definitive stamp on this relationship revision. She had awoken screaming, and Lael and I raced into the room to provide comfort. We reached her simultaneously, picking her up in a kind of awkward three-way hug on the toddler bed. After a fair amount of tickling and mugging and giggling, she beamed at both of us and said, in a timid voice, a word we didn't even know she knew: *family*. Actually, it sounded like "famiyee," but we understood what she meant. We chuckled uncomfortably, and our daughter did what she always does when she finds a word that produces a reaction. She said it again, louder. "Famiyee." We said it back to her and she said it again, this time bouncing on the bed and saying it in three emphatic syllables: "Fa-mi-yee." We laughed and bounced with her, all three of us in a warm messy jumble of pillows and blankets, all laughing and chanting our new word and feeling quite intoxicated that it was five in the morning and the rest of the world wasn't up yet. They were sleeping, poor fools.

not perfect but lovin' him anyway

· Lisa Earle McLeod ·

Were we blindsided by a diaper?

Speaking for myself, I think I was bonked over the head with one, and it was full at the time—full of prime-time dads, storybook endings, and feminist fantasies that I had swirled together into such a little bundle of unrealistic expectations, I can now only laugh at my naïveté.

Others may have begun their parenting journey with a positive pregnancy test and parenting book, but I started mine in front of the television. Years of senseless sitcoms and empowering perfume ads had convinced me that I knew exactly what the perfect family was supposed to look like and I was determined to create one.

My own perfectly planned pregnancy occurred when I was twenty-nine years old. We'd been married for eight years, since the fall after I graduated from college. My career was well under way, and after checking off the Get a Good Job, Get Married, and Buy a House boxes on my perfect little life plan, I was ready for phase two—a family.

As a big-bucks-earning consultant happily wed to an enlightened modern man, I assumed that our prebaby fifty-fifty workload split would continue after we became parents. After all, my charming man had enthusiastically cooked and cleaned during the entire ten years I'd known him without ever uttering so much as a murmur about woman's work. Being nine years older than I am, he actually began our marriage as the more domestically skilled member of the family. He'd lived on his own for several years, grocery shopping, doing his own laundry, and watering the plants. He continued this delightful behavior after we married, and so I naturally assumed that his transition to fatherhood would be just as smooth and easy as his conversion to being a husband.

On the surface, our parenting journey actually did start just like a sappy movie: the happy couple joyously watching the little blue line show up on the little white stick and then breaking the good news to Mom and Dad over the phone before we headed out to Barnes & Noble to pick up some best-selling expert advice.

But unbeknownst to my poor husband, by the time we made it to the bookstore aisle, I had already been crafting our parenting story for years. And my version was decidedly different from his. In my version, he, the dad, would come home every night in as good a mood as Mike Brady and as eager to jump in with the kids as Cliff Huxtable. We would be totally "equal"—an interchangeable mom and dad, who would share all parenting duties and household chores equally. And of course there would still be all sorts of time for us and the white-hot passion we have for each other. It's clear to me now that I spent way too many of my formative years parked in front of the boob tube.

I was also convinced that our perfect little family was going to be entirely different from the one in which either of us had been raised. He comes from conservative parents in the Deep South who gave big huge parties and were often served by maids. I grew up in a boisterous family outside Washington, D.C., that made a regular practice of passing out Save the Beaver Pond leaflets during soccer practice.

Both upbringings had their merits, but after eight successful years of marriage, we were convinced that we had completely left our own parents' lifestyles behind and were creating our own. Our parents may have slid into traditional roles that left Mom in charge of it all and Dad as the good-time guy, but not us. And while we'd seen other lesser couples derailed by a baby, we knew that we were going to be different.

Or rather, I should say, I thought we were going to be different. I'm not sure he had given it much thought at all.

My first clue that there might be trouble ahead came when I was three months pregnant. I was at lunch with two friends, and as I announced my impending arrival, one of my friends burst into laughter and told me that she was actually due on the same day. What an unbelievable coincidence.

As the two first-time moms-to-be giggled and twittered about how wonderful life was going to be after our babies were born, talk naturally turned to the subject of husbands. When we both launched into descriptions of how things were going to be so different for us than other mothers because we had men who were already skilled at domestic duties, it was our other friend's turn to laugh.

An experienced married mother of two, she shook her head knowingly and said, "You two don't have any idea of what you're getting into. Your husbands may be smiling and nodding now, but just wait until after the baby is born." At the time I assumed she was a cynical jaded woman who was married to one of those lazy guys who never did a thing.

Little did I know that one year later I would reflect back on that conversation and think that she was probably one of the wisest women I ever met.

It wasn't so much that my husband didn't help. I can honestly say that he did almost everything I asked. The trouble was I always had to ask.

Yes, he made a few unsolicited runs for Pampers and he sometimes remembered to bring me a glass of water when I was nursing. But for the most part, I was the master keeper of the "list"—the mental Rolodex of what the baby needs, when she needs it, which neighbor or book to consult when there were questions, when she was supposed to be doing what, how long she needed to nap, what foods she could and couldn't have, and how many times she had pooped each day.

All information was possessed by me, and no matter how many times I repeated it, it never seemed to become integrated into my husband's brain.

As the baby grew, the list gradually morphed from bodily functions to signing up for Gymboree, hiring a sitter, and figuring out which shots she needed. I had expected my husband to be a coparent, but I got a reluctant assistant instead.

Control freak that I am, having an assistant wouldn't have been so bad if he had acted like one of those chop-chop, think-ahead, on-call-24/7 assistants Donald Trump hires. But my husband seemed to think that parenting was a part-time job only done when the boss made a specific request. And if the boss didn't ask in just the right way or show enough appreciation when he was done, he acted like the most put-upon man alive.

Stay home and watch the kid while *he* traveled for three days? No big thing. But one twenty-four-hour round of child care while I was on a business trip wore the man out for three days.

Now he wasn't some Neanderthal who thought watching his own flesh and blood was a charitable act on my behalf. But there was the distinct feeling in the air that much of what he did for the house or baby was a favor for me.

In the beginning it was cute to give him some positive reinforcement. We were both nervous and I wanted him to know how much I appreciated his stepping out of his comfort zone. But one month into the job when he was still expecting kudos for giving her a bottle, my energy for being his personal rah-rah girl had begun to fade. Two months later when he was bragging about being the only guy in the office who rolled up his sleeves and gave his own kid a bath, my resentment had reached a slow boil.

And by the time I went back to work full-time and happened to overhear him boasting to the neighbor that *he* was home first to relieve the sitter two days a week, I about murdered the man.

To make matters worse, my husband wasn't the only one who thought I should be grateful. On business trips people told me how lucky I was that my husband would actually watch our baby while I was away. The other moms at Baby Gymboree fawned all over him because he was the only dad who regularly came to class. And his family thought the fact that he knew which end of the baby to wipe made him a candidate for Father of the Year. I could change thirty-seven dirty diapers in a row without anyone batting an eye. But let him change one in front of his mother and I had to hear her brag about it for a week.

It was like my mothering bar was a hundred, his fathering bar was zero, and any deviation off his preset mark was a gift from heaven above.

Looking back, I feel like a bit of shit for not being nicer to a guy who was doing his best and only wanted a little praise from his wife. I now have a clear vision of an eager husband taking his baby out for a walk and coming home hoping that the woman he loves might boost his ego a bit with some heartfelt thanks. But instead he found an evil witch who wondered why he wanted a medal for something she did without notice every day.

There were many times during that first year in the stressed-out mommy zone when I felt like screaming, "If it's going to be such a big f—ing favor, don't bother." Now that I think back, I realize I didn't just *feel* like screaming that, on several occasions I actually did.

In the words of Charles Dickens, "It was the best of times, it was the worst of times." I had a beautiful baby and motherhood had been the greatest gift of my life. But I was beginning to wonder if my marriage might bite the dust. I may not have been actively considering divorce, but the high hopes I'd once had for my husband to be the perfect coparent had been dashed. And I wasn't sure if things would ever be the same again.

If he wasn't going to adhere to my vision of partnership and parenting, where the heck could this marriage possibly go? I wasn't sure I could embrace another script so different from the TV one I had clung to long ago.

One day, down in the dumps about the whole thing, I found myself back in the same bookstore where we had delightfully purchased *What to Expect When You're Expecting* a mere eighteen months before. This time I sneered at the happy little pregnancy tomes and found myself in the relationship section instead. I've always believed that the right books come to you at the right time. So when I saw the *The Transition to Parenthood: How a First Child Changes a Marriage,* by Dr. Jay Belsky, I immediately grabbed it off the shelf. And when I read the book jacket describing how so many men and women felt alone and adrift inside their little families of three, I knew this book wasn't just for me, it was *about* me.

I took it home and read the entire thing in one long tear-filled night. Couple after couple had experienced the same pain and disillusionment we were feeling. And I didn't just weep when I read the woman's side of things. What haunted me most were the voices of the men, father after father describing with great passion the kind of dad he wanted to be. Men who were determined to be better fathers than their own dads, but who felt criticized by their wives every time they even tried.

One of the book's most interesting insights was that while a woman measures her husband's efforts *against what she is doing,* most men measure their contributions *against what their father did.*

No wonder my husband expected to be treated like such a big hero. His dad might have taken him on great camping trips when he was ten, but I don't think he ever gave him a bath in his entire life. Using this criterion, if my husband did thirty percent of the household chores and his father only did ten percent, then he feels like he's doing three hundred percent because he's doing three times more than his dad ever did.

Meanwhile I, the overworked wife, am doing the other seventy percent, and spending my time dwelling on what I perceive to be his halfhearted effort because his thirty percent is still less than half of what I'm doing.

Talk about a wake-up call. Measuring yourself against a man who's been dead for ten years (and who's fathering you personally thought was bit lacking) might not make much sense to me, but a quick conversation with my husband revealed that was exactly what he had been doing.

As I recall his comment was "I do so much more than my dad ever dreamed of doing, and yet you never seem to notice."

Ouch.

Of course I didn't notice how different he was from his dad. I wasn't around when he was growing up, so I never knew how his dad behaved. His father died the year before we were married, so I barely knew the man. Just like the other wives in the study, I had been comparing my husband to me, not his long-dead 1950s dad. All of a sudden my lens on the situation changed. Instead of being angry that he wanted so much praise, I got off my high horse and realized how easy it was to give it to him.

Thinking back to my own upbringing, I also realized how hard it is to change course from the parenting you received as a child. I might not have wanted to emulate my mom's version of mothering, but judging by how often her words kept coming out of my mouth, it was a little harder for me to adopt a different mommy model than I wanted to admit.

Applying that same principle to my husband helped me see that compared to his dad, he had evolved faster than a pig who learned to fly.

And here's another thing that hit me like a ton of bricks. Apparently there are two primary factors that determine whether a marriage will improve or worsen after a baby. The first is the husband's ability to put his own needs aside and support his wife in her new all-encompassing role. And the second is the wife's ability to forget about the baby now and again and pay attention to the man.

Truth be told, my husband might not have been doing as well as I thought he should on task number one, but at least he was trying.

I, on the other hand, was making no effort whatsoever on task number two. I was waiting for him to perfect his part before I even started on mine.

I still don't completely understand why men need so much praise. And why doing stuff for the kids counts as doing something for the woman. It must go back to some primitive caveman instincts. Perhaps if it wasn't for their innate need to please women, men would have bagged hunting altogether and just sat around eating grubs all day. The cave kids would have starved, and Mom would have left Dad for a guy roasting a good juicy yak over his fire pit.

Is the male need for approval survival of the fittest or hopeless immaturity? Who knows and who cares? I have different answers depending on which day you ask me. But I do know that when I started thanking my husband with a smile on my face, things began to get better.

And while I'm still the keeper of the master list, I've come to realize that with my multitasking brain, life works better that way. We don't divide things equally. For the most part, I figure out what needs to be done and then decide who's going to do it. It's sort of like powerful monarchy and indentured servanthood at the same time.

Is it the happily ever after I scripted for myself when I was a kid?

No, it's not. Cheerful Mike Brady is nowhere to be seen, and my husband's job doesn't pay nearly as well as Cliff Huxtable's. My husband works harder than his dad did, and I put in more hours each day than my mom. Why two people who are doing more than their parents did aren't further ahead is something I can't explain. Sure, we may have nicer furniture and fancier cars, and our kids have seen a few more museums than we did growing up. But neither of us ever remember our parents frantically measuring their time in minutes. But then again, who knows what it was like for them. When you're a kid your perception of your parents, not to mention life, is never an accurate picture.

We were both blindsided by the effect a child had on our marriage. But now, our notions of equality have changed and so have our perceptions of each other. I can honestly say that I love my husband more now than when we first had the baby. But now I love him like a grown-up. Someone who knows that the other person isn't ever going to conform to her TV-influenced version of perfect, but who has decided to love him anyway.

Five years after baby number one, we had baby number two. The challenges weren't as surprising that time, but they were still just as hard. In fact, in many ways, becoming a family of four was even tougher on our marriage than becoming parents for the first time.

But we do have a happy marriage, and we're raising a great family. It might not make for a memorable sitcom, but it's happy enough, for today.

confessions of a sugar mommy

· Amy Sohn ·

A few days before my wedding, I got a call from a reporter at the New York Times *saying she would be writing about the event for the* "Weddings" pages. She had to ask me a few background questions, like "What first attracted you to your husband?" As I packed my dress into its garment bag, I told her that Jake and I met through a mutual friend, shortly before my twenty-ninth birthday party, when Jake, an artist, came over to lend me some paintings. I was pleasantly surprised when he turned out to be a six-foot-six-inch redhead with tattoos up and down his arms, and we fell in love soon after that.

The reporter pressed me some more. "What makes you two work together?" she said.

"I think it's a case of opposites attracting," I said. "We're both unusual for our gender in different ways. I have some masculine qualities, he has some feminine. I had always imagined myself with a man who would be the primary caregiver in terms of children, and this is what Jake saw himself doing, too."

What I was really saying was that my choice to marry a struggling artist, a guy without a lot of money, was deliberate. I was investing in the welfare of my yet-to-be-conceived child by marrying a man who wanted to be a stay-at-home father.

Though I was drawn to Jake for many reasons, what seduced me the most at the beginning was the way he took care of me. I had dated a lot of guys who needed taking care of and I was never very good at it. I didn't bring chicken soup when they were sick or nod emphatically when they said things like "I'm a better monologuist than Eric Bogosian, don't you think?" When I met Jake I knew he would never ask me questions like that.

He was one of those people who always put those he loved first. It came naturally to him, which made it all the more endearing. On our second date I suggested dinner out and he suggested I come over to his place instead so he could cook breaded chicken and tortillas for me. I brought an egg for the batter and some wine, and we ate and talked and fell to his mattress. From then on, on the nights that I went over to his place, he cooked, and on the nights he came over to mine, we dined out since, like many New York women, I cannot cook.

As much as I enjoyed all the home-cooked meals, both Jake and I knew that one of the reasons he was so quick to cook for me was because he couldn't afford to take me out. He had a graduate degree in architecture but hadn't practiced in ten years because the hours were so punishing and the money so terrible, he figured if he wasn't going to make any money, he might as well do something he enjoyed: paint. At the time we met, I was making a good living writing for magazines and he supported himself by selling his paintings. I earned about five times as much as he did.

When girlfriends asked if this difference in our incomes both-
ered me, I always cracked jokes about how I was an alpha male anyway. But as Jake and I got more serious this became a source of
tension. When we moved in together, I paid the rent, electricity,
cable, and credit bills, while he cooked all the meals and did the
dishes. On one level, the trade-off seemed fair. After all, how many
generations of men and women had cohabited just this way, only
with the genders reversed—the man bringing home the bacon, the
wife frying it up in a pan? I was no good at cooking and he was. He
wasn't good at making money and I was. As a couple we were a
whole.

But there were months when the phone bill would be high and
I'd harangue him about his long-distance calls, or I'd get a credit
card bill with a lot of meals out and he'd say that it was *me* who
always wanted to eat out, he was happy just to stay in, which was
true. One night we saw an *Odd Couple* episode where Felix keeps a
log of all the money Oscar owes him, and we laughed at it in that
loaded uncomfortable way you do when art imitates life just a little
too much.

When I met Jake I was being treated by a ninety-two-year-old,
white-haired Austrian analyst on the Upper East Side, and whenever I expressed concerns about the financial inequity, Dr. Berger
would shake his head gravely and say in his thick accent, "For za
relationship to survive you must be za voo-man, not za man." But I
never knew what exactly he meant and when I asked he would
answer in psychobabble I didn't understand.

Then I switched to a brown-haired, fiftysomething Buddhist psychiatrist in Tribeca and when I told him of the financial inequity he
said, "Sounds like it works. Someone's got to devote themselves to
the cooking and house care, so you should be grateful you met a
guy who can do it." This made me feel much better. But there was a
part of me that didn't really think the arrangement was fair.

When Jake and I began talking about having children, I realized that a child, which we both wanted anyway, could have a side benefit for the relationship. Once we had a baby, I would continue my writing and he could become a stay-at-home dad. Suddenly he would be providing care that would otherwise cost us twenty-five thousand dollars a year. He wouldn't have to take on the small jobs he hated like landscaping and carpentry, and I could stop nagging him to make more money. We wouldn't have to leave our child with a stranger, and I could feel secure in the fact that she would be in the care of a capable and loving father.

In this radical-feminist vision, I was little more than a vessel for the baby. "I'll just pop it out and you take care of the rest," I would joke, enjoying the idea of myself as a professionally ambitious, unmotherly mother. In this fantasy, I was a carrier, a Sherry Lansing–esque ball buster (how I morphed myself from a messy-haired writer into a power-suited 1980s Hollywood exec I do not know) who would squeeze out a kid and promptly hand her off to her husband for safekeeping so that she could get back to what she really cared about: work.

What I didn't count on was that once my baby came out, I might actually feel something for her. I had thirty agonizing hours of back labor in which nothing seemed to be going right, but after she was born and the midwives put her to my breast, she latched on easily, willingly, with no fuss at all. Looking down at her, pressing my nipple away from her nose so she could breathe (which I later learned was completely unnecessary), I felt not peace but something close. I wasn't a vessel, a surrogate mom. I was a mother. I didn't feel love yet—that would come later—but I felt the instinct to care for and protect this tiny helpless thing that was, miraculously, my child.

I looked over at Jake. He was curled up in the bed with us and he was looking at Alice like he had never seen anything so beautiful. His brow was furrowed in a mix of exhaustion and intense feeling and I realized how badly he had wanted this baby. I saw the adoration in his eyes and it frightened me a little. This was no glib, out-of-it dad lighting a cigar and cracking jokes about what he'd witnessed. This was a changed man. He was in love. I had married a nurturer but now I was going to have to pay the price: competition in that role. Alice was going to have not one, but two, overweening, intense, opinionated, and thoroughly obsessed parents. And I never like having competition for anything.

The first few weeks of Alice's life I nursed and slept, while Jake took care of the household. He went grocery shopping, cooked (when we didn't eat takeout), and rotated loads of laundry. He ran out for extra burp cloths and a breast-feeding pillow and when guests came, he put out hors d'oeuvres and wine and straightened up, glowingly snapping photos and telling the long story of how she was born. When the apartment felt claustrophobic and messy, he made us walk to a nearby pizza place to eat at the bar. When she woke at night and I fed her, he simultaneously fed me yogurt and fruit to fill my ravenous body. When I had trouble sleeping because I was so pumped up from the intensity of new motherhood, he went out and bought an herb called motherwort, safe for women who are breast-feeding, and I dozed off.

I look back on these months now, one year later, and I'm incredulous that I had so much help. Without Jake, I could not have gotten through those first formative weeks. And yet, a part of me had wanted to be left alone with my child. On the street we would pass other new mothers alone with their infants, the fathers long-ago back at work, and I would envy their autonomy. Sure, some seemed exhausted, or bored, or shell-shocked, but others seemed proud to be managing the bottle and the baby sling all at once. I wanted to feel that kind of pride in being able to care for Alice myself, but Jake wanted to be around her every second, too. One night when he heard about a gypsy jazz concert nearby, he packed her in the Bjorn and took her with him. I wished it were he and I at the concert, and Alice home for an hour with my mother. Then I wished it were she and I at the concert, all the audience members envious of my beautiful, well-behaved baby. I wanted him to myself and I wanted her to myself, too. I was triangulated both ways.

I went to see my Buddhist psychiatrist. "Try to spend a little time alone with her every day," he said. "You need to do that in order to gain confidence in yourself as a mother, and if you don't do it now you'll have a lot of problems later on."

I came home. "I'm going to take Alice for a walk," I announced.

Jake spun around from his chair by the computer, where he was uploading photos. "Did your shrink tell you to do this?"

"N-no," I said in a high-pitched voice.

"Do you really think I'm that dumb?" he said. "Go ahead. Take her out. Nobody's telling you not to."

"Sure you are. Every time I try to get away with her you say you want to come with us. Why does it always have to be the three of us?"

"I love it when it's the three of us!" he said.

"Well, I don't! I like you and me the best, then me and her, and then the three of us!"

I wrangled Alice into my arms, went downstairs, and put her in the stroller, even though she couldn't sit up yet. I heaved it down the front stairs myself, huffing and puffing, and then we walked to the bus stop. I had to exchange a few onesies at a batik store and I thought this would be a good excuse for a trip. The bus came and I struggled mightily to get Alice up the stairs, took out my wallet and Metrocard, pushed the stroller to a nearby seat, put the brakes on, and collapsed with a sigh. "You have to fold your stroller," said the driver.

I took the brakes off and tried to hold her in one hand and fold the stroller with the other. When I finally got her into my arms I was shaking, half from exhaustion, half from nerves.

"Your baby's too cold," said a woman next to me.

I covered Alice with her blanket, gritting my teeth. It was a cool air-conditioned bus and the blanket probably *was* a good idea, but I was quickly discovering that this was the downside of mothering alone. Everyone you passed told you you were doing it wrong.

On the ride back Alice was fussy, but when it was over I felt an enormous sense of accomplishment. Jake never even tried to take her on a bus, but I did, and I could. I could take care of her myself. All I really needed were my boobs, a diaper, and some patience. I began to take her on excursions, every day, an hour to the park or a stroll through the neighborhood. And I was surprised to find that I loved it. She was tiny and she didn't talk and all her smiles were really farts but I loved taking her out when she whimpered, peering over the stroller to be sure she was okay, putting her on a picnic blanket and cradling her in my arms.

Just as I was starting to feel bonded, we had to go to Los Angeles for a business trip. Before Alice was born I had gotten a script deal with a television producer named Ernie that required me to try to sell an hour-long drama about precocious teenagers to a network. Since the meetings were only five weeks after Alice's birth, Jake and I had decided that all three of us would have to go.

When we got to the hotel, we put Alice right in her port-a-crib, then ordered room service and turned on the TV. I felt like we were on top of things as parents. How many people could take a five-week-old across the country without any drama? We'd gotten through it with only a little bit of fighting, and Alice was adaptable enough to be able to fall asleep in a strange environment. I yawned. "I'm gonna turn in," I said.

"Don't you think you should pump?" he said. We had brought a manual breast pump because I didn't think an electric one was necessary, so reluctantly I curled up in the armchair and began squeezing that goddamned white thing, feeling the beginning of carpal pumping syndrome.

After half an hour, I had only a quarter of a bottle and I was falling asleep in my chair. "You'll be fine with this," I said.

"How long are you going to be gone tomorrow?"

"Four hours."

His eyes bugged out. "You've got to pump more in the morning!"

"All right, all right," I said. "I will. But I've got to stop now. I can't feel my hand." In the morning I pumped, gobbled down room service, breast-fed Alice, reread my pitch, showered, dressed, did my makeup, stuck two enormous nipple pads in my bra and then checked to make sure they didn't show through my shirt, kissed my family good-bye, and got into a waiting cab.

Somehow, it worked. Sure, there were problems—during my first meeting, Jake realized he had brought the wrong bottle nipple, Alice wouldn't eat or stop crying, and he had to drive with her to a drugstore to buy the right one. But we got through it. Sometimes she took a long time to fall asleep, it was hard for him to go outside with her because there wasn't much to do near the hotel. I felt a jolt of guilt that I hadn't been there to help, but I reminded myself that I was doing this trip so I could make money for my family, even if Jake was turning out to be a far more frenzied version of Mr. Mom than Michael Keaton.

And I have to admit, after five weeks of nonstop baby contact, I loved the simple pleasure of getting in a taxi and being driven away. I put on my sunglasses and watched the traffic and the tourists on the hot streets, touched up my lipstick, and enjoyed the temporary silence. I had been granted an opportunity for separation from my child that I never would have taken if it weren't for this deal, and it wasn't so bad. I even enjoyed it.

I also felt gratified that I could do something creative so soon after she was born, something that gave me a sense of self-esteem completely separate from the kind I got mothering. When I was in the room pitching I felt exhilarated and high. I wasn't just a mother,

I was someone who could go into a room and sell a show on the basis of nothing but enthusiasm.

Or not. Unfortunately, I didn't sell the show. It turned out the networks didn't want another show about teenagers, no matter how good it was. So when we got back to New York, I set about brainstorming another concept with Ernie, for a drama about a group of college students. One afternoon while I was working on the pitch and Jake was at the playground with Alice, he got a call from a friend of his, a father of two girls, who said their baby-sitter was looking for two days a week of work. She was a Tibetan woman who had worked for them for eight years and though they adored her, their kids just didn't need as much baby-sitting anymore. "So what do you think?" Jake later asked.

"I don't think we need someone yet," I said. "She's not even three months."

"But we're going to need someone soon," he said.

"I thought you wanted to be a full-time dad."

"That was before I knew how hard it was."

"But you're so crazy about Alice!"

"Of course I am, but I find child care very stressful. And I'm old. At the end of the day I'm tired. I couldn't handle seven days a week. Besides, if I paint I can sell some work, but if I don't put in the time I won't be able to."

I felt my *New York Times* "Weddings" section vision, where I was the man and he was the woman, begin to evaporate. Now I was going to be out eleven thousand a year for part-time child care *and* supporting three people.

A few days later, Sonam came to meet Alice. She was warm, doting, calm, and kind, and when she took Alice in her arms Alice blinked at her calmly, peaceful. We hired her on the spot and when she came for her first day and left the apartment to take Alice to the park, I felt a surge of relief that she would be in good hands. "I'm a little nervous," Jake said. "What if she just runs off with her?"

"You wanna go to lunch?" I said.

Over the next ten days, with help from Jake, I came up with the characters and story line for my next show concept. Ernie loved it and set up meetings with three networks. This time Jake and I stayed at a boutique hotel in West Hollywood, and when we got to the front desk I felt like we were seasoned travelers, a hip New York family with a good, beautiful baby.

In the morning I nursed Alice and got in a cab to ABC, site of my first meeting. Ernie hadn't arrived but his agent, who would be sitting in on the meeting, had. She knew I'd just had a baby and she congratulated me and said she was a mother of two. Then she took out her BlackBerry and typed something into it. "You must be making a lot of deals this time of year," I said.

"Oh, this is about a play date," she said. "My son needs to reschedule and I'm not getting the mother on her cell."

"Oh," I said. It was all so efficient. Was this the type of working mother I would be, one who e-mailed about play dates on a Black-Berry? Would I approach motherhood with this kind of organized efficiency?

Ernie arrived and we pitched the show to two young male development executives and the female head of drama development who was on speakerphone, since she was nine months pregnant and on bed rest. When we finished I felt good, and energized, and optimistic. Ernie and I walked out to the elevator and while we were waiting, one of the execs ran out and said, "Sold," and stuck his thumb up. Ernie pumped the air and then threw his arms around me. The agent congratulated us and began BlackBerrying and I knew this time it wasn't about a play date.

I called up Jake. "We sold it!" I said.

"Honey, I'm so proud of you," he said. "I knew you would." He sounded muted and stressed, like it had been a rough day.

"I couldn't have done it without you!" I said. "How's Alice?"

"She was fussy this morning but she's sleeping now. When are you coming home?"

"Ernie wants to know if I can have lunch with him. Is that okay?"

"Sure," he said. "Go out and celebrate."

Ernie took me to lunch at Mori Sushi, a hot sushi joint with the décor of a hole-in-the-wall Greek shish kebab place. We ordered sake and he toasted me and said, "Congratulations. You're going to have a hell of a busy fall." Then we both did sake shots.

"The breast-feeding mother is drinking before noon," I said. I felt on top of the world. This was the best time in a writer's life: after you got the job but before you had to draft a single word.

Back at the hotel, I raced into the room, where Jake was resting on the bed. Alice was sleeping in the port-a-crib and he put his fingers to his lips. I hugged him and started to tell him about the meeting. "I'm exhausted, honey," he said, whispering.

"Why's that?" I said, too loudly.

"As soon as you left she started wailing," he said, and then gave me a minute-by-minute play-by-play of the entire day, including the brief walk to the pharmacy to get diapers, the lunchtime room service order, Alice's poop consistency, mood, and the amount of milk she took at each feeding. I wanted to tell him about the meeting, the jar of Hershey's miniatures in the office and how they gave me the energy I'd needed to pitch. The way I realized, as soon as I walked in, that I'd gone to college with one of the executives. The way it felt when the guy came out to the elevators and said, "Sold."

"So anyway," I said, "the meeting was amazing." Jake put his arm over his head. I lay down next to him. "There was this jar of—"

"I want to hear all about it," he said, "but now I'm tired. I just want you to watch the baby for a while so I can sleep." I nodded but felt rejected.

I realized this was the price I would have to pay for having an involved husband: I wouldn't get as much me time. Gone were the days where I could go on and on about a passive-aggressive editor or difficult assignment, with Jake hanging on my every word. He just didn't have it in him to nurture both of us, at least not so early on in Alice's life.

I cuddled up next to him and leaned over to check on Alice in the crib. She was sleeping peacefully, her arms splayed out, above her head. I had just scored a deal with a major television network that would support my family for the next two years. I wanted a dry martini and a massage, but instead my husband and kid were sleeping and no one would talk to me. I went into the other room and took out my cell phone. "Dad?" I said. "I have good news."

Back in New York, I started writing the show and for the next two months, on the days Sonam wasn't working, Jake did about eighty percent of the child care. Sometimes I'd come home and there was only time for me to nurse Alice, put her to bed, and gobble down dinner before I had to lock myself up in my office and write for another four hours. One day I walked in and he was giving Alice her first bath in the bathtub. Until then we'd given sponge baths on her changing table. "I wanted to do that," I said, and started to cry.

"Honey, she was dirty and she needed a bath. I couldn't wait for you to get home." I wondered how many other firsts I would miss because I would be too busy working. I didn't know then that I would administer a thousand more baths on my own. I didn't know then that someday I would beg Jake to take over and do it himself, so trying was the witching hour between supper and bedtime.

In the winter the job ended and over the spring I began taking her out more alone and things evened out again. Jake got a studio and began to paint, Alice got on a nap schedule, we moved her to the second bedroom, and I made some friends on the playground.

Our arrangement is not what I imagined it would be. I do far more child care than I thought I would and I am surprised to find that I enjoy it. I like pushing her on the swings, taking her to the sprinklers, visiting the fat tabby that lives in the copy shop. And I have found that baby wrangling is a writer's best friend: fun procrastination.

I like the slow pace of baby care in contrast to the stress of writing on deadline. It allows me to get a taste of the stay-at-home life without having to live it every day. And the fact that I can support my family *and* spend time with my baby makes me feel lucky to have it both ways.

As a breadwinning mom, I very rarely feel guilty about working. Many of the other working moms I know are married to men who make great money. They could choose not to work and so they agonize over their choice to continue working. I will never be in this predicament because for me, work is not a choice but a necessity.

But do I worry about all the responsibility? Like any breadwinner, of course I do. I freak out that I'm not good enough, the work will dry up, we'll run out of money, have to sell our apartment, become destitute, and it will all be my fault. I don't like having so much financial weight on my shoulders, but I also have faith in Jake's work and have noticed that he's made more money in the years that he's known me than he made before he met me. When I get really paranoid, I ask Jake if he would go back to architecture to support us if he had to, and he says yes. I remind myself that, as the old Jewish saying goes, "When there is a baby, there's always an extra loaf of bread."

The other day while she was cruising in our apartment, Alice lost her footing and landed flat on her back, her head thumping loudly against the floor. (Why is it that the worst accidents happen when both Jake and I are a few feet away?) I rushed to her to comfort her and she reached for him. I handed her over and watched as he stroked her head, kissed it, and told her she was okay. A year ago I would have been wildly jealous and blamed myself for not being around enough, not nurturing enough. I would have castigated myself for being a failure of a mother.

But a year of motherhood has made me secure enough to know that it has nothing to do with me. She is in a daddy phase, and it is just that, a phase, one of many that she will go through in her childhood and a testament to how safe she feels with her father. As he sat in the armchair and held her, I watched from the floor. Then I reached for her again and this time, she came to me. I rocked her and kissed the same spot he had kissed.

breastlessness

· Elisha Cooper ·

I think my wife and I share the responsibility of raising our children in the most equal, enlightened, and perfect way, and I usually think this when she is giving our children a bath and I am sitting on the couch watching football.

Elise is an academic. I'm a writer. Our schedules are pretty flexible. During the days we both spend time with our children, taking them to the playground or the zoo. Around our home, we share the duties of cooking and laundry and cleaning (yes, we're perfect!). And yet, there are certain times, usually in the evening, when the responsibility is all Elise.

Women have breasts. Men don't. All the trouble starts there. Sometimes I think if women had one breast, and men had one breast, there would be no trouble in the world. At least, no trouble in the world of parenting. Think about it. Breasts, and the milk that comes out of them, provide that initial comfort from which attachment flows. Men, even the best-intentioned ones, are always one step behind, playing comfort catch-up (I don't count the three babies in America who turn to their fathers for comfort, or those with gay or single fathers). As the baby grows, even if both parents evenly divide the child rearing, there are still those moments—skinned knees, scared nights, soap in the eyes—when the mother takes over. This imbalance leads to resentment, then resentment of the resentment. Mothers often think fathers don't do the heavy lifting of parenting, which reveals itself in a condescending dismissiveness of men's parenting abilities, eye rolling comments like "Oh, just give me the baby." Fathers respond with dumb rationalizations about breasts. So, I take that back, the part about the breasts, even though it's true.

So we're a little stuck, warily circling each other. Young mothers and fathers, trying to even things out. And while balancing responsibilities is not a big issue for much of the world or the country—where raising children is woman's work and that's that—for an increasing number of parents it seems to be *the* issue that causes friction. It's confounding: If we imagine our relationships as equal, what do you do when they're not?

Before Elise and I became parents we had the idea that we'd do everything together. And then things like reality happened, and specifically, baths.

When our daughter was an infant, Elise and I both gave her baths. We lived in Berkeley, in an Arts and Crafts house that had an ancient blue-tiled bathtub the size of the bed of a pickup truck. It was easy for us to swim around in the pickup (though less easy filling it with water). There we were, four soapy hands washing our child together. It was great. But, if something happened to make our daughter cry, she would dive toward Elise. Elise's breasts always won out. I would stumble out of the tub, dripping. I likened the first months of fatherhood to being a sous-chef. Elise did the real cooking—the nursing, the bathing, the soothing—while I was scurrying around the house doing little chores, taking out the trash, scrubbing dishes. I suppose that if Elise and I were truly equal, we would have given our daughter baths on alternate nights. We would have insisted on dividing bath time. But on the few occasions where I did bathe my daughter, there always seemed to be that critical moment when I'd get soap in her eyes and she'd start flailing around and shouting an SOS to the mother ship. It was disconcerting. And it is precisely at moments like this that men retreat.

Of course, surrendering ground (or having it taken) is loaded and complex. After being dumped from the bath and finishing up my sous-chefing, I was able to sit on the couch and watch football highlights on television. And though I was needled with the sneaky suspicion that I wasn't trying as hard as I could with the baths, it didn't stop me. I was okay with not being needed. Was I incompetent, or was it that I wanted to be incompetent? The answer to both is yes.

Over the next two years our bath time routine solidified until it became fact. Elise had her responsibility. I had mine. Then we moved to Chicago. We said good-bye to the blue-tiled bathtub. We got another couch, another daughter. I spent the days with my daughters, taking them for swims in the great big bathtub of Lake Michigan. Since Elise was away for a larger part of the day now, she felt, like many working mothers, even more adamant about taking on nurturing responsibilities like bath time. That was fine with me. I cleaned up from dinner, then sat on the couch and watched sports. The couch was my little island of irresponsibility. There I had twenty minutes alone, barely aware of the rest of the family happily splashing around in the next room.

The arrangement worked well, until this winter. Elise had a bunch of trips, job interviews in Minneapolis, New York, Boston. Two days, two nights, she was *gone.*

Bath time would be up to me. At first I thought about not bathing the girls at all, but that didn't seem right (and Elise would notice). Then I thought about just spraying the girls with a hose out on the sidewalk, but it was February. So, on the first night that I was in charge, at seven o'clock, I started running the water, getting the water temperature just wrong.

I put the girls in. I took them out. I put them back in. Then I put my foot in, stubbed my toe on the hard hoof of a plastic giraffe, yelled, "*Fuck!*" I could tell this was not going to be pretty. The girls could tell, too. They huddled at the other end of the bathtub looking me wide-eyed, heads tilted to the side as if to say "Who invited *him?*"

It was as if their little oasis of female tranquillity had been inter-rupted by a loud and clumsy hippo. As I eased myself uneasily into the water, sending one tidal wave over the edge of the tub, another one in the direction of the girls, both of them started clambering over the sides to safety. Ten seconds later the "bath" was over.

The next night there was no bath. We jumped on the couch instead.

A few weeks later, Elise flew away again. I figured I should try to get back in the swim of things, so to speak. So I filled the tub, checked the temperature, put in the girls, got in myself, and started soaping them up. But as I was scrubbing one girl, the other one dove underwater. Then they switched places. The next five minutes were a blur of slippery bottoms and near drownings. Soap was everywhere, but nowhere it was supposed to be. More water was outside the tub than in it. There was a lot of shrieking, some of which came from my daughters. Finally, I gave up and placed one girl out on the wet floor, where she promptly fell. When I leaped out to help her she started doing pirouettes across the floor like an ice skater who couldn't land a jump, and her sister back in the tub took that opportunity to do an impersonation of an upside-down synchronized swimmer. I was stranded between the two of them, arms reaching in one direction, legs in the other, in an awkward and naked yoga position, unable to help either.

That evening could not have been worse, which, if you think about it, was not a bad place to start. After the bath, I wrapped the girls in towels and we sat on the couch. Their crying slowed and they leaned into me and I was able to comfort them, despite the fact that I had been the one causing them discomfort to begin with. As often happens in parenting, you go with what you've got. And I was all they had.

Over the course of Elise's next trips, something else happened. Maybe I learned the finer points of shampoo management or how to hold a slippery body. Maybe the girls relaxed, or maybe it was me. Because there were fewer tears. And when there were tears, I was able to soothe them away. On the last night of Elise's last trip, the girls and I had a calm twenty-minute tidal wave–less bath, followed by jumping and dripping in front of the television, watching football and shouting, "*Goooollllaaaa!*"

This was about the time that Elise walked in the door. After some wet hugs, after she brought the girls back into the bath to rinse the shampoo out of their hair, I felt sort of proud. I felt competent, or at least less incompetent (next time I will remember to rinse out the shampoo).

In the following days, we settled back into our old routine. Elise gave the girls baths, I cleaned up from dinner and watched television. As I sat there on the couch, I realized how initially I had given up too easily. And that while I was okay with Elise doing baths now, it was good to learn how to do the things you didn't know how to do. To be able to help in an emergency, or on the weekends: sort of like the National Guard.

the roles we play

Figuring out how to balance responsibility is ultimately a negotiation every couple must make. It won't always be equal. But it should be equally acceptable, so that neither parent feels like they're underwater, or, to switch the metaphor, getting kicked in the shins.

I should mention that the football I was watching was the kind where you use your feet. As a sort of reward for the winter days I had spent with the girls, I flew in the spring to England over a long weekend to attend two English Premier League soccer games. I saw two wild matches, one of which even ended in a brawl with fans from both teams streaming onto the pitch and punching each other. It was fun to watch, though I kept an eye on the exit behind me in case the fight on the field moved into the stands. Standing there, surrounded by burly guys with beer guts hurling insults at each other in odd accents, I was fully aware that I was enjoying this because I was a man. Not because of the swearing and the anticipation of violence, though that was pretty cool, but because I was here at all. Because, as a man, I could be away from home for four days. Elise could be away only for two (that's all she wanted and all our daughters would tolerate). There's just an inherent imbalance. It comes back to breasts. Women have them. Men don't.

As mothers and fathers struggle toward equality, the argument about how to divide responsibility in raising children will continue. But it is the wrong argument. Because it is *children* who should bear more responsibility. Think about it. Children are cute and lazy. They get away with everything. I suspect their whole act is a ploy, that they're fine with their parents arguing about responsibilities as it distracts us from their own idleness. This must stop. It's time for children (hey girls, I'm talking to *you*) to carry their own weight. To carry *our* weight.

Imagine. Young parents everywhere, relaxing in bathtubs the size

blindsided by a diaper

of pickup trucks, having their backs soaped and scrubbed and rinsed by little fingers. Afterward, warm towels. Then, a bottle of wine, a favorite book read out loud, tucked into bed with a song, another song, another song. Now *that's* a division of responsibility that women and men can agree on.

PART TWO

seeing
each other
differently

*M*y son's delivery was the usual grueling marathon. You don't need to know the boring details. What came *after* is what's important. I was beat, spent, bent. Back in my hospital room, my roommate was leaping cheerily out of bed to get her baby from the nursery, after perhaps having squatted in a corner to give birth and then celebrated by eating the placenta with some gal pals. She made it look that easy. I hated her.

It wasn't so easy for me. I couldn't even sit up—it hurt just to *think*. When the nurses brought Levi to me, he wouldn't latch on. He screamed, I cried. *You poor, poor thing,* I thought, looking into my darling baby's miserable face. *Could you have been born to two more clueless parents? How will you survive?* You notice I included my husband, Bill, in that reverie. That I assumed he was as uninformed about the parenting thing as I was. Because up until then, he was.

Oddly, I found that comforting. We were always pretty much on the same page about everything. Finished each other's sentences, held the same political convictions, ate the same pizza toppings, went to bed at the same time, wanted to leave parties at the exact same moment, blah, blah, blah. You'd have wanted to puke on us, we were so adorable. We were one of those obnoxious couples you hear about who meet on a Thursday, flirt at a party on Saturday, have lunch on Tuesday, and move in together by Wednesday. Done deal. Five years of total symbiosis later, we were in our twentieth hour of labor and he knew just by the mad glint in my eye that if he breathed his acid coffee breath in my face one more time, I would take his coffee cup and jam it up his . . . never mind. But *that's* how in sync we were.

Now, this is the key part, so pay attention: Enter Bill, the supposedly equally clueless father. Enter Bill, into my hospital room, who looked into my wild, frightened eyes . . . and proceeded to instruct me on how to care for Levi's belly button, swab his eyes, and wash his cradle cap; who showed me how to change diapers and explained what meconium was. Enter Bill, with lists and schedules and plans and routines and proper infant seat adjustments. He was as cool and unfussed as if he were just picking up dry cleaning instead of his half-demented wife and starving newborn son. All I could manage to do was traipse along behind, bleary-eyed, going uh-huh, uh-huh, yup, got it, okay, whatever you say, nooooo problem-o. And become filled with confusion.

With one ferocious push of my womb, I no longer knew my heart's twin. Where and when did he learn all this? What other surprises did he have up his sleeve? *Who was the tall guy and where did he come from and why did he think he could get away with telling me what to do?* Of course, it didn't help the matter that I didn't quite know who I was anymore, either.

"Oh, I picked it up somewhere," Bill said airily, with a shrug, and then went back to instructing me on the difference between the football hold and the cradle hold in breast-feeding. And when and where exactly had he gleaned this knowledge? Seemed to me he spent my pregnancy right alongside me, eating cherry-dip Dairy Queens and shouting out answers to *Jeopardy!*

In fact, when I first became pregnant, I very much wanted my husband to be a hands-on father, to share the child-care duties with me fifty-fifty. I had had a good chance of getting my wish. Since we are both freelance writers who work out of our house, neither one of us was ever going to be more than a hallway away from our baby. Still, I was taking no chances. I had indeed given Bill a copy of *The Birth of a Father*, a book that a male friend had gotten quite misty eyed over. Bill's response wasn't quite so moist. He read two pages and placed it on his bedside table. It now earns its keep in life by propping up our TV. Apparently, he didn't pick anything up there.

What have I gotten myself into? I had thought back then, more than a little panic-stricken. *He isn't going to help at all. This parenting thing is going to fall all on me.*

Ha. HA. And may I say HA once again? There's that old saying about being careful about what you wish for because you might get it. And in my case, I got a husband who was involved, creative, energetic, and instinctual in his parenting. The problem was, I wasn't expecting this. I wasn't prepared for this personality transplant. When I was at my lowest right after Levi's birth, thinking I had fallen down the rabbit hole, I reached for my Bill, expecting he would agree with me and say, "You're right. This is nuts. Who is this child? Do you think they're going to let us keep him?"

Instead, he became not just Mr. Capable but Mr. Super-Capable. We had a hired a nanny to help for a month after Levi's birth. Bill wanted to fire her immediately because, mainly, he felt he could do a better job. After a week, the nanny was gone. With Bill around, what was the point? Before I got up in the morning, Bill had already boiled the bottles and nipples. Breast milk I had expressed during the night had been labeled and stored in the refrigerator in date-appropriate order. Occasionally, he rearranged the hanging toy setup on the baby gym so Levi would have something new to play with. "It's stimulating for a baby's brain," Bill said with authority. As a former theater major, he was killer at creating new games and songs. And no one could make that baby laugh like Bill could.

Is it any wonder that Levi preferred Bill right off the bat? He must have sensed that the tall one knew what he was doing, as opposed to the short, tense one who kept poking him while he was trying to sleep. (I wanted to make sure he was really breathing. Was his stomach really rising or was it just a trick of the light?) This brought a whole new wrinkle into our relationship, a very attractive chapter I like to call Competitive Baby Raising, or Who Does Levi Love Best?

Was I complaining about Bill's aptitude, energy, and focus? Good Lord, no. Heaven forfend. I knew those exhausted mothers whose husbands left at 6 A.M., returned at 7 P.M., and thought they deserved a prize if they actually handed their wives a washcloth during the kids' evening bath time. I knew what gold I had.

And yet . . .

If Levi cried in the middle of the night, Bill calmed him. If I got to him first, Bill would lift him out of my arms to walk him around. At first, I was grateful for the chance to slip back to sleep. Then I became resentful of missing the chance to snuggle with my baby, to have my baby need me. But what was I going to do? Have a tug-of-war over an already crying child?

I'm not saying I didn't have a good relationship with Levi. There was nothing dysfunctional going on. We had a fine time. Sometimes babies just prefer one parent over the other. At least for a while. But in the beginning, when you're new to this parenting thing, what mother wouldn't have her soul knocked to her knees in those vulnerable moments—when her baby has bumped his head, woken up disoriented in the middle of the night, shied away from a stranger—seeing those little arms go up for comfort and reach not for her, but for someone else. For Daddy. So I lost confidence in myself, and by default, let Bill run the show, cowed by his seemingly unassailable confidence.

And what did this do to the "perfect couple"? Oh, we of the same pizza toppings, the single breath rising in complete harmony? I wouldn't say Bill and my relationship took a truly serious hit because of this. We were too close for that. But yes, it threw me. And yes, Bill did get a wee bit full of himself. And yes, I got a bit tired of being ordered around. I will confess to one or more unseemly crying fit and tantrum, ending with my stomping away from Bill and Levi, thinking, *Well, I hope you two are very, very happy together . . . assholes.*

As weeks went by, however, and Levi seemed to survive having me as a mother, the old me started to reemerge—and the old me wanted in on the game. The old me had a few things to say. Here is what I figured out:

1. Bill and I were not the same person after all.

2. Some of Bill's parenting ideas were actually kind of anal and stupid.

3. Some of my parenting ideas were not stupid AT ALL.

And most important of all: After watching Bill agonize for far too long over which brand of diaper would best wick away moisture, I realized what would've been obvious to me all along, had I been in my right mind:

4. My poor husband was just as nervous and anxious as I was about being a parent. He just dealt with it by compulsive organizing.

And with that, I got my groove back. I knew who I was: I was not Bill's shadow, I was Mama. And *no one* was going to take that away from me. I never actually shared these brilliant insights with Bill, but with those in my hip pocket, it was a whole new ball game.

One day, I picked up Levi and his breath smelled funny. I said, "There is something wrong with him. I'm bringing him to the doctor." (There seems to be a bad breath theme running through this.)

"For funky breath? Don't be ridiculous. You worry too much," Bill said dismissively. Something told me to override him (maybe it was that dismissive tone, which is always so charming), and I ran the baby to the doctor's walk-in hours. Turned out, Levi had a horrendous case of strep throat.

I found out that day that I was the instinct person. I've been right every time since. About Levi's asthma. About his iffy motor skills. About a lot of things that call for hunches and observation. Every time Bill said, "I think you are making too much of this," later on he had to apologize because it turned out I'd been right on the money. Bill lost that dismissive tone. Bill learned to take notice when, like Miss Clavel in *Madeline's Rescue,* I rose to exclaim, "Something is not right!"

I knew also when to let something go. When Levi spent most of his toddler years throwing up — hmmmm, there's a vomiting theme here as well — and relatives insisted he had food allergies, I knew he was a kid who just threw up a lot. Which indeed he was. Not an attractive trait, mind you, but not worth getting your knickers in a twist either.

As I found confidence, the family scales balanced a little more evenly. Levi no longer searched only for Daddy. Mama became a welcome sight, too. And with that, Bill and my relationship balanced out as well. Now that we could shed this silly pretense that we were the same person, we could separate and appreciate each other's strengths and weaknesses, and come back together in a stronger complement. We knew then to end the competition and to just send in the best man or woman for the job at hand.

Bill is the organizer. Let him put up his lists and Post-it notes, let him demand order and schedules if it makes him feel better. Don't get me wrong, there are times when Bill's rigidity gets to me: If he calls for one more family meeting, both Levi and I will pull out his nose hairs one at a time. But his organizational skills certainly make our world spin easier. Our kid slept through the night at six weeks and don't tell me Bill had nothing to do with it.

Thirteen years later, Bill does the homework brigade while I hide in the bedroom, because we all know that Levi and I will end up screaming at each other within minutes. I am the point woman in the schools (meetings, volunteering, glad-handing the teachers and administrators). I am the one who knew that Levi needed extra help in school and made sure he got it before his minor struggles became major issues. Bill shares his love of Broadway and theater. I find the books that keep Levi reading until 1 A.M. I am the one who says, "You are not quitting"; Bill is the one who says, "Give the kid a break." I know when to push and Bill knows when to back off.

I think it's fair to say that the previous pukers around us would all agree that we're no longer quite so adorable. There is more air and light between Bill and me these days. We no longer finish each other's sentences. Half the time we don't even know what the other is working on. We may no longer think exactly alike, we may crab at each other a lot more than before Levi came on the scene, and there may be times when we wonder just who it is we married, but we're definitely on the same team. For keeps. We've learned to trust each other, which is important. Even more key, we've learned to trust in ourselves as individual entities. We no longer need to be attached like lichen on a rock.

blindsided by a diaper

So this is the story of a couple that used to think that they were one. A baby split them apart, and made them see each other—and themselves—with new eyes. It turned out to be not so bad. In fact, they are a lot stronger for it, because they liked what they saw after the baby forced them to grow up. The End.

debunking the myth of the angel and the goon

· Andrew Corsello ·

A couple of months back, my wife gets on a plane to spend a week with her best friend from childhood. Back at home, me and the boys go a little wild, as we tend to do when Mom's not around to police things. We eat what and when we want, leaving the spoons and pans we use for cooking in the kitchen sink (without washing them, since we know we'll be using them again), and the spoons and pans we use for banging on the kitchen floor. Change our underwear and diapers when we feel like it, leave 'em where they fall; if Quincy, age three, declares while noodling on the piano that "I wanna be naked butt!" and then sheds his drawers, that's where they stay, next to the pedals, along with the pair(s) he dropped there the day before, and the day before that—as a testament. We go to sleep when and where we feel like it. As a convenience, we leave every bed in the house unmade, because, you know, there's no telling when somebody might want to jump in, or on, this or that mattress.

But I don't let the household devolve into *complete* anarchy. We are not animals. I get the boys nourished, dressed, bathed with enough regularity that their hygiene won't call attention to itself either way. I get Quincy off to preschool and his one-year-old brother, Casper, ready for the nanny. And I take care, as always, to gauge what's going into the ears and eyes with as much care as I gauge what's going down the gullets. That's why I make sure the boys are soundly asleep—Quincy on my left and Casper on my right—before I flip on the tube to catch an old episode of *Deadwood*.

Goddamn, how I love that show, its baroque obscenities, its unabashed celebration of *fucking* (the word) and fucking (the act). Toward the end of this particular episode, the show's preeminent vulgarian, Al Swearengen, spits out his disgust for "that bloated tick . . . that cocksucker, Claggett!" The way he makes a meal of the words, those furious alliterations, is just too much. I snigger.

Something in my peripheral vision. A subtle motion. An angling: Quincy's head, assuming the forty-five-degree left-to-right downward tilt that signifies rapture. And absorption. The boy isn't anything close to asleep. *How long . . . ?* He's upright, alert, soft-eyed, still. His palms are pressed together in his lap, as if in prayer. His hair, as ever—since I've never allowed it to be cut, and never will—is a psychedelic white cloud of curls.

I will provide no cue, no indication, I think. *Nothing to remember.*

I mute the tube. Though the boy's head reassumes an even plane, the eyes remain affixed to the television. I click the power button. The picture vanishes. We sit silently for a time in the weak light that comes in from the street. The eyes remain on the blackened screen.

"Hey, Q," I whisper. "What's up?"

Time passes. Has he heard me? At last, a tiny, faraway voice.

"Daddy?"

"Yes, Q."

"I need to tell you something, Daddy." His eyes are still on the screen. "Daddy, your balloon is going to pop."

I have no idea what the kid is talking about, but I run with it.

"Don't worry, sweet prince," I say. "My balloon is safe."

The next afternoon, while Casper naps, Quincy and I read in the living room. I'm halfway through Frank Rich's column when Q closes his book, points at me, and grins.

"Hey, you fuckin' man!"

No cue, no indication, nothing to imbue the word with power.

"What's that, Q?"

"Fuckin' man!"

His execution is gorgeous, with a heavy landing on the *f*— *fffffff*uckin'! — that constitutes its own syllable.

My son, it is true: It really is the funniest word in the world.

"Hmmmm. I don't think that's a word." I return to the *Times.* "You must have heard it wrong."

"Yes, it is a word, you *fffffffffff*uckin' boy!"

When Casper wakes, I take the boys to Barnes & Noble hoping in some vague way that books will undo what TV wrought.

"I wanna see the birds," Quincy announces.

Next door, at PetSmart.

"After Daddy gets his Philip Roth."

"I wanna see the birds."

"Duly noted. Hold on a minute."

"The birds. The birds."

"You know, Quincy, patience is a virtue."

It is then that Quincy sees fit to let the beast out of its cage.

"*Fffffff*uckin' boy!" he hollers. Three times in a row.

He not only understands the abstract music of the word, but how to employ it! That's my boy!

Those who stare (everyone) can't be blamed. Who's ever heard the F-bomb out of the mouth of a three-year-old? All those eyes, all those pointed thoughts, the silent and screaming imperative to *do something*, register as an unpleasant pressure in my ears. Quincy, too, feels the eyes, feels the judgment, that sour cloak gathering about both our bodies, and responds with a rousing take on "The Muffin Man," replete with a little skip step. His notes are pitch perfect, though the lyrics are a bit off:

Here comes the *fffffff*uckin' Man!
  The *fffffff*uckin' Man!
  The *fffffff*uckin' Man! . . .

DO SOMETHING.

Now here's the thing: Mine is an extreme temperament. Always has been. For whatever reason, in the face of great emotional or psychic pressure, I either *do* or I *don't*. There is no deciding. It's at the core of my character, this tic, and it's a real character flaw, too. There's the ghost and there's the machine, and when the shit starts flying, the machine takes over. Which means one of two diametrically different responses: either some kind of pointless, pyrotechnic, Tourette's-like display, or psychic vapor lock—an utter freezing up. Both are invariably out of proportion to what needs to be done. It's in large part the reason I do what I do for a living—or rather, how I do it (at home, alone). It's also the reason I've lost an impossible number of terrific girlfriends, and the reason I could lop off a couple of fingers and still count my good friends on one hand. I gave up on trying, or even hoping to change this . . . *thing* about me some two decades ago.

So here in Barnes & Noble, it's a foregone conclusion that my balloon won't weather this trial. The only question is whether it's going to pop or slowly hiss itself away. (Quincy's clearly placed his bet on the former.)

And yet, and *yet,* here's another thing. The *next* thing. I don't know how to describe it except to say that my balloon begins to rise. Up it goes, to a height of about ten feet. Then it stops. There it is; I am below it and it is above me. Yet, somehow, the reverse is also true. I'm also *up there,* an observing specter. There are my boys. There is their father. There are all those amazed strangers. This warm third-person hoveringness is not unlike what people who undergo near-death experiences sometimes describe. While everything I behold slows to a crawl, I myself feel as light and alert as a bat.

A man who looks like me, but isn't, lays a reassuring hand atop my older son's pretty head.

"Q," he says with a rueful smile, "you know better."

Some tone, some message inside or beyond the words themselves—*You are my son, you are my boy, you are all right, there is no reason to panic*—passes into the boy, dissolving his rage.

I ought to be shocked. This calm flies in the face of everything I have ever been and felt. But it's been available to me now for more than three years—since Quincy's birth. Until he, and his brother in turn, showed up and drew it out of me, I'd have scoffed at any suggestion that it was there, dormant. But it was. It's been growing, too, both in frequency and strength.

Nobody who knows me believes me when I try to explain the *thing,* by the way. They know my story. Even my wife, who lives with it, who has seen it time and again, who benefits from it, doesn't quite buy it. But then, how could she? She knows my story better than anyone.

So here's the story of my wife and me. I'll start with her.

When Dana was a very young girl, her cousin ran away for two weeks. Several days into the search, Dana had a clarifying moment.

Sitting with her aunt and uncle, beholding their terror and grief, she made a vow.

I will never cause such grief. I will be . . . good.

An astonishing ambition: Not just to act good, which is merely goody, but to *be* good, intrinsically. But she did it. Anybody who knew Dana as a child, or a teen, or a young adult, or who's in her life now, will tell you the same story. Hell, anybody who just *meets* her can tell you her story. With that big old pie-plate face of hers (her college roomies called her Pumpkin Head), she's as emotionally open and readable a human being as you'll ever meet on this earth. The woman radiates a goodness (a goodness less sweet than deep) and a motherliness that neither competes with nor diminishes her sex appeal. People want to be near Dana. It makes them feel, and want to be, good. There's an iconic childhood picture of her that I had framed a few years back when she was out of town and I felt like reminding myself why I missed her. In it, she's four years old. She's seated, clasping her hands, leaning forward, and in that smile, in that befreckled, beaming-moon face of hers, is a look of such giddy and innocent embrace of everything before it that it breaks your heart. It now greets visitors as they enter our home.

She's a priest, you know. An Episcopalian.

My backstory: I was an unpleasant child. Ferocious temper. Quick with the coldcock. Two refrains soundtracked my early years: "You're so immature" and "You have a *dirty* mind." I was less interested in questioning authority than terrorizing it, and I wasn't above employing my own poop to this end. In church, I pocketed cash from the collection plate. On the soccer field, my dirty tricks inspired parents (opponents', teammates', and once, my own mother) to howl for my ejection. After a couple of decades, I managed to mold the foul clay of my immaturity and sourness into a functioning self. (For a host of reasons, my college roommates called me Greasy.) There's an iconic childhood picture of me, too. In it, I am—as Dana is in hers—four years old. I'm sitting atop a large, flattened cardboard box and leveling a bitter squint at the cameraman (my dad), as my stumpy schlong pokes rudely through the fly of my cutoff shorts. This picture does not greet visitors as they enter our house.

Obviously, then, *our* story, Dana's and mine, the story of our marriage, is an opposites-attract affair: She's the angel, I'm the goon. The relationship draws its sustenance not from amity and unity but from constructive friction. ("Baby, you put the ho' in holy," I told her the day she was ordained; "Jesus," she responded.) Yes, that's it: My contradictory needs to be good enough for her on the one hand, and to corrupt her on the other, create a tension, the story goes—a tension from which a strong and sustaining current flows. Without my loogie-hawking antics, our relationship would wither. Does the way I'm rendered in this story bother me? Hell, it *affirms* me. Every time some friend remarks, "He married a priest, yes, but he's still an irresponsible pig," a deep and pleasurable *Yes* takes shape within me.

There's a funny thing about these kinds of stories, though. Once they start, they're hard to stop. They acquire momentum. They *metastasize*. Which is to say that other people began to expand the story of our marriage—the angel and the goon—to our children years before we actually had children. In the years preceding Quincy's birth, how many times was I subject to the punchline "God help us when Corsello becomes a father"? Not even half the number of times someone quipped, "Has that child been baptized?" or "Doesn't the court injunction say fifty yards *minimum*?" whenever I took somebody else's infant in my arms.

Jokes, all of them. Good jokes. I laughed every time. But were they *just* jokes? Of course not. Like all stereotypes, these jokes were based on a *there* there—that's what made them funny. That *there* presupposed a clear picture of what kind of parents Dana and Corsello would be. Dana, a called person, a person who knew exactly who and what she was, who always knew the right thing to do in any situation, would be the patient parent, the nurturing and responsible parent, the parent who would create structure in the lives of her children. Corsello, forever steeped in his own self-regard and studied ambivalence, prone to temperamental surges, would be the fun parent, the one who (yes, indeed) would let the house descend into a Fresh Killsian dump of pizza, poop, pans, and *Deadwood* profanity whenever Mom left town for the week. Fun, but . . . not a "real" parent. Because, as anyone familiar with the story could tell you, Corsello's a congenital flitter and fleer, a man-child with the attention span of a three-year-old. Capable, in love and work, of inspired bursts, but no good for the long haul. The unglorious *commitment* that constitutes ninety-five percent of good parenting (and, more generally, good love) would fall to Dana. When the going got tough, Corsello would do what he always does when the going gets tough: blow up or freeze up.

I'm not complaining. This is just something the human brain does, this reducing of the infinite complexity of other human beings into single, straight narrative lines. It's the only way human beings can comprehend and deal with the hellish enormity of other human beings. Those who have siblings come face-to-face with this phenomenon earlier than those who do not. "Johnny is the *X* one and Jimmy is the *Y* one." In the case of my older brother and me, it was always "Jack is the studious one and the athletic one; Andy is the rebellious one and the musically inclined one." *One.* One thing. One dimension. One story. By itself, that refrain was benign and more or less true. Repeated regularly over the course of our childhoods for friends and relatives and teachers, however, it posed the danger of determining, rather than reflecting, the story. We tend to rise or fall according to expectations, after all. (Incidentally, as aware as I've tried to make myself of this pattern, I often find myself realizing after the fact while tickling or hugging or playing with my children that I've just exclaimed, "Quincy, you are a *wild* man!" or "Casper, you are a *sweet lamb!*" for the umpteenth time.) They stay with us, these *X*s and *Y*s, these masks created for us in our childhoods. Even if we eventually strike through them—becoming who we are in spite of, not because of, what our parents told us we were—we still end up taking on, inhabiting, and dramatizing new stories devised for us by our friends and lovers.

So it is that Dana and I, without ever really thinking about it, have not only accepted but embraced the premise of the angel and the goon. In part, this is because that premise is endearing, and makes for merry conversation at cocktail parties. But mostly it's because, after a certain age, it's just too damn time and energy consuming to attempt to present one's self and one's marriage, in all their respective complexity and self-contradiction, to somebody who isn't your spouse, or something damn near it. Who can possibly process all that data anyway?

But then our babies came along, and yes, they changed everything. They changed the way we spend our time, of course. We saw that one coming. But the sheer *pressure* of their presence did something we didn't expect; it challenged and, in important ways, debunked the premise of our story. As with everyone who procreates, we discovered that who and what you are prior to parenthood by no means guarantees what kind of father or mother you'll be. In a way, fathers and mothers are like soldiers: No matter how well prepared, there's no telling whether they're fighters or fleers until the bullets start flying.

Without Quincy and Casper, I could have spent the rest of my days lazily (and happily) accepting and living out the cartoonish reduction of two souls that is the angel and the goon. But now that we're parents it needs to be said: Corsello *is* as capable as the next guy of spiritual transcendence, of *goodness;* and the halo-headed Dana *is* as prone to the flaws of the flesh as the next gal. Our friends *are* going to have to stop disbelieving Dana when she tells them that I spent my summer vacation singing evensong services in Westminster Abbey and Canterbury Cathedral with my church choir. And they *are* going to have to stop disbelieving me when I tell them that Halo Girl is a shopaholic and an occasional vulgarian willing to end a debate about whose turn it is to change a diaper, or get up with the baby, by snapping, "Oh, munch my [epithet too goonish to print]."

So you know that bit a few paragraphs back where I said I wasn't complaining? Well, fuck that. I *am* complaining. Because I've been slandered, Swift Boated as a dad even before I got into office, so to speak. And now I'm setting the record straight.

There's nothing complicated about it, really. This probably has something to do with the fact that in the first year or two, there's nothing intrinsically complicated about parenting. It's *demanding*, of course. But the challenge is quantitative, not qualitative. There are no decisions to make about what to do or not to do. There are only things to do.

The test—of our parenthood and therefore of our "story"—was immediate. From the instant he burst, ululating, from the womb, Quincy was ferocity. His first gesture was an emphatic, arcless jet of urine into the face of the doctor who'd delivered him. He refused to eat. He refused to sleep. He found all positions and locations unsatisfactory. Even the maternity ward nurses, those old pros, found the frequency and volume with which he expressed his displeasures to be "remarkable."

Now, when I say there's nothing complicated about it, I'm simply saying this: I did it. The tortuous work of getting up and staying up, night after night, week after week, doing what had to be done: I did it. In the first week or so, my ability to do it went without saying. The novelty—a boy! a wonderful, rowdy, screaming, suckling, pooping boy!—created its own momentum. But even as I did it, a subterranean fear began to rise, slowly and surely, to the surface: *Corsello's a flitter and a fleer, good for a show now and then, but incapable of the long haul.* I knew the story. Everyone knew the story. When the novelty wore off, when the boy was no longer headline news, when the well-wishers and casseroles stopped coming, the oppressive mundanity of it all would force Corsello to snap. Or freeze.

I don't know what else to say except: It didn't. I didn't. That is, snap or freeze. I just . . . *did.* Quincy didn't start sleeping through the night until he was two, and throughout that time, I did. And Dana? She did, too. She did. But can I be frank here? Not to the degree that I did. When it came to taking the boy for walks or drives from three to five in the morning, she didn't quite have what I'll call an *aptitude.* It's not that she wasn't a good mother. She was and is tremendous. It's that the burden of being endlessly pooped, in every sense, was just that: a burden. To me, it turned out to be something else. And something more. And, oddly enough, that *more* has to do with sin.

This is no story: In this life, my greatest sin is that of things left undone. I won't detail this sin here, except to say that my awareness of it takes form as a shrill and sinister voice, as ever present as the Brownian hum, that tells me that there is something else, something more, I should be doing.

Something else. Something more.

And yet on our first nights back from the hospital with Quincy, when everything fell to me (Dana was recovering from the cesarean), a different voice, calm and quiet and persistent in its own way, came into my head as I bathed and swaddled and comforted and fed bottled breast milk to my boy. *There is nothing else I can be doing. Nothing else I should be doing.*

Despite the *I* in that thought, it felt external in nature, less a voice from within than a blessing from above.

There is nothing else.

There was a hallucinatory disproportion to this voice vis-à-vis Quincy's. The boy's shriekings sometimes went on for hours. (In ensuing weeks and months, there came to be a fairly predictable point, around the half hour mark, where his mother would snap, "God*damnit*, I can't take this shit anymore!" and flee the house.) But the louder and longer he shrieked, the less I could hear him—and the more clearly I tuned in to that mantra.

Nothing else.

God, the immunity and impunity conferred by that voice!

And simplicity, too. Because what was to figure out about a screaming baby? There was an *entirety* to it, an objectivity, that I've never encountered before.

I have the attention span for this. I can stay up as long as it takes. I can take it. I can do it.

I am doing it.

Here's the truth: There is nothing like dealing with one's own screaming, shit-slathered spawn at three in the morning that better puts one *in one's place.* Because when Quincy was delivering his worst, there was nothing *else* for me to think about. For the first time in my life, I shed my own poisonous third-person regard, stopped looking at myself doing whatever it was I was doing and passing judgment of one kind or another. How strange: Taking care of Quincy in those first years was, objectively, a very loud and very unpleasant experience. But subjectively? It was quieting. And is, still. Fatherhood has quieted the furious mouse-on-a-wheel motions of my brain as nothing else ever has.

There was a time, before our children were born, when it seemed a certain kind of mystery had gone out of half my marriage to Dana, and out of half of our story. The reason was plain enough: I'd used up all of *my* stories. Being both an egomaniac as well as a professional storyteller, I'd served up . . . all of myself to my wife. I'd excavated everything from my past and left nothing to be discovered.

Dana, on the other hand, always had, and always will have, the mystery of her stories—precisely because she is *not* an egomaniac, and not a person for whom stories are the very currency of existence. It simply *doesn't occur* to her to tell this or that story about her past, because it doesn't occur to her why anyone besides herself would find them of value. Which means that living with Dana (especially if you feast on stories, as I do) is like living with the knowledge that here and there, under your house and in your yard, there are buried treasures that, once in a while, you'll be lucky enough to stumble upon.

Every three or four months, some gem from her past will plop out of her mouth and I will be astounded—despite my elation, I'll actually feel angry and even *betrayed*—by what she's been "withholding." I'd known the woman five years before I learned that in high school, she was the number-one-ranked cheerleader (not as part of a team, but *individually*) in the state of Colorado. I'd known her six years before learning she'd quarterbacked her school's football team (in *Texas)* until the seventh grade, when school officials decided such a thing was inappropriate. And only last month, after ten years, did I hear about the endless and ingenious fuck-yous her dear, departed mother, Reba, devised for her wayward alcoholic husband when Dana was a young girl. (Exhibit A: The night Reba unscrewed the shower head, filled its insides with red food dye, then screwed it back on; when the old man inevitably stumbled into the house at three in the morning and then, still fully clothed, into the shower, a minute passed before the screams began. "Jesus! Reba! I'm dyin'! I'm *dyin',* Reba, I'm *dyyyyiiiiing!*")

"How could you keep this from me?" I've whined whenever she's unearthed these gems, marveling all the while at the renewed mystery of the woman I married, and ruing the fact that I've got nothing of the kind to offer her in return.

But then our boys came into our lives, and with them, my unexpected capacity for calm. Just when she thought there were no mysteries left when it came to Corsello, when it seemed that no part of his story remained to be written, out came this new chapter. What Dana's cheerleading and quarterbacking, and her mother's shower-head tampering, have been to me, the storm-eye remove that comes over me whenever my kids are covering the two of us in screams and shit, or barking "Fuck!" in the middle of Barnes & Noble, has been to her. It mystifies her, my new evenness. Her experience of it isn't overt, or exclamatory, like my experience of her childhood tales, mainly because this *thing* of mine involves an absence rather than a presence. She feels it in the form of *assurance*—that I am capable of handling not just the everyday stress of parenting but, if necessary, actual calamity; that there resides within me a kind of insurance policy for myself and my family that has nothing to do with money.

For a long time, this role reversal of Dana's and mine, this debunking (or revising) of the angel and the goon, went unacknowledged. But then, about a year ago, we had one of those perfect storms. Quincy brought a stomach virus home from day care. It was terrible, terrible. Within twenty-four hours, the home was an epidemiological hot zone, with both boys and both parents voiding from both ends, racked with body aches, feverish, sleepless. There was much gnashing of teeth, much pulling of hair. On the second night of this, while Dana slept alone in another room, Quincy, Casper, and I spread out on the bed in the guest room. Then, just after two in the morning, and with spectacular synchronicity and symmetricality, both boys vomited upon me. Then began to shriek in horror. The stench, the screams, the steamingness—I found it all . . . weirdly calming. Eventually, from the adjoining bedroom, Halo Girl, sounding like a wounded gibbon, joined the screaming.

"*Goddamnit, I can't take it anymore! GODDAMNIT! GODDAMNIT! GODDAMNIT!*"

By the time she roused herself from bed, the boys and I were in the tub, devomiting. Their shrieks had ebbed to rueful moans. She stood in the doorway. She studied the three of us. She pieced together what had happened.

"God," she finally said. "How do you do it?"

I'd never actually heard the words out loud until I spoke them then.

"Darling," I said, "there's nothing else I can do."

where the bruises are

· Susan Maushart ·

I *met a life coach a few years back who promised he'd help me* "become more of who I was." He said that as though it were a good thing. I'm not so sure.

I never hired the life coach. But I did have three babies in four years, and in that time, you might say, I became so much of who I was I went into surplus production. On the down side, my marriage became more of what it was, too. Turbulent. Tense. Exhausting. Full of passionate ambivalence.

Nora Ephron says having a baby is like tossing a hand grenade into a marriage. When I first read that, I was still hoping for a negotiated settlement. Now that I'm divorced I know a baby doesn't really blow things up. (Grown-ups can do that all by themselves.) A baby *italicizes.* It takes what is there — a self, a pair, a family — and underscores it, amplifies it. Pushes it to its logical, and also its absurd, extreme.

The presence of a baby can no more destroy a relationship than it can save one. But it can and will enlarge it to the point of pixilation.

He was a doctor with beautiful, strong hands that smelled of soap. On our first date, I had three gin and tonics—for medicinal reasons only, you understand—and ended up outlining my history of infertility (if two years can be said to constitute an epoch) in clinical detail. His bedside manner was exemplary. "Perhaps you and your ex-husband didn't have sex often enough," he said. "People sometimes don't."

Two months later, I was pregnant.

He had two girls, eighteen and nine, from two previous, unwanted marriages. When he used the word *termination,* I honestly didn't know what he was talking about. He would not say the word *baby.*

"You don't love me," I said.

Two months earlier, we had gone swimming, stupidly, in a stormy sea and gotten caught in a rip current. We could have died, and we both knew it. We went back to my bedroom and made love seven times. And on Valentine's Day, he'd written me a poem—it was funny, and clever, and extravagant—to go with the chocolate and lingerie. We'd spent the day in bed, drinking ginger beer floats and watching *Casablanca.*

"It's *because* I love you," he said. "Terminate the pregnancy and, later, we can have as many babies as you want. I promise." His eyes were pleading.

"Just a blood sacrifice?" I taunted. "Well, why didn't you say so?"

Getting pregnant made me more of who I was, all right. Fifty pounds more. I hated that version of myself (me: the supersize pack), hated feeling rubbery and taut, like an overinflated pool toy.

I'd always expected pregnancy would feel ripe, but somehow or other I'd skipped ripe and gone straight to rotten. And I was not only disturbed by my body, I was disturbed by being disturbed. As a feminist, I felt duty bound to embrace my fecund woman-self, whether it made me gag or not. Rhetoric or no, what I saw when I looked in the mirror frightened me.

Would I have taken the changes better if I had been with a partner who welcomed the pregnancy, or even accepted it? Perhaps. But within the context of an already fragile relationship, the unexpected body blow to my self-worth made me vulnerable to a degree I would never have imagined possible. The balance of power between us—a transaction (I now realize) disastrously tied up with his status and my desirability—lurched.

He was Australian. I was American. Two nationalities that, on the face of it, seemed a match made in multicultural heaven: similar enough to be sustaining, different enough to add spice.

But once I became pregnant, and the deeper I advanced into parenthood, the more we were . . . *italicized.* The differences—in accent, in outlook—that had initially attracted us inverted, like some cheap optical illusion, in the blink of an eye. What was once enticing and exotic was now simply alien.

I realize now that I had fallen in love with an Australian archetype: the dry humor, the cheerful contempt for authority, the insistence—not always convincingly—on a "fair go" for all comers. But you can't have a baby with an archetype. And God knows you wouldn't want to marry one. I thought I knew what I was getting into, though; I had lived in Australia long enough to have also encountered the darker side of the Australian way of life—the parochialism, the arrogance, the sexism so unexamined it was almost exuberant. Yet when those same qualities revealed themselves in the father of my child, I was shocked.

While we were dating, he had seemed genuinely delighted by

my career success and the financial independence that went along with it. He was proud that I was a "serious" academic. (As opposed to what? I used to wonder. The kind that does stand-up?) It never occurred to me that I wouldn't have an equal marriage, that we wouldn't approach parenting as a fifty-fifty proposition. I was aware that the rest of the country was experiencing—now, how can I put this diplomatically?—a noticeable developmental delay in these areas. But we were different. Weren't we?

From his perspective—a perspective drawn from a harsh working-class childhood in an Irish Catholic family of ten—parenthood wasn't a "lifestyle option." It was more like a terminal illness. A life sentence. Children swallowed you up, like a great maw. And once over the threshold, there was no going back. Especially if you were a woman. One day you were Murphy Brown. The next you were the mother in *Sons and Lovers,* crooning mournful lullabies and blacking the hearth.

"We never talk to each other anymore," I'd begin. "Talk?" he'd reply. "You have your girlfriends for that." (This from a man who loved Joyce, who listened to Puccini and Fauré and Gregorian chants, who wrote poetry along with prescriptions.)

In truth, we both became flattened into paper dolls. He was The Man, who worked hard all day and expected "a bit of consideration" for it at night and on the weekend. I was The Woman, too distracted by love for my child—and too exhausted by the demands of caring for her—to mount an effective protest. It was as if having a baby released in him not his own inner child, but his own inner father: a man he'd feared as much as he'd loved, whose anger had smoldered like a damp fire in a too-small house.

Our experience was unusual in its intensity. But in other ways it was textbook stuff. New parents are often astonished—and appalled—at their own regression to gender stereotypes after the birth of a child. I certainly was. Family patterns I was sure I'd rooted out years earlier reasserted themselves with dismaying vigor in those early months, like some hardy, noxious weed. At times, I felt as if we were literally reading from a script of 1950s family life: "Not another meeting?" "You call that dinner?" "You're never here when I need you." "But what do you do all day?"

For any couple, the birth of a first child—no matter how joyously anticipated—constitutes both a culmination and a crisis. Which is why, as newborn parents, we experience delight and apprehension in roughly the same degree. A heightened sense of danger is an adaptive response, reminding us that our babies (and ourselves) need special protection. At the same time, it can close us down emotionally.

No wonder the issue of trust looms so large. A kind of structural paranoia seems to be part of the package, and whoever or whatever is not entirely with you is perceived as entirely against you. Perhaps there is simply no energy for discerning shades of gray.

Fear makes us "rigid," as we say. Which is why in a time of crisis we instinctively seek refuge in the familiar, the predictable. We become not only more of who we are, but more of where we come from. More gender bound, more role fixated, more hostage to class and culture. After all, there is safety in stereotypes. And in our craving for emotional comfort food, anything too novel, too challenging, too highly spiced may prove impossible to assimilate. Thus does parenthood make cowards, or at least conservatives, of us all—especially at the start.

It's all so very understandable once you think about it. The problem is, at the time, so very few of us do think about it. We are so focused on childbirth, we forget about the labor it takes to push a family into the world. And then we wonder why the mortality rate is so high.

"You never really know someone until you live with them," my mother used to warn. I used to think she was being dramatic. Now I

know she wasn't being dramatic enough. In fact, you never really know someone till you have a child with them.

Maybe you never really know yourself. In my own case, my sense of who I was culturally underwent a deep shift after my first child, and I was bemused to find myself becoming more and more "American" with each passing milestone. Even my accent became stronger. American, suddenly, was no longer a geopolitical designation but a question of identity, of tradition. Almost (I am tempted to say) of destiny.

I consciously sought out other Americans, for the first time since moving to Australia. My mothers group—the women who formed a human life raft for me in those early months—consisted of three Americans, a Brit, and a Rhodesian expat. I realize now that, in part, our group solidarity was all about *not* being Australian.

Before the baby, I hadn't really noticed how, or whether, I fit into the cultural landscape. Now I was conscious of feeling "foreign" for the first time. The local lingo—formerly a source of fascination—grated now. "Nappy" for diaper, "dummy" for pacifier, "pram" for stroller or carriage. Having to remember that babies didn't spit up, they "sicked up." That they went "down" for naps—like prize-fighters or drowning men—and woke up for "feeds." That, instead of a pediatric nurse, one visited the ominous "clinic sister," with her sensible cardigan and gleaming stainless steel scales. ("Why is your child crying?" she demanded to know during one early visit. "Possibly because she's a baby," I replied icily.)

I could have assimilated. Over time, indeed, that's exactly what I have done. What I have had to do. But my initial response was to cling to my sense of differentness. To wear it like a flag.

Having a baby did not create irreconcilable differences in our relationship. But it did expose them. It did rub them raw. Our relationship had always been all-consuming. Even at our best, we'd had a tendency to be emotional demand feeders, draining each other with a frequency and an intensity that excluded others, and exhausted ourselves. With a baby to care for, such profligacy was no longer possible, or even thinkable. Now, I came to the relationship premasticated, as it were—chewed up and spat out by the demands of new motherhood.

There were times when I longed to get both of them, husband and daughter, onto a schedule. But I never succeeded. It was a case of constant nurture on command, with both stakeholders vying loudly and indignantly for attention.

Yet, compared with the primal, urgent tasks of infant care, my partner's requests for service (as I then construed them) seemed so petty, so beside the point, so *babyish. Who cares if your shirt is wrinkled?* I'd fume silently as he huffed and puffed his way through the wardrobe each morning, sighing ostentatiously. I felt much the same way about his not-so-subtle hints about sex and "proper meals," which is to say, disinterested to the point of wonderment.

I realize now he was looking for a sign that I valued his contribution, as breadwinner, to our life as a family. I knew, even then, that he felt taken for granted. But the truth was actually worse than that. I was beyond not being grateful that he went out to work and I didn't. I was resentful. Not because I really wanted to be in the workforce. (I was so desperately bonded to my daughter at that stage, I could barely journey to the basement to do laundry without misgivings.) But because I understood the workforce. I knew who I was there. At home, I didn't . . . not yet.

But then I'd always loved my job and considered it a privilege. He'd despised his and felt "real life" happened elsewhere. The result was we both felt aggrieved. The *Who Has the Harder Job?* show had begun—and it ran for more seasons than I care to count. Inevitably, we both ended up losers.

And yet the possibility that we might have switched roles was beyond imagining. That's a fact I find, in hindsight, both tragic and telling. I can't help but wonder what life might have been like for us had we been able to cast off the deadweight of our own unexamined assumptions.

I resented his hands-off approach to parenting, but I can't honestly say I encouraged him to be a more active father. I never exactly withheld the baby. But I did have a habit of taking her with me wherever I went: shopping, the office, the bathroom. It just felt safer that way. In the evenings, if she had been fed, cleaned, and snugly wrapped, he would hold her for perhaps an entire local newscast at a time, till she drifted off. But that was all.

In retrospect, I can see I was in some ways what the literature calls a "gatekeeper"—someone who subtly but unconsciously discourages a partner's help in a bid to retain control. It was a perfect way to punish both of us—all of us, really.

He'd made it clear at the outset he'd never really wanted us. On some level, I was making clear that the feeling was mutual.

When our daughter was a few months old and settled into what seemed a predictable sleep pattern—waking only once in the night—I started rising at 5:30 to take the dog for a run on the beach. I remember the shock of recognition the first time I threw myself headlong—cracked nipples aquiver—into the surf. I surfaced with the transfiguring assurance that I was, despite it all, still me. The sun was the same old sun, and Jack—still barking at the temerity of the Indian Ocean to advance and retreat without permission—the same old Jack.

One day, perhaps a week or two into the new routine, I came home to find the baby awake and the man colicky. "She woke up, and you weren't here," he said coldly. "She's hungry." The next day it happened again. And that, as we both knew without having to say it, was that. My run on the beach was his ironed shirt: a small gift, the withholding of which was so pointed (or so it seemed), so disproportionately wounding.

It was as if the fissures in our relationship, which, when viewed from above, had made such interesting patterns, now deepened into chasms. As far as empathy for my partner's plight goes—and "plight" was exactly how he experienced our child's infancy—frankly I had none. I was so totally "with" my daughter in all the minutiae of her newborn life, nothing and nobody else stood a chance. "Try to see things from my point of view," he'd plead. *What?* I'd think. *Why?* Now I can see what he was getting at. He'd already been through this transition, twice in fact. He was forty years old, in a job he despised, clinically depressed and numb with self-loathing. I can see all that now. Then it was as if my emotional intelligence had dried up like spilled milk on a hot day. And I still don't know why.

We had two more babies together—astoundingly, it seems to me now—before we split up for good. When I ask myself why on earth we stayed together as long as we did, the answer is as clear as it is utterly mysterious: Those children could not not have been born. And everything else is just conjecture.

It is a truism that trust is at the heart of every strong relationship. My experience taught me that, where there are gaps in that trust, new parenthood—like some powerful ultraviolet light—will cause them to fluoresce. And the flaws that were hidden from ordinary sight loom up unmistakably in its glow.

I suspect that every relationship, regardless of its tensile strength, must bend under the weight of new parenthood. Some exhibit remarkable resilience. Others sag, or scar. And a few, inevitably, give way entirely. My own was the last kind.

So having a baby, I am convinced, doesn't really change a couple for better or for worse. It simply makes you more of who you are. Peeling you back like a piece of fruit and showing how all the sections fit, and where the bruises are.

to jealousy and beyond

· Elizabeth Larsen ·

My *y husband, Walter, flipped our two-year-old son, Peter, over* his shoulder and ducked and spun, Tilt-A-Whirling across the nursery. Peter's head bobbed against Walter's back, oblivious to both the potential whiplash and the pulsing of his cheeks and ears, now hot and wet and red from bouncing upside down. As the path of their orbit shot them dangerously close to a lamp, Walter slowed down.

"More, Daddy," Peter yelled. "Spin more."

Walter sped up, and Peter's laugh broke apart into a cackle. Finally, when it seemed as though Peter might pass out from so much excitement, Walter flopped him onto his new big boy bed and spread kisses all over his delicious little body. "I love my boy," he cooed. His voice was high and singsongy and completely uninhibited.

I watched my family from the doorway. It would be obvious to anyone that these two were father and son. They had the same slender torsos, the same tea brown hair hanging straight across their foreheads. But beyond the physical similarities, there was an invisible current buzzing between them, an understanding I could feel from across the room.

It's a connection between father and child I'd fantasized about when I was pregnant and Walter refused to read a single pregnancy book or sing to my belly or engage in any late-night fantasy sessions about who our child would one day become. In fact, the only time Walter ventured into any what-ifs was when I admitted that I hoped the baby's hair would be curly, like mine. "That's not genetically probable," he explained as he set to work on a diagram of *X*s and *O*s to prove that our baby's hair would be straight. (The ungovernable blond ringlets of our now-middle child, Henrik, proved that Walter might want to retake tenth-grade genetics.) I interpreted Walter's unwillingness to depart from the safe facts of science as a sign that he was too detached. That maybe he wasn't cut out to be a father.

Now that he is a father, and it is clear that my worries were unfounded, this tender scene should have delighted me. Instead, I felt like an intruder. Adrenaline blasted from my chest to my cheeks as I imagined pulling Walter off our child so that I could be the one to lose myself in kisses.

I willed myself to get a grip: *This is my family,* I reasoned. I decided that I just needed to join in on the fun.

"How are my guys?" I asked as I jumped on the bed. Walter turned his chin up and kissed me on the collarbone. He seemed happy to have me there. Peter peeked out from the cocoon of Walter's body and grinned. He looked at me again, and then at Walter.

"Mommy away," he said. His words weren't mean, or delivered in a tantrum of frustration. There was no unspoken agenda, no attempt to soothe his message through euphemism. Peter was simply stating the obvious: He wanted to be alone with his father.

seeing each other differently

I looked at Walter. "Mommy away" had been an occasional refrain for about a month. We were both bewildered by it, but all the toddler books reported that preference for one parent (usually the mother) is a normal stage. It was important, the books counseled, that the rejected parent not make the child feel guilty for expressing what he wants. Because I was still relying on those books to help turn me into what I hoped could pass as an actual mother, I took this advice seriously.

"Daddy's great," I chirped, a smile pasted to my face. "It's great to want to play with Daddy." I wasn't sure why I was pretending to not be upset. Perhaps in my insecurity I was still unsure about whether or not it was okay to tell my child (without making him feel guilty!) he'd hurt my feelings. Regardless, I was fairly confident that "Fuck you both" wasn't a response sanctioned by those friendly baby and marriage experts.

I retreated to our bedroom and buried my head in a pillow. Even though I was ashamed of this miniature tantrum, part of me knew that many a mother—trained as we are to expect most-favored-nation status—would be jealous if her child preferred his father. As much as I wanted to believe all the cant I recited about coparenting, I couldn't help stewing over how Walter had stolen my inalienable right to an exclusively passionate relationship with my child.

Unfortunately, Peter's preference was only the topical sting of a deeper burn. The truth I didn't want to admit was that I was also jealous of the way Walter unabashedly worshipped our child. Loving Peter exposed a hidden chamber in Walter's heart. When I watched them play, a piece of my own heart smarted with the same intensity that I imagine I'd feel if I walked in on Walter making love to another woman.

That Walter adored our child wasn't the problem. It was that he loved him with an over-the-top abandon that he never showed me. I married Walter secure in the knowledge that he was a good man and that we were a good couple. But after we became parents, I realized that good wasn't enough for a lifetime together. I wanted more. The truth was that I had always secretly hoped for more passion and openness in our relationship, but had reconciled myself to the fact that the man I adored would never become a sensitive new-age guy. Finding out that he was should have made me hopeful. But it wasn't with me! Instead I feared that we really didn't know each other, that our love wasn't that strong.

I also worried that the reason I was excluded by the two people who know me most intimately was because I deserved to be. I might have appeared to the rest of the world as a competent and caring wife and mother, but perhaps my husband and son understood the truth: Maybe I was the rusted, wobbly tire on an otherwise well-oiled tricycle. I felt invisible, like I could float to the outer reaches of the galaxy and hang there, alone, for infinity.

Jealousy and I were never strangers. Before Walter, a hang-up call or a woman's phone number crumpled up in a boyfriend's pocket sent me raging through address books, journals, even the alleys behind suspected lovers' homes. But even though I may have let myself go too far in my reactions, my jealousy was never delusional. Rather, it was like a carbon-monoxide detector warning that an unnoticed but lethal danger lurked. Part of why I was attracted to Walter—in fact, the reason why I instinctively knew we could get married—was that our relationship always transcended that unruliness. I felt safer with Walter than with any man I had ever known because he was startlingly honest. In fact, Walter was the first man I'd been with romantically who was unwilling to have me see him as more than he was. For instance, after work, he drummed in a band. A mutual friend had told me Walter was an exceptionally talented musician, but when I trolled for this information, Walter pulled me back down to earth. "I'm pretty good," he said. "But no one makes it in that business. It's really just a hobby."

Two years after we married, when studying for his music teacher's license required weeknights in a practice room with Miraslava—a Ukrainian pianist with more than a passing resemblance to Botticelli's Venus—I knew he would never do anything to jeopardize our marriage. Our relationship, as I saw it, was a loving and sturdy miracle built out of mutual respect and a bullheaded determination not to go the way of our own divorced parents.

Now, when I watched Walter with Peter, I couldn't help but feel cheated. Cheated of the love I felt I deserved but didn't feel I had. And cheated of the affection I had perhaps hoped for as a child. My father's love for me is something I never questioned. But the truth is, he traveled and worked eighty-hour weeks to provide my three sisters and me with the kinds of opportunities that he—a child who was raised during the Depression by a single mother—could only fantasize about. I didn't experience the same kind of hands-on love with him that Walter gives our children. I was questioning everything, past and present, and became very afraid that my paranoia and discontent were going to send our relationship skidding into a ditch.

In her 1957 essay "Envy and Gratitude" Austrian psychoanalyst Melanie Klein wrote that jealousy "is mainly concerned with love that the subject feels is his due." According to Klein, jealousy is based on envy, or the angry feeling that another person possesses and enjoys something that you desire. "The envious man," Klein writes, "sickens at the sight of enjoyment."

While I never actually *sickened* at the sight of Walter and Peter's enjoyment, Klein's insights cut deep enough that I could see we were not living out a feel-good story. Mostly, I blamed myself for our predicament. What mother and wife, after all, would want to deny her child and husband the magical bounty of each other's love simply so she didn't have to feel bad about not having it all to herself?

One night after Peter had fallen asleep, Walter practiced a Scarlatti sonata on the piano. Between songs, I calmly asked him why he wasn't as demonstratively *out there* with me as he was with Peter. His hands went limp on the keyboard, and he stared at the music, his tongue not even attempting to form a word against the roof of his mouth. I could tell by the way his lips were pressing together that he thought the question was preposterous. When I turned to storm out of the room, he looked up.

"You can't compare the two," he said. "They're completely different. Loving a child is so one-way that it's almost like loving a pet. It's not so complicated. It's safer."

Satisfied with his answer, Walter returned to the sonata. His rhythm was smooth, but occasionally he hit a wrong note, and it carried through the room with the energy of a cavity touching tin foil. He kept trying, every version a little less jarring than the one before it. His fingers searched the keyboard for the answer to our unresolved conflict. When he finally found the perfect note, even the furniture appeared to sigh in relief.

I, however, was in a rage. A *pet*? "How could you compare our child to an *animal*?" I broke in, not owning up to the fact that what I had really wanted Walter to say was that he loved us both equally.

"That's not what I meant," he answered. "And you know it."

"How would I know?" I was yelling now. "How do I know anything about you when you keep it all tucked away inside?"

Walter closed his music. "What do you want from me?"

The answer was suddenly obvious. And for the first time since we became ensnared by jealousy, it seemed neither selfish nor unattainable.

"I just want *more* of you," I said. My face wrinkled into a long, aching sob. "I don't want you to love me the way you love Peter. But I want you to trust me enough to let me see the parts of you that neither of us knew were there before he was born." I was so pleased with this answer that my tears stopped. I almost smiled.

Walter shook his head, and closed the piano lid with enough of a thud that a few stray notes vibrated in the air. "I'm not sure I get what you mean," he said. "Loving you and Peter are so different that I can't compare them." His tone was so rational that I swung to the opposite extreme. I wished he would stand up and call me a bitch, rage out of the room, throw a chair. I wanted him to do something, anything, to prove to me this argument raised his pulse above sixty.

Before this exchange, I thought we were battered but unshakable. Now, less than five minutes later, I worried that we were the most fragile, mismatched couple on earth.

Walter and I didn't resolve this fight. Or the one after it. Or the one after that. It took years for Walter and me to wrangle our way out of this stranglehold. Years that involved both of us brooding on opposite sides of an uncomfortable couch while a well-intentioned woman jotted notes and asked mortifying questions about our sex life. And then still more years of my lying down on another couch, confiding my secrets to a disembodied voice behind me. For months at a time, my jealousy eased up, like a braid being freed from its elastic. And then suddenly it was back, not only replaited, but twisted and pinned into a tight bun.

If there was any single moment that made me understand our family dynamic differently, it came in the fall of 2002, when Minnesota senator Paul Wellstone and his wife, Sheila, and daughter, Marcia, died in a small plane crash while campaigning for Wellstone's third senate term. By then Walter and I had two children—Henrik was now six months old. Like most Minnesota Democrats, I revered Wellstone, and I coped with the raw shock of his death by watching every possible television program related to his life, his work, his death. At the memorial service, held in a sports arena, over twenty thousand people raged with a grief that felt more like a crate of fireworks that accidentally caught a spark than the tightly somber rituals of a funeral. The crowd booed when prominent Republican faces flashed across the JumboTron and cheered when Democrats encouraged those assembled to "fight for Paul." Minnesota governor Jesse Ventura stormed out when the tenor of the eulogies started to sound more like campaign rallying cries. For weeks, Washington experts theorized about the effect the memorial would have on the election.

What moved me most, however, was something not a single pundit mentioned. When eulogizing his father, mother, and sister, David Wellstone—one of Sheila and Paul's two surviving sons—made an unconventional choice. "I saved my mother for last," he told the crowd, "because she held everything together for us. My mother was *everything* to us." His voice catching, Wellstone went on to describe the cold washcloths she wiped across his hot forehead when he was ill and dinners cooked specifically to suit her children's picky tastes. And while he made it clear that he also wanted her to be remembered for her professional accomplishments—after her husband became a senator, the former librarian went on to distinguish herself as an expert on domestic violence—his most important point was that simply by being his mother, she defined him. The Clintons and Al Gore and Ted Kennedy didn't fly to Minneapolis because of Sheila, but to her remaining children, her loss was perhaps the most devastating. It was then that I realized that mothers provide an almost unnameable core to their children's existences. Hearing the broken tenderness in David Wellstone's voice made me finally understand that I, too, am at the core of my children's lives; I don't need to fight a popularity battle within my own family. My children love me. And so does my husband. I know this now even if it's not always shown according to my predetermined specifications.

seeing each other differently

That's not to say that I don't still get those green-eyed pangs every once in a while. In fact, just the other day the sight of Walter snuggling with our youngest child, Luisa, began to stir up those unattractive emotions. The difference is that now I know that their affection isn't occurring at my expense. And that my yearning for my husband is instead a sign that we need some time together away from the three young souls who have colonized our hearts.

confessions of an FP

· Rick Marin ·

Men underestimate women. When I was single, my girlfriends were all charming, intelligent women whose careers were still in the "promising" stage. They were assistants, cub reporters, subeditrixes—entry-level media slaves of one kind or another. I recognized their intelligence and ambition, but could never picture them rising above their station. Years later, I would be surprised, shocked even, to see one become a high-powered literary agent, another be appointed editor in chief of a magazine, still another win an Emmy Award.

Clearly, I lacked vision, impaired as I was by the vodka goggles I wore throughout my late twenties and early thirties. When, finally, I married the woman who saved me from those days of whine and poses, I made the same mistake all over again. Not about her career prospects—of those I had no doubt. I thought she'd be a bad mother.

seeing each other differently

Ilene and I put parenting off as long as we could. We'd been together five years before getting engaged, seven before the arrival of our first child. "Why mess with a good thing?" was our flip defense of our happily unmarried, child-free life. But clocks were ticking. If we waited much longer, it was going to take a team of cloning specialists, science-fiction writers, and some form of time travel for us to reproduce. We got pregnant under the wire, and after the initial shock and elation was over, the fear set in.

Not quite the mortal terror I experienced with my first marriage, which was filled with pregnancy "scares." I'd wake up with night sweats every time my child bride was late. She was—how shall I put it gently?—somewhat eccentric. Her idea of familial bliss was to move to a trailer park in Oklahoma. I'd picture our diapered infant staring through a rusty screen door as his mother trotted off in her Diary Queen uniform each morning while I eked out a living on my dusty laptop.

It wasn't that kind of fear with Ilene, more like a localized anxiety. And so I don't come off like a total bastard, I should mention that my worries about Ilene being bad mommy material were based on her self-avowed babyphobia. She was a scowler at screaming infants on airplanes. She liked to point out that the happiest couples we knew seemed to be the ones with no kids. I'm not sure she'd ever even *held* a baby before, much less fantasized about having one. Her view of parenthood was more than a little fatalistic. The word *doomed* was thrown around. She couldn't help seeing childbirth as the beginning of one life and the end of her own.

Then along comes little Diego and, within minutes of the blessed event, Ilene was nursing, swaddling, making up songs to lull the baby to sleep. Her predicted resentment of Baby D as a drain on her time, energy, and milk supply never materialized. If anything, she suffered from postpartum elation. As did I, not only at the sight of our dimpled little lad, but also at being proven wrong about Ilene.

I loved watching her surprise herself, and me, with her mothering skills, Diego on her stomach moving his tiny arms and legs to James Brown's "I Feel Good."

I especially loved watching her feed, bathe, and play with him, as I was useless at all these things. I loved him, but I had absolutely no idea what to do with him. The best I could do was shake the occasional stuffed animal in his general direction. The only time our baby nurse left him in my charge for an afternoon, I hovered over his bassinet for two hours praying he wouldn't wake up, because then what would I do? I couldn't even get *myself* up in the morning, much less cobble together a bowl of rice cereal for him.

How was I rewarded for my third-wheel incompetence? By becoming the Favorite Parent, the "FP," as we came to call it. Ilene planned all our lucky offspring's home-cooked meals, ministered to his every ailment, assiduously tracked his motor and mental development. But a few months in, it became clear Diego was a daddy's boy.

When he cried, he reached for me. When I left for the gym in the morning, he'd stand by the window on tiptoe looking for me. When we came home at the end of the day, the one he toddled to was me. Ilene woke at the crack of dawn to get him up and changed and fed, always with a smile on her face, and the first words that greeted her were "Dada? Dada? Dada?"

As his vocabulary grew—"ball," bubbles," "uh-oh"—so did his myriad iterations of Dada. From the short, inquisitive "Where is he?" to the demanding "Come here, please!" wail to the appreciative "He's up to his old tricks again" chuckle when I performed some piece of shtick that had become one of our running jokes. He had what Ilene called a "symphony" of ways he'd say Dada. But still no "Mama." And it was starting to get to her.

I realize that the FP phenomenon—choosing one parent over another at certain ages—is not uncommon. I've read the UrbanBaby .com posts from disgruntled mamas complaining that they do all the work and dada gets all the love. How do you think it makes us FP's feel to be put in this position?

Well, good, of course. Great, in fact. Who wouldn't want to be the FP? You're a hero just for walking in the door. As I basked in the glow of his adulation, my parental confidence soared. I came into my own. I worked up an entire stand-up act of running jokes involving Indian accents, Jonathan Winters' old "Big Fig Newton!" commercial, and a new martial art called "baby fu." Diego's laughter was like crack, and I was as single-minded as any junkie about my score.

I milked my FP status, even though I knew deep down it made Ilene feel worse. He still wasn't saying "Mama"—at a year-plus—and she was starting to lose it. A notation in my diary from September 18, 2005, says, "When IR is changing D for bed, he hits her."

This was when she said for the first—but not the last—time: "He hates me."

"He doesn't hate you," I said. "He loves you."

"No he doesn't. He hates me."

I said she was exaggerating. She said I didn't know what I was talking about.

On September 19, the next morning, my diary reads: "IR gets up with D, reports that he's still mad at her. Says he looked 'sullen' when she came into his room to get him up. Yelling at her during breakfast as she was reading the paper."

After Diego's breakfast, Ilene came into our bedroom, where I usually was at that hour: sleeping.

"Now I know why people beat their children," she said.

"This is getting too weird for me," I said, jumping out of bed and into the shower.

"Sorry," Ilene said, seeing she'd freaked me out. "Bad taste."

I felt the old anxiety coming back—the bad-mommy fear.

A month or so later, Diego and I were playing in his room when he slammed the door on Ilene. I'm still not convinced he knew she was coming in when he slammed it. If there was an open door, he had a primal urge to close it. But this pushed her over the edge. She stormed out to the grocery store.

I gave him his bath that night, because Ilene was "on strike." I began to wonder darkly about what would happen if she crapped out and left me a single dad. Bath time I could handle. But I dreaded the prospect of changing a diaper in a public restroom. So I definitely wanted us to stay together, at least until toilet training.

Some days Ilene didn't think her son hated her.

"He tolerates me," she'd say. "He loves you."

I began to believe her. Not that Diego hated her, but that she felt like he did, which was all that really mattered. The eternal male-female struggle is between fact and feeling. In arguments, men are always trying to parse the objective truth of *what* was said and *when*. Women deal in the subjective: how whatever was said made them *feel*. Empathy was not an emotion I suffered terribly from in my dating days, and this was the first big test of it in my married life. Ilene was afraid she'd hate being a mom, ends up loving it, and in return she gets slammed doors and swats on the nose.

One day, I saw the hurt look on her face when she tried to console our crying Diego after he'd taken a spill and he turned to me instead. That look made me stop worrying about whether she was a bad mommy and how many diapers I'd have to change as a single dad. I stopped reveling in being the FP and tried to figure out how to be the GH—Good Husband. Which is never easy.

First, I tried to spin. I vouched for the intensity of a son's love for his mother. One of life's great givens! It's why sailors tattoo MOM on their biceps. Why football players caught on camera say, "Hi, Mom!" Why Norman Bates . . .

That didn't work.

Next, I argued that the mother-son bond is closer than fathers and sons ever get because boys see their mothers as an extension of themselves. (I was cribbing from the breast-feeding part of our birthing class here.) I told her I'd say things to my mother I never would have dared say to my dad, how I'd mock and abuse her if she neglected to correctly butter my toast.

That didn't work either.

Then I suggested being more physically affectionate. Neither of us is the smothering type, and Diego was never a cuddly baby. No sooner do you scoop him up in your arms than he says "Down" and wants to play. Still, Ilene followed my advice and tried being more huggy.

That *really* didn't work. It only made the rejection sting more.

"I've lowered my expectations," Ilene said with a bitter sigh of resignation and tristesse.

This was getting bad. I didn't see a way out. And there were ramifications for the FP, notably a disturbing development called "alternating mornings."

If Ilene wasn't going to be appreciated for rising at 6:15 A.M. to make her son french toast and freshly squeezed OJ, then I could damn well start doing my fair share. Regrettably, this was impossible.

No matter how much Diego cried or called for me in the morning, no matter how much Ilene tried to shake or shove me awake, I'd still try to buy five more minutes. Shameful, I know, but I'm functionally useless at that hour. Rather than let her son starve in his crib in a wet diaper, Ilene stepped back up to the plate. Getting up early, sorting out his meal and changing his clothes. Overcoming her own hurt feelings to care for him when he was sick. Firing the bad nanny. And in general showing the patience and strength of character it takes to be a truly good mother. This from the woman who once suggested airlines should have a separate class for babies, somewhere near cargo.

Half—maybe more—of being a parent is just to keep going. That's what I did with Ilene. There were no magic words. I just kept saying the same things to her over and over. She says that's what helped her keep going with Diego until, in time, the "he hates me" phase phased out.

He now bleats "Mama!" if she's not around. As she sings him to sleep at night, I hear the two of them giggling over their own inside jokes. And two years after Diego was born, along came another little boy: Kingsley. Ilene once again proved a natural in the mothering department. This time it was reciprocated—and then some. In Kingsley's early months, I'd go for days without a smile, while he beamed and cooed whenever Mama was near.

Once again, I'm guilty of underestimating the woman in my life. Bad enough she turns out to be a superb mother. Now she's the new FP.

*I*t's a glorious moment steeped in atavistic ritual. The groom stands anxiously at the altar resplendent in black tie and tux. The dewy young bride glides down the aisle to join him. The wise officiant earnestly asks whether they will love each other faithfully . . . for better or worse, for richer or poorer, in good times and bad, until death does them part. And then, after each says "I do," they are bound together inextricably for life. . . .

Or just as likely, until one of them wants out. Our young newlyweds are not married for life at the point of walking down the aisle. Not yet. Not when their marriage could easily succumb to a wandering eye, the seven-year itch, or irreconcilable differences. Not when they could walk away from their solemn rest-of-life vows for half their assets and seven to ten years of alimony. And not when nearly half of all American marriages crash and burn long before death becomes the issue.

No, you cannot be bound together for life by a priest, a rabbi or a minister, a judge, a ship's captain, or an Elvis impersonator. There is only one person in the world who can truly and fully bind two people together forever, even against their will. And that person can't talk, poops in diapers, and weighs about seven pounds.

So over the likely objections of childless married couples—or more vexingly, childless married couples who infantilize their dogs—I submit to you that you are not really married, or more accurately, you are not fully married, until you and your spouse create a child together. And after that, um, seminal moment, you can never ever be fully divorced, no matter how badly you want to walk away. Listen, childless marrieds can leave each other anytime they want, and yes, it's very sad. But except in cases of wanton abandonment or gross negligence, couples that create children together truly are bound inextricably. So just as children fundamentally alter the nature of marriage—as many other writers in this book will tell you—I contend that it's just as important to recognize that children affect the end of marriage even more profoundly.

My ex-wife and I were married by a wild-eyed Unitarian minister (if you can imagine such a thing) on the pitching deck of a rented forty-foot sailboat off the coast of Waikiki. It was sort of a spur-of-the-moment elopement. But in my mind—actually, in both our minds, we intended a genuine lifelong commitment. As I used to say quite often, believing it every time, I couldn't possibly get divorced, because I don't even have a model for that. My own parents, who have grown progressively closer for fifty-three years until you can hardly tell where one ends and the other begins, instead gave me a wonderful model for a lifelong marriage.

And in my own marriage, I fully intended to emulate theirs. On our wedding day, I already imagined our three children, not yet born, and even their children. I imagined how my beautiful young wife would grow old gracefully by my side, and how we would finish each other's thoughts and sigh tolerantly in the face of each other's peccadilloes. We would be a cute older couple. I imagined my wife and me, old and retired—not rich, but comfortable enough—well-dressed, strolling New York's Fifth Avenue visiting museums and taking tea at four in the salon of an Upper East Side hotel. We would have big Thanksgivings with all our children and grandchildren, and travel to Paris while we still could. I even imagined how sad my wife would be when I finally passed because I knew I would go first.

And some of that came to pass. We did have the three kids. Our fair and beautiful daughter was born just ten months after the wedding and our feisty dark-haired son followed fifteen months later. Five years after that, we were surprised by another son who was born a happy old soul and, for the most part, has stayed that way. Unlike some men, I instinctively understood that when children join a marriage, the husband inevitably ceases to occupy the center of his wife's world. And that made sense to me. If anything, our children brought us closer together. And when our baby daughter needed an operation to close a hole in her heart, that brought us even closer.

So if our marriage contained the seeds of its own destruction, I was either too insensitive or too dim-witted to see it—even in retrospect. My ex-wife may well tell another story about all of this. But in my opinion, our marriage with children was just fine—more than fine—for more than a decade. And everyone who met us said they couldn't imagine us apart.

In fact, I was so confident about the strength of our marriage that I put it to what I assumed was the ultimate test. One day, I suggested to my wife that we sell our house, cars, and furniture; pack our clothes in a suitcase; and take our three children on a sixteen-month trip around the world. And she said yes. We were both confident enough in our marriage that we looked forward to spending more than a year together, 24/7, in small hotel rooms with three young children. And you know what happened? It went very well. It was the trip of a lifetime. And I drew all the wrong lessons from it.

Because when we came back to real life, bought a house, and settled back down, I made a mistake. Then my wife made a bigger mistake. Then I made an even bigger mistake. Then she made the one last mistake that turned out to be the deal killer. And that was that.

My initial mistake was to believe that since the family spent so much time together in close quarters on the road, we could replicate that at home. While we traveled, I spent nearly every minute of every day with my wife and kids. I enjoyed it. I thought it was a privilege, and I didn't really stop when we got back. I was always a very involved father—before, during, and after the trip—but when we returned, I took it to a level where the basic family construct changed. It was no longer Dad goes to work and Mom takes care of the house and kids. Now we both took care of the kids, and in retrospect, I think that helped to push my wife out of her space.

My wife's mistake, in response, was to draw a false conclusion from this intensive coparenting; namely, that the bulk of her work as a mother was substantially done—even though our children were only still in grammar school. In her mind, she had spent more than a decade pregnant and taking care of kids. She was about to turn forty, had attended a top university, and wasn't satisfied with what she had achieved in life. I had a satisfying and exciting career under my belt. What had she done, except support me and take care of our kids? In her view, the light shone brightly on me, and she stood in the shadow. Now, it was finally her time in the sun. It was only fair.

So with a husband and nanny to help take care of our kids, another woman to clean the house, and a third to do the laundry, my wife devoted herself, heart and soul, to becoming the world's greatest middle-aged, female, off-road triathlete. That was the dream. And over the course of several years, it became a single-minded obsession. She showed up less and less when the kids came home from school because she was "training." She traveled around the country—and eventually the world—ten to twelve times a year to participate in off-road triathlons, hundred-mile bicycle races across the Rockies (no, really), marathons in distant cities, and half-Ironman races. One day she actually told me, in all seriousness, that we both had jobs: My job was to write, produce, and edit books, and her job was to be a triathlete. I retorted offhand that her job didn't actually meet the two basic requisites of a job—i.e., it didn't produce any income (and after our globe-trotting that was definitely an issue for us) and it didn't help anyone but her.

From that too-clever response, you can probably intuit my next big mistake. I did not sufficiently understand or respect my wife's deep need to accomplish something significant, something that would bring her self-satisfaction and recognition as she reached middle age. I didn't get that managing our house, taking care of our children, exercising, gardening, and taking long lunches with her friends just wasn't cutting it. To me, it looked like a dream job, but to her it seemed like a support function.

Also, as a natural-born dabbler, I did not fully realize, even after ten years, that whatever my wife did, she did singlemindedly, to the exclusion of everything else. So when she became a mother, she was one hundred percent a mother. She read every parenting book, went to parenting lectures, gave it her full attention, and was great at it. But now as a triathlete, she was one hundred percent a triathlete, and most everything else fell by the wayside. As an illustration of how focused she was, we had subscriptions to both *Swim* and *Swimming* magazines, and she read both cover-to-cover every month.

Finally, I did not adequately respect the basic nature of the quest itself. At the time, I didn't see any difference between my wife training for triathlons five hours a day (and reading and talking about carb loading and bicycle-tire pressures another five hours a day) and some guy who golfed every day because he wanted to win his country club tournament. I thought it was more than enough that I supported her quest by making an income for our family and leaving work early to take care of the kids. Why did I also have to be interested in the minute and, let's face it, excruciatingly boring details of handlebar configurations and GU energy packets? And why did I also have to be happy about the situation? (And, believe me, I wasn't.)

But—and you probably saw this coming a full Ironman away—the understanding, respect, and enthusiasm for her sport that my wife didn't get at home, she found elsewhere. Yep, all those trips to Tahoe and Kona with her male training partner (whose wife brought home the bacon, by the way) weren't just about the endorphins— or, anyway, not just about the endorphins generated during triathlons. It turns out they were generating even more endorphins back at the hotel. I don't know the exact dates, but I believe this went on for well over a year while stupid, crotchety old me stayed home with the kids, unwilling to face the truth, getting sick instead.

Just for the record, I was a one hundred percent loyal husband for fourteen years, and I couldn't even contemplate my wife cheating on me. I wouldn't have thought it possible, which is why I brought it to the surface very slowly. Strangely, one aha moment came when I found a Prince CD in our car. I knew my wife would never buy that for herself.

As I gradually figured it out, I became increasingly hurt and pissed off, and my reaction included a very public end-of-the-marriage affair of my own. (I know. There's no good excuse for that.) But really, my principal reaction was that I no longer trusted my wife. I didn't trust her blandishments as she tried to win me back. I didn't trust her motives for wanting me back at all. I thought it was just about the financial security. Don't get me wrong, I am convinced that my ex-wife would never have had another extramarital affair. She always wanted her affair to remain a deep dark secret (even her best friend didn't know), and she never wanted to get divorced. But for me, it was more about what it must have taken to successfully pull off a yearlong, small-town affair in the first place. How many well-crafted deceptions it must have taken. I couldn't get past that.

So after months of cruel and excruciating waffling, I finally decided to leave her—for better or worse, for richer or poorer (definitely poorer). And believe me, when I did finally walk out that door, I would have preferred to have never seen nor heard from her again—at least not for a very long time. I have never wished her harm. She's the mother of my children. But I didn't exactly want to talk to her every day either.

But guess what? As it turned out, we couldn't just leave each other. It wasn't that simple. We are parents. And our children now spend half their time at my house and half their time at my ex-wife's house a few miles away. And two of those children are now teenagers. They get into a little trouble every so often—occasional traffic accidents and all the other usual hormonal teenage stuff. And that takes cooperation on the part of their parents, no matter how we feel about each other.

So once you have children, leaving your spouse forever is a very relative concept. Like it or not, I am obliged to talk to my ex-wife at least three times a week about pickups, drop-offs, doctors' appointments, report cards, child-support checks, who gets the kids for Christmas or Thanksgiving, and every other thing that parents must discuss about their children. Only now it's more so, because the logistics are more complicated and far less pleasant. You call that leaving?

But that's the least of it, the very least. And if you've read this far, and take anything away from this rant, let it be this: Once you decide to have children with your spouse, you'd better recognize a very uncomfortable fact of life before the fact—if you ever decide to leave, for whatever reason, no matter how justified, the exit price will inevitably include inflicting great pain on your innocent children, the people you love most in the world.

After I decided to leave, we of course had to tell the kids. We gathered our three children together in the living room and broke the news. They were fifteen, fourteen, and eight at the time, and they sat quietly, side by side, on the couch, while we gently told them the news that would irrevocably rip up their childhoods. In preparation (hah!), I read a book that, among other things, advised us to repeatedly stress that the divorce was not the children's fault, since they tend to think that way. So I did that over and over during the course of the conversation. And then I actually walked out of that room thinking, *Well that went as well as could be expected.* Right? You fool. You idiot.

Do you want to know how well it went? Two weeks later, my wife found our eight-year-old, the happiest kid on earth, the old soul, standing in a hallway at three in the morning crying softly and saying quietly over and over, "It's not working. It's not working." That's how well it went.

Collectively, the kids had many other negative reactions to the divorce, including lower grades, which I always consider the canary in the coal mine. So I decided to step up, work fewer hours, and devote myself to getting them back on track. After two years that has more or less happened. Thankfully, all the kids are doing well now. My daughter recently left home for college. My older son completely turned his high school career around with four back-to-back 4.0 semesters, all achieved while he worked part-time at Best Buy and served as editor of the school yearbook. And our youngest son seems to have reverted back to his normal happy bodhisattva self.

But I don't fool myself into thinking that this makes everything all right or that it exonerates me in any way. Every single time my kids have to pack their bags and change houses, twenty-six times a year to be exact, a pain shoots through my heart, and I desperately want to think of some way to adequately apologize to the people I love the most and hurt the worst. Some way to say, "I am so sorry about what I did to you. It is the greatest regret of my life." But, of course, it would never be enough.

travelers

· Ariel Gore ·

In Tuscany, when a woman hopes for a baby, she goes to the priest and gets an apple that's been blessed. She recites an incantation to Santa Anna, seduces her husband, eats the fruit, and, mystically, she is with child.

I'd simply run out of birth control pills.

We tripped into the central Italian province in early summer—a couple of vagabonds chasing a rumor of free shelter in an old stone farmhouse. The vast glistening fields and dense vineyards reminded me of northern California. *Home.*

Our medieval hill town rose up from the landscape like a fairy-tale castle.

"People live happily ever after in places like this," my boyfriend smiled.

And I believed him.

I was weary from harsh travels and drawn in easily by the smells of fresh bread and garlic, the friendly staccato chatter of the old women in the village piazza. They were gossiping about us, surely, but the unknown language sounded like poetry to me, and even if they only hoped to spread stories, they offered us red wine, offered to help my boyfriend find work, offered to teach me to make soup in their broad-tiled kitchens. We could make a life here, maybe.

We found our free-shelter farmhouse, but it had no amenities— no kitchen and no bathroom, no running water and no electricity. Maybe it wasn't much of a farmhouse, after all. Maybe it was more like a barn. *No matter.* I was eighteen years old. A high school dropout. Expecting my first child. Not a penny to my name. But poverty seemed romantic. Life on the road had been stormy, but what was life if not fiery and chaotic? My boyfriend—twice my age and fresh out of a London jail—had been steadily losing his charm since we left Spain, but if I'd learned anything from traveling it was that the right place could make all the difference. A place could be healing, I reminded myself. A place could change everything.

As evening fell on that first night, I opened the only window in our dirt-floored new home. Outside, the fireflies flickered in the warm summer air, promising a whole new life. And I believed them.

Stella arrived midmorning, led me to her ancient house, let me use the shower. She spoke English. "Today we make summer soup," she announced when I emerged from the bathroom, shampooed and clean scrubbed but back in my dirty jeans and T-shirt.

Bean and Sausage Soup with Summer Vegetables

"You add the vegetables last," Stella told me. "And you just use anything you have. Today we have squash and zucchini."

Begin by sautéing a pound of sausage in a saucepan for about five minutes, until it's heated through. Remove the sausage and most of the drippings from the pan, leaving just about a tablespoon of drippings behind in which to sauté your onions. If you can't afford the sausage, just start with a tablespoon of olive oil.

Now add a cup of diced onion and a cup of chopped fennel and sauté for about ten minutes until they're soft. Add a clove or two of garlic, finely chopped, and sauté for another minute.

Stir in four cups of broth and two cups of diced tomatoes—canned or fresh. Add a teaspoon of black pepper and a teaspoon of sage. Cook it up for ten minutes, then add three cups of cannellini beans—either canned or dry that have been soaked and cooked.

Add your cooked sausage and drippings and bring it all to a boil. Reduce heat and simmer for five minutes, then add the cubed summer squash and diced zucchini or any other summer vegetable you have. Simmer for five more minutes until your vegetables are cooked.

Serve with thick-sliced bread.

My boyfriend found work tending a nearby olive grove.

"Honest work," he beamed when he got the news. "Honest work can make all the difference."

I inhaled hope.

He talked dreamily of building us a little house in the valley, but he spent all his wages on grappa. He came home singing, but when I asked after the money, his face flushed. He clenched his fists, punched the stone wall next to me so that I wouldn't forget whose paycheck it was, and that he'd taken my passport "for safekeeping."

I'd sobered up as soon as I got pregnant. He said he'd do the same when the baby was born. Women and men were different this way,

Stella assured me over iced lemon tea in her airy kitchen. And it made sense, if you thought about it. The woman holds the baby in her body for nine months before the man welcomes that new life into his house. Parenthood strikes the mother at conception, the father at birth.

As for money, who needed it? I'd been a hippie kid myself. I'd met children all over the world who lived without the luxuries of running water or electricity. I had love to offer.

In the fall I sprinkled water on our dirt floor, to settle the dust, make it a home. I took a bucket and went out alone to pick the wild blackberries that grew along the paved roads and dirt paths. They stained my fingers purple. The neighbor woman had watched me silently from her window for weeks. As I got home that day, she finally spoke. Her voice was shrill, but she enunciated each Italian word carefully, and I was proud that I understood. "Be careful, American," she said, "or the baby will be birthmarked with berries." She had deep worry lines across her sunburned forehead. "You mustn't eat fish when you're pregnant, either," she told me, "or the baby will be dumb. And you mustn't eat snails, or the baby will be slow. You should drink coffee and eat bread; prepare warm autumn soup."

"Thank you," I nodded.

And she smiled at me, baring a mouth full of brown and rotting teeth. "Come in," she curled her fingers. "My name is Signora Melina."

Warm Autumn Tomato and Bread Soup

All these ingredients can be easily begged or borrowed, Signora Melina pointed out. And the soup can be prepared on a camping stove.

Take about a half pound of stale bread and break it into little pieces. Put the bread into a big bowl and pour about four cups of warm broth over it. Set it aside.

Now heat a couple of tablespoons of olive oil and sauté four cloves of garlic, finely chopped, and two cups of peeled, diced tomatoes. Add some salt and pepper, and simmer for twenty minutes.

Go back to your bread, which should be mushy now, and add that to the pot.

Cook it all up for a good fifteen minutes and serve warm, with fresh torn basil as garnish.

Winter arrived like some stern high school principal.

We needed heat, water, light.

"Where's the baby going to sleep?" I wondered out loud.

"It'll sleep with us," my boyfriend assured me. "We're warm."

But I felt cold.

The earth didn't offer so many fruits now, and I hadn't canned up more than a few jars of tomatoes with Stella as the generous seasons ended.

I walked the same roads, barren now. I hitchhiked the fifty miles to the hospital in the next province for checkups. The doctor jellied up my belly with ultrasound goo and showed me blurry black-and-white images of the baby: a girl.

I begged change on the corner outside, bought square slices of pizza. There was a hippie college in California that had accepted me the year before — I'd applied on a whim as I blew through my home state over the holidays.

If I'd stayed on that road I'd be finished with the first semester of my freshman year, I thought. *Would they take me now?*

At home, I told my boyfriend the news.

"A girl?" Tears of joy streamed down dusty cheeks. He gripped the edge of the table, closed his eyes.

"I was thinking about going back to school in California after she's born," I said.

Now he narrowed his gaze. "What business do you have in California? We're travelers."

"He's just afraid," Signora Melina assured me. "The men get scared just before the baby comes."

But I was getting scared, too.

There wasn't any more work in the olive grove for my boyfriend. The property owner's wife invited me over to make soup and to break the news. They'd noticed my boyfriend had a temper. They didn't want to upset him. Would I be so kind as to be the one to tell him he was no longer needed?

Hearty Potato Soup

"Potatoes are cheap," the property owner's wife reminded me. "You can live on them."

Take about a half a pound of spicy Italian sausage meat and crumble it into your saucepan. Add a chopped onion and sauté until the meat is cooked. If you can't afford sausage, just sauté the onion in a tablespoon of olive oil until it's translucent.

Now add about six cups of chicken or vegetable broth and three large potatoes, cubed. Boil until the potatoes are soft.

Add a full bunch of fresh spinach, washed and torn, and keep boiling for a few more minutes — until the spinach is cooked.

Now remove your soup from the heat and stir in a quarter cup of evaporated milk. Add black pepper and sea salt to taste.

○○○

The baby was born with wide, dark eyes. I named her once, and then again. I stayed in the hospital for days, not wanting to go back to that cold, cold home; not wanting to be alone with just the baby and my boyfriend. He hitchhiked to the hospital every day, brought yogurt, cigarettes, and whiskey. "You can smoke now," he told me. "You can drink."

He held the baby close to his chest, looked as if his heart would break, but that sudden vulnerability seemed to spook him. "She's. Just. So. Small."

I sipped the bitter brown liquor, but it tasted like poison now.

"When are you coming home?" my boyfriend wanted to know.

I shrugged. "I'm not well enough," I lied.

I'm sure the nurses knew I was faking the lasting pain. They seemed sympathetic when my boyfriend stumbled and fell down the maternity ward stairs, but after a week they couldn't cover for me anymore. "You'll have to go," the grandmotherly one whispered. "You'll have to go today."

I strapped the baby to my chest with a red checkered scarf and hitchhiked to Rome to apply for new passports. By the time I got back to my fairy-tale village, my boyfriend was drunk in the piazza.

The old women gossiped that he'd finally gone crazy. He drank longer in the bars now, Stella said. He broke furniture, smashing chairs against walls and doors. "You need help," Signora Melina whispered. "You need to bathe in *l'erba della paura* to gain courage."

I needed a whole new life.

"Hit the Fear"

Stella came to my house on a Saturday evening when my boyfriend was at the bar. Signora Melina held the baby. The olive grove owner's wife watched the door.

Take a fist of the wild herb *erba della paura,* preferably harvested in midsummer, dried and saved for such an occasion. Slowly bring it to a near boil in a liter of water, then steep for twenty minutes. Cool and strain.

Immerse one hand in the water and quickly wash your face, using downward motions, as if brushing the fear away from your body. Wash the front of your neck in the same way, then your ears, your arms, your legs, and your feet—including the soles.

Repeat the washing three times on three consecutive nights, then pack up as much as you can comfortably carry on your back, fasten the baby on your front, and walk away slowly, without looking back.

the communication challenge

the 3 A.M. marriage

· Hope Edelman ·

We meet in the middle of the night like clandestine lovers, creeping down a dark stairwell, careful to avoid waking the littlest household members, who would surely intervene. We speak in tender whispers, or hurt ones. We vent, review, inform, apologize, share, and repent before the sun rises. The television room—small, womblike, and farthest from the stairs—is our preferred rendezvous spot, but if it's too cluttered, the living room will do. On either couch, we run the risk of getting a My Little Pony up the butt, but we're willing to overlook such details. We need these early morning hours, so we take them, however we have to, whenever we can.

From 9 A.M. to 3 P.M. every day I'm a writer and a teacher. From 3 P.M. to 9 P.M. I'm a mother to two girls. I'm too exhausted by their bedtime to be much of anything to anyone else, but after just three or four hours' sleep, I wake with a clear head. So the middle of the night is my time to be a wife.

Those hours are often the only time all day my husband and I get alone. Without them, we'd be two adults who gave up romance to run a chaotic day-care center. With them, we can be partners, lovers, and friends. This is the truth: If asked to visualize my husband as a lover, his face comes to me in shadows. I can draw all the bumps and creases of his moonlit profile with my eyes closed. This is the even bigger truth: Without these stolen hours, I don't know what kind of marriage we'd have, or if we'd have one at all.

The exhaustion was what nearly did us in. Nearly did me in, to be more accurate, which would have done us both in before long. It was the kind of dramatic limbs-pinned-to-the-bed exhaustion, a cement-helmet-pressing-down-on-the-top-of-my-head exhaustion, that engulfed me like a physical tsunami as soon as our first daughter, Maya, was born. The kind of exhaustion that keeps you glued to the sheets with your eyes closed, wondering in a panic, *Chronic Fatigue? Lupus? Cancer? Cancer. Oh my god . . .*

My entry to motherhood was ten weeks with a colicky infant who never slept more than two hours at a stretch. Only breast-feeding could calm her; she wouldn't take a bottle at night and shrieked without pause if anyone rocked her other than me. Those first months I averaged about five hours of broken sleep a night, slightly better than the new-mother average of four and a half, but still nowhere near the zone of proper functioning. I'd always been a solid eight-hour-a-night sleeper, able to function on seven in a pinch but cranky, headachy, and forgetful on anything less. But this postpartum period was another solar system entirely. I would lie down at 10 P.M. thinking, *What's the point?* knowing I'd be awake again in two hours' time to comfort a squalling infant for the next hour, eventually to lie down and wonder again, *What's the point?* My days became a series of weird and cyclical déjà vus. I would start the morning feeling that I'd never even slept, haul myself through the daily tasks of new motherhood, and collapse on the bed again at 10 P.M., my mind whirling from lack of sleep. *What's the point?*

This kind of sleep deprivation does evil things to a person. I was bitchy. I was despairing. I was depressed. Even the simplest chores— folding a load of laundry, paying the electric bill, blow-drying my hair—felt like magnanimous efforts, so impossible to master that I couldn't muster the energy to try. Now I know that profound and prolonged sleep loss puts women at serious risk for postpartum depression, but I didn't know it then. I just thought something had gone terribly wrong with me. It was as if some essential cord of humanity inside me had snapped. All of my previous desires— for food, for intimacy, for companionship, for sex—had become focused into a hard little knob of longing for just one thing: sleep. Sometimes in the middle of rinsing dishes I'd lean my forehead against the kitchen cabinet and close my eyes, daydreaming about four hours of uninterrupted rest. Just four hours, damnit! Was that too much to ask?

"Maybe you can try to sleep while you're breast-feeding," my husband, John, said, trying to be helpful. "You could feed her lying down."

The other me, the me who until just recently was a normal sleeping person, would have thought, *Sweet idea from someone without breasts.* But this new me, this ugly, desperate me, didn't give a shit about good behavior. This one had lost her filter. "And maybe *you* could sleep through an hour of constant, tiny tugs on your penis?" I spat back.

"Sorry!" John said, lifting his hands in the air in defeat. "Sorry!" He retreated backwards from the room.

My poor husband. He really had no idea what hit him. Just one month earlier he'd been an eager, expectant father with a ravishingly pregnant wife who prepared dinner every night. Now he had a beet-faced, squalling alarm clock of an infant and a wife who couldn't aim milk into a cereal bowl without splashing it all over the counter. And then spun around and yelled at him for not helping her more when he tried to wipe it up.

My husband became the focused object of my despair, the one person who had what I wanted but couldn't seem to get. Because he wasn't the one breast-feeding, and could somehow sleep through Maya's nighttime cries, *he* was getting something that resembled enough sleep. I, by contrast, had developed a kind of bizarre maternal radar that now woke me thirty seconds *before* Maya started to stir in her bassinet, reducing my sleep time that much less. This hardly seemed fair. It *wasn't* fair, but I had begun to realize that profound sleep deprivation is something only mothers have to suffer, and I would be lying if I said I accepted this with any degree of grace.

Things would get better between us, we decided, if we could get some time away together, without the baby. We'd remember what it was like to be a couple, instead of an ineffective problem-solving team. So when Maya was five weeks old and my mother-in-law came to visit, we left the baby in her care for an evening to attend a costume party at the home of one of John's business acquaintances. It was the thirty-fifth birthday party for the wife of an elegant, educated man who had started and sold a large high-tech company. We drove up to find a squadron of valet parkers at the curb of a Brentwood estate. I'd never seen a party like this before, let alone been invited to one. The house was full of antique furniture, oil paintings, and ten-foot potted plants. The guest of honor was showing off her new chandelier to a group of women friends when we arrived.

Most of the guests were outfitted in costumes that looked custom-made by Hollywood wardrobe designers, and probably were. I hadn't had the energy to put anything festive together. Nothing I owned with a zipper or buttons fit yet, so I went dressed in black stretch pants and a long maroon velour shirt that successfully hid my nursing bra. "I'm a new mother," I explained to anyone who looked my way.

There was a poolside buffet. There was music. There was dancing, I think. I spent most of the party sitting at an outdoor table, pinching my cheeks to stay awake. While John—dressed as a farmer in overalls and a straw hat—carried on a conversation with a high-tech mogul wrapped in a linen toga, I rested my cheek against the tablecloth and closed my eyes just as Nefertiti drifted by with Napoleon. For the next half hour I slept with my head alongside a half-eaten plate of couscous. When I woke up I saw John across the lawn stealing glances at me with a sympathetic smile. I didn't blame him for pretending not to know me. I didn't know me anymore, either.

Why hadn't anyone warned us about this? Maybe they had. Probably, they had. Nine years and another daughter later, I'm still too tired to remember.

That's the most insidious part of maternal fatigue. *It doesn't go away.* Even when the baby starts sleeping through the night, and glimpses of your old self reemerge with increasing frequency and duration, it's too late. Your sleeping patterns have irrevocably changed. Once you're a parent, you never really sleep again, even when you're sleeping.

I skate across the surface of sleep now, gliding between one episode of wakefulness and the next. If it's not someone's monster in the closet that wakes me, it's a stomach flu that comes on without warning, or a small body crawling between our sheets. Or it's an owl on the roof, a toilet running downstairs, or John closing the bedroom window to keep the cold air out, the kind of things that never would have ruptured my sleep in the preparent years. Now I've got the nocturnal third ear, ever on the alert for upsets or danger.

Still, even on such fractured sleep one can manage to make it through most of a day with reasonable amounts of good cheer. At least that's what I like to believe. On a typical morning the blue alarm clock next to my bed goes off at 6:40 A.M. From that point on, I'm on the hamster wheel, starting with the morning breakfasts-lunch-boxes-backpacks-hair-brushing-clean-up-the-kitchen routine. I do the school drop-offs, followed by a six-hour workday, finishing in time for the afternoon pickups. Then I chauffeur the girls to their various afternoon activities and play dates, until it's time to return home to cook dinner, serve dinner, clean up dinner, and supervise homework and baths. At 7:20 P.M. the automatic garage door goes up, signaling John's return. Then it's divide and conquer time, with him reading one child's set of bedtime stories and me taking over the other. On a good night we've got both kids in bed with lights out by 8:45, and I'm just about ready to join them.

Except. That's precisely when John wants his time with me, too.

He's such a good man, my husband. Honest. Loyal. Hardworking. Kind. But there's the small problem of his libido, which kicks into gear every night at about 9 P.M. Or maybe it's more like his libido is in gear all day, and 9 P.M. is the first chance he gets to exercise it with me.

Unfortunately, my libido is somewhere in the vicinity of Antarctica by that time. Touching parts of my body that would normally make me pant and quiver feels about as arousing as having my kneecap rubbed through the sheet. Nothing, truly nothing, compares to lying down with my husband under a down blanket at the end of the day, but by 9 P.M. that's really all I want: ten minutes to myself to read a few pages in a book, and then the heavenly sensation of turning out the light and closing my eyes for the night.

If you're wondering how often a married couple manages to have sex under these circumstances, the answer would be, oh, 'round about never. Does this make my husband feel dejected and rejected? Sometimes. Does this twist me up inside with anxiety and guilt? Always.

That's when you have to start getting creative.

I can't remember the first time it happened. There have been so many nights since then, they've blurred together in memory. Still, it's easy to imagine the inaugural event going something like this:

The loud yipping of a coyote pack pierces the dark. Or maybe the cat starts doing his inexplicable cat things on the hardwood floor downstairs, or Maya shouts, "My sunglasses! My sunglasses!" in her sleep, and I wake up. John is curled up next to me, his body a small, bumpy mountain in the night.

The blue alarm clock on my night table reads 2:02 A.M. I stare at the ceiling, wrapped in a cocoon of calm wakefulness. I know I haven't slept enough for the night, but I don't feel like I need more right now. I reach over and lay my hand on John's shoulder. He stirs slightly under my touch.

"Are you awake?" I whisper, softly. It's an irritating question, I know, but I wouldn't ask it if I thought he was really sleeping.

"Yes," he whispers back.

"I can't get back to sleep."

"Me, neither."

We roll to face each other. I lay my hand against his cheek. It's the gentlest sustained touch I've been able to give him all day.

"Do you want a back rub?" he asks.

"Mmm," I say, rolling over. I can't think of anything that sounds better at this moment. John has hands that can push the tension right out of you.

Once or twice a week we wake like this. Sometimes we'll stay in bed, making love in the darkness, luxuriating in the found hours together. If we need to talk, we'll creep downstairs in the dark and sprawl across a couch. Removed from the *rat-a-tat-tat* of the morning school routine or the evening homework-dinner-bath-bed sequence, we finally have time to discuss something—*anything*—without interruption. It's in these hours that most of our connecting takes place, reminding us that we're alert, intelligent, sexual partners with a passion for each other's bodies and minds. Then we go back to sleep for a few hours before the alarm clock rings.

We decided to refinance our house in the middle of the night. It's also when we chose Maya's school, grieved the loss of my father, developed an Internet marketing strategy for my last book, discussed how to give me a year off work, and planned all our family vacations. We sleep this way during vacations, too. When Eden, our younger daughter, eventually asks how she was conceived, I'll tell her, "In a pension in the Old Town of Prague, local time 3 A.M."

Half our friends think we're crazy to live this way. They suggest baby-sitters and earlier bedtimes, and a moratorium on lying down with the kids at night, as if we haven't thought of this already. The other half thinks we've landed on a brilliant, innovative idea. "I can't believe we didn't think of it ourselves," one of my girlfriends said.

I, too, might view it as a unique solution, if it weren't so quaintly retro. Apparently, all preindustrial families slept in segments like this, with a first shift between about 9 P.M. and midnight, followed by a few hours of calm wakefulness and then a "second sleep" until dawn. In the middle of the night they brewed beer, smoked pipes, conversed with neighbors, or stayed in bed and made love. (Think about it: how else could families expand to seven or eight children when everyone slept together in a teepee or a single heated room?)

Take away artificial light at night and the way it messes with our melatonin levels, and we'd all sleep in intervals, like wild animals do. Some sleep researchers view insomnia as the body's attempt to reassert its natural, primal pattern. I prefer not to think of John and me as so desperate for time together we have to bisect the night to get it. Instead, I like to think of us returning to our animal instincts, getting back in touch with our ancestral, biological roots.

One night, I dream my younger daughter's eczema flares up red and raw on the front of both legs. Beneath it, I find sparkling jewels embedded in her skin. When I try to take them out, I discover they're attached to her legs with tiny gold safety pins I have to remove carefully, one by one.

I wake with my heart beating fast at 3:23 A.M. When I reach out with my right arm for John, the sheets are flat.

I find him downstairs, partially illuminated by the glow from his laptop screen. When he hears me coming down the stairs, he looks up and smiles.

"Hi, sweetie," he says, extending his hand. "You were sleeping so deeply, I didn't want to wake you."

I scoot over against his shoulder and sneak a look at his computer screen. It's a detailed and complicated spreadsheet. Next to him lies a sheet of scrap paper where he's been scribbling notes and arrows.

"What are you working on?" I ask, snuggling up against him.

"Oh, just this presentation," he says, and then he starts to explain.

We talk about the pros and cons of his approach, and agree that his greatest skill is as a strategist. That's why our marriage works so well, I say: because in our house he's the idea person, and I'm good with implementation. This segues into a discussion about the amount of energy it takes for me to do most of the executing, and he comes up with some good ideas to lighten my load.

"Thanks," I tell him, and I mean it.

"No problem," he says.

We look at his spreadsheet some more, and it reminds me of Maya's last math test.

"She's having trouble with multiplication tables," I say. "The teacher is timing the kids, and she can't think of the answers fast enough."

"Maybe we should make her some flash cards," he suggests.

"And quiz her in the car on the way to school in the morning," I add.

This is how it goes, until nearly 5 A.M. I sit up straight and pat him on the thigh. "I'd better get some more sleep before the morning rush," I say.

"I'll be up in a couple minutes," he says. I kiss him on the side of the head and go back upstairs.

Sometimes, if I'm honest, these early morning conversations are better than sex. Or maybe what I mean to say is they're even more essential, allowing us to reconnect with the parts of each other we love most. Here, in these stolen hours, we're freed from the roles that define us so stringently during the day: mother, father, home-owner, husband, wife. Here, we're just two people, rediscovering each other in the dark. It's in these hours that I remember all the reasons why I chose my husband, why I will never leave his side, and how he makes my life complete.

Rip my nights in two, if that's what it takes to remind me. Rip them in three or four. The magic of our marriage lies in the sum of these parts, all of the scattered pieces working so efficiently together, this collaborative, postmidnight miracle that keeps our marriage whole.

harried with children: communication breakdown

· Kermit Pattison ·

*F*or the last few years, I've been carrying on a relationship with a married woman over the Internet. We exchange e-mails laced with evocative code words and whisper intimacies over the phone at work.

It would all be very erotic if the woman weren't already my wife. But my wife she is and, sadly, there's nothing arousing about this whatsoever. It's an office affair born out of grim necessity: we have no privacy at home.

We began as lovers. Then we had children and quality time vanished as surely as my short-term memory. I liken my marriage to a once-great civilization that was sacked when a horde of Viking dwarfs came ashore and had their way with us. And ever since, our marriage has been a saga of trying to communicate while the barbarians are at the baby gate.

We were talkers before we were breeders. We discussed books and actually found time to read them. We lingered over coffee and the Sunday paper and didn't worry about someone shredding and eating the pages. We talked over candlelit dinners with no inkling that someday we'd end every meal down on all fours to see how much of it wound up on the floor.

Somewhere in an upstairs closet lies a time capsule. There, behind the cartons of toys and children's clothes, sit boxes of love letters. Words united us, then held us fast through years of separation as we moved around the country between jobs. When we wed, we read aloud passages from our letters. "Someday down the road, I want little ones bouncing into our bed and waking us up in the morning," I wrote in one. "I want to raise brilliant young kids in the most unorthodox ways. I'm counting on your genes for a little help."

Nature took its course, the children arrived, and now we really need help.

Fourteen years later. Dawn. I shuffle into the kitchen and find a note from my wife on the counter. *Put out recycling, empty trash, pack school lunch, put laundry into dryer. I'm going to sleep in. PS, I love you.*

This is as close as we come to a love letter these days. The night shift has left a memo for the day shift.

More like the graveyard shift, actually. A few minutes ago, I was ripped untimely from the womb of the warm bed. The first scream came before dawn.

"A fire truck can't fly!"

"This one can!"

"No! That's not real!"

The Viking dwarfs had awakened. Our two sons, ages three and six, were locked in a full-throated ideological debate about the aeronautical capabilities of a toy fire engine. Then my older son proved the toy in question really could fly by hurling it at his brother's head. *Thunk!* Another high-pitched wail.

My wife emits an exhausted groan from beside me. The message is clear: your turn. She's eight months pregnant and needs to sleep. She flops over with her back to me and restacks the pillows, which have multiplied over the course of her pregnancy and come to resemble a sandbag dam. Personally, I'm willing to give it another couple of hours to see if the kids go back to sleep on their own. Another scream comes from the next room. Another groan from the next pillow, in the imperative. Go!

I haul myself out of bed and shuffle into the boys' room. I try to coax them into their clothes, but from their protests you'd think I was trying to stuff them into straitjackets. They have yet to embrace one of the fundamental rules of civilization: no tantrums before coffee.

I hustle the boys downstairs and begin the first negotiation of the day: breakfast. My oldest flops on the floor facedown and bawls when forced to eat cereal instead of toast. Apparently, I've ruined his life. Sliced banana with that? When I turn around, my younger son has disappeared. Moments later, he begins shouting from the upstairs bathroom.

"Wipe!"

Uh-oh. He's violated the quiet zone. I rush upstairs as the hallway echoes with chants of, "WIPE! WIPE! WIPE!"

Too late. A door opens and my wife emerges from the bedroom. Another rude awakening.

A few minutes later, we're all crammed into the kitchen. My wife is heavy with our latest Viking dwarf, and nobody has grown accustomed to the size of her belly. We keep getting pinned against each other in the narrow passageway between sink and fridge.

We download information in a quick burst. We're like two satellites that must take advantage of the brief time when they are orbiting within range. Doctor's appointment this afternoon, school meeting tomorrow, grocery list, basement pipes getting replumbed. There's no such thing as a non sequitur: As soon as you think of anything that must be communicated you must say it before you forget it.

"Sharon called you last night. PUT DOWN THE BASEBALL BAT AND EAT YOUR CEREAL."

"There's a squirrel nesting in the garage, and it fell on the windshield when we came home last night. Is the milk gone?"

"LEAVE YOUR BROTHER ALONE. You already poured it in your bowl."

"That shirt doesn't match your pants."

The phone rings repeatedly. Each time it's another parent with kids screaming in the background. Over the last few years, our circle of friends has been reduced to other couples with kids, and I have a nagging suspicion that when their lives get out of control they call us just to reassure themselves that somebody else has it worse. The boys take advantage of each distraction to slip away. My coffee gets cold. *Now what were we just talking about?* It's like trying to carry on a conversation with a person at the other end of a crowded subway car. Subway . . . transportation . . . *the school bus!* I stuff my son into his coat, grab my laptop, blow my wife a kiss, and we run to the bus stop.

That's our family time.

Everybody has a moment in their youth when they see an older couple eating in silence and vow to never be like them. Our generation has solved that problem by packing our lives so full that we rarely have the opportunity for silence.

The sexual revolution mandates that we both work and share

responsibilities around the house. The communications revolution bombards us with electronic chaff all day long. With all these so-called revolutions, it's no wonder we're so turned upside down. The art of conversation with my spouse is kind of like the Spanish I took in school: I used to be fluent but now . . . *¿Que?*

Family dinners are no longer occasions for adult conversation; instead, Mama and Daddy refer to themselves in the third person and more rice winds up on the floor than did at our wedding. After the kids go to sleep, it's time to clean up, pack lunch boxes, put out clothes for the next day, pay bills, return phone calls, or finish work assignments.

We take turns playing GOD. In our house, that stands for Grown-up On Duty. Having more than one adult minding the kids is considered an inefficient use of time and resources. It means dishes aren't getting washed, phone calls aren't being made, and laundry is composting in the hamper. Virtually all of our child care is scheduled to enable us to work. But quality time as a couple to talk? Somehow that gets forgotten.

We tag off as often as a team of professional wrestlers, and we're just as absurd. It's the Viking Dwarfs vs. the Old Farts, and we're getting our asses kicked. I wake and get the boys dressed and fed. My wife wakes and—*Tag!*—I go to work. I pick up our younger son from school, go home, and wait for the nanny. *Tag!* My wife comes home from her job. *Tag!* I bolt out for a run. After dinner, I wash dishes while she gets the boys in their pajamas. *Tag!* I brush their teeth. To her for the first book. Back to me for the second. My wife leaves for an outing with her moms' group. *Tag. Tag. Tag.* . . . I fall asleep with *Curious George* on my chest. I'm tagged out.

All this craziness courts trouble. Since becoming a dad, I've spent more than my share of weekends as the family handyman, and I've learned that one principle of husbandry applies to both house and marriage: a little maintenance now prevents a lot of decay later. It's the broken-window theory: neglect breeds more neglect. And, believe me, with children there will be *lots* of broken windows. A marriage, like a house, will last a lifetime with proper care. Without it, it fails with alarming speed.

Words are the foundation of our relationship. When we don't make time to talk, the foundation cracks and alienation fills the void. Our sense of family citizenship turns into zero sum individualism. "I've washed the dishes every night this week, and you went out with your friends to some wine bar. And who spends twelve dollars for a plate of artisanal cheese?" "I stayed up until midnight sewing Halloween costumes, and all you did was buy a couple bags of crappy candy. Which ran out." Small interactions become proxy wars for larger struggles. You feel you're not getting enough love, so you're going to make damn sure you get the front section of the paper at breakfast.

But maintaining communication keeps the foundation patched up. It predisposes us to be generous instead of critical. Even a brief check-in about the banalities of our workdays inoculates us against the disease of estrangement. Some sort of chemical shift occurs so that the things that made us boil with rage a few hours ago suddenly seem hilarious examples of our own pettiness. *Did I really snap at you just because you left your house keys on the roof of the car, where they miraculously remained during the three-mile drive to school? Joke's on me.*

The trick, of course, is finding time to talk amid all this chaos, before the foundation of our marriage starts to crack.

We try to cope. We cram conversations into the margins of life. We leave Post-it notes on the bathroom mirror and memos on the kitchen counter. We call each other at the office and share details inappropriate for the workplace. One night I work late and my wife calls to say good night while giving our son a bath. Even this conversation is cut short. "Oh my god," she says. "He just pooped in the tub!"

It gets to the point when my wife and I have to *schedule* conversation days in advance. We institute the Sunday night family meeting, when we sit down with our day planners and talk through the coming week. And on one such night, we open our calendars and realize we have achieved a new milestone of harried with children: We've forgotten our own anniversary two days before.

The sad fact is our memories ain't what they used to be. What do we expect? Most of the time, we talk while doing something else, like sorting mail or fixing whatever toy broke that day. My wife has become a ferocious multitasker who copes with midlife stress by having a raging affair with her to-do list. I regard any such list as a multiple-choice test: *choose one.* Look, if you're going to demand that we sort Legos while we talk, don't expect me to remember what we actually said. She insists that we had conversations that I cannot recall. I can see her rage gathering as she recounts details to jog my memory while I continue to stare at her blankly. I don't think I've got Alzheimer's yet. But I do have children.

Ah yes, my children. In their eyes, a parental conversation is like a mud puddle. It looks so peaceful they can't resist stomping right in the middle of it. The trick is not to let them know you're having a conversation in the first place, and this requires cryptography. We teach our children to be honest, and they teach us to be sneaky.

First we tried the old trick of spelling out words, which only ensured that our firstborn became literate by age five ("That spells ice cream!"). Next we developed a code that I call "obtuse obfuscation," or using words outside the child's vocabulary. If we're returning home late and I want to say, "Let's drive around until these guys fall asleep"—a statement guaranteed to ignite howls of protest in the backseat—I phrase it as, "Shall we continue our operation of the vehicle until certain parties succumb to accumulated fatigue, at which point they may be conveyed inside without protest?" My wife responds in kind, and pretty soon we sound as pompous as classical music announcers on public radio as we drive aimlessly, mile after mile, glancing furtively in the rearview mirror and waiting for the kids to fall asleep so the person riding shotgun can flash a thumbs-up and we can revert to adult conversation. Then our date can last as long as the gas. Call me pathetic. Call me whatever you want, just as long as those kids go to sleep.

Still, we believe it's important for marital security to find communication techniques that aren't dependent on Middle Eastern oil. So we begin writing to each other by e-mail. In the effort to rekindle the spark in our relationship, we've resorted to using a marital aid made by Microsoft.

This next act of desperation comes when I change jobs, and my wife and I are both on the computer for eight hours a day. We're five miles apart, but suddenly our communication is the most efficient it has been in years. We can dash off an e-mail message before the thought evaporates. It doesn't matter if the kids are screaming or one of us is reading the paper. The message will sit highlighted in the in-box until opened and read.

In fact, this works so well that it soon replicates all the problems of verbal communication. I want succinct, actionable information. She wants *connection.* Soon my wife's messages grow into a virtual blog. She sends me musings about child rearing, office gossip, recipes, and copies of stuff she's read in the newspaper. I send her bulleted lists. Bang bang bang. Out.

One Monday, I'm rushing to catch up on work when my computer chimes with an incoming e-mail. My editor? No. My wife. The subject line: "bird feeder info—we should fill it."

Huh?

"This time of year, keeping that bird feeder full is very important to the little feathered ones . . ." I scroll through the message in disbelief. There's page after page of stuff she's copied from some bird-watching website about the morning feeding rush of nuthatches, purple finches, chickadees, and titmice. She's making a case that we must add another item to our ever-growing to-do list. Our bird feeder has been gathering dust in the basement for two years, yet suddenly she's acting as if failure to deploy it immediately would be the moral equivalent of making pesticides in *Silent Spring*.

Then it hits me: I married a spammer.

Being a male, I react predictably to information overload. I filter. That's my version, anyway. She would say I just tune out. It becomes just another piece of electronic chaff that bombards me all day long.

"Did you get my e-mail?" my wife asks me over the phone.

I look at my computer. There are so many messages from my wife that her first and last names form perfect, uninterrupted columns in my in-box.

"Which one?"

"About picking up the kids tonight."

"What did it say?"

Her voice takes on a sharp edge. "Someone has to get them in half an hour."

Panic.

I mumble something to buy time as I scroll through her messages. Nuthatches, chickadees, Thanksgiving menus . . . Normally I'd say she never told me, but everything is in writing. If only I could find it. . . .

A few weeks before the baby is due, my phone rings.

"I was halfway through an e-mail and realized that it's probably not the most efficient way to communicate," says my wife. "We'd have to go back and forth five times. So I thought I'd just call you."

We make a pact: That night, we'll catch up.

It's nearly midnight by the time we collapse into bed. Most nights we try to read a few pages to keep up the illusion that we still have a life of mind. Tonight we just snap off the light.

The house remains silent except for the snoring of our two boys in the next room. A trapezoid of moonlight falls on the quilt and silhouettes the bulge of my wife's belly. She slides her hand across the sheets and touches me. "Feel this," she says.

She lays my palm across her skin. The baby is kicking.

And, lo and behold, that night, we talk.

how i became a nag

· Pamela Kruger ·

I really am hating my husband right now. *Yes, I know that this* feeling will pass—I love him, he loves me—but at the moment, I am so angry that little billows of steam should be shooting out of my ears.

David promised me that he'd find an orthodontist for our ten-year-old daughter, Emily, after her dentist warned that she might end up losing a couple of her adult teeth if we didn't get her in treatment soon. Since I was facing a work crunch and had more than my share of household and child-care tasks, I'd asked David if he'd do the research to find an orthodontist and then ferry Emily to whatever appointments were necessary. He agreed.

Okay, maybe he had agreed a little reluctantly, and I had pressured him a bit ("I do so much around here, can't you just do this?"). But given that David is the son of a dentist and knows the difference between an incisor and a canine, and has a genuine interest in such issues as whether palate expanders need to be removable, I figured he was better suited for this task anyway. Maybe, I reasoned, he'd even get enthused about handling it.

It's weeks later, though, and David admits he hasn't made a single call.

"But I sent you an e-mail yesterday and you said you'd do it that day. What happened? Why didn't you do it? You said you were going to do it!" I say.

"I forgot," he bristles. "You know it's not so easy for me to make calls during my workday!"

"But I reminded you yesterday and you said you'd do it then," I repeated. I'd also reminded him six times before, but who's counting? "I even sent you a list of a few orthodontists and phone numbers. Why say you are going to do it if you're not going to do it?"

"I am going to do it. This week."

"You've been saying that for weeks! Why can't you just do this one thing? Emily's teeth are going to be a mess if we don't do this! Do I have to do it? Do I have to do everything?"

I know I am repeating myself, but right now, I am like a dog with a bone—I can't give up. I start talking over my husband, who is saying he is overworked, he just forgot. He says I'm acting as though he does nothing in this house, and why am I making such a big deal of this, he is going to do it tomorrow!

But I don't stop talking until he suddenly lowers the boom. "Stop *nagging!* You're *nagging.* I said I'm going to do it!"

Suddenly, my face gets hot. I'm furious, and embarrassed, as the image of a nag—housewife in curlers, barking orders at her beleaguered husband—is conjured in my brain. "I am *not* a nag. I'm not nagging!" I sputter. "Why don't you . . . can't you . . . just do it when you say you're going to do it?"

He says this time he will, and we both get very quiet.

the communication challenge

I am not exactly sure what is going through my husband's head, but I am thinking, *How did I – or we – become a stereotype?*

"Shrewish, complaining, constantly finding fault, usually a woman" – this is how *nag* is defined in my dictionary. I am appalled and ashamed to admit that the definition fits at times, while my husband is also playing the companion role: checked out, sometimes maddeningly indifferent to his wife's requests.

I don't remember exactly when this dynamic developed in our marriage, but I am pretty sure it was after we had Emily. Perhaps I'm romanticizing our prechildren marriage years, but I remember us as having one of those effortlessly egalitarian relationships, in which chores were divvied up easily and often wordlessly, according to who was willing, available, and able to take on a task.

Since David enjoyed being Mr. Fix It, he became the one to unclog the bathtub, put together the Ikea furniture, and install new lighting fixtures. And because he also loved to cook, he prepared all our meals. I took on the traditional female task of making all our social plans, and since I was interested in business journalism and chronically worried about our finances, I made our investing decisions (some quite poorly, as it turns out, but that's another story). But whenever one of us was too busy at work to handle a chore at home, the other would just step in; if we were hit with one of those minor domestic disasters, such as a flood from a brand-new dishwasher that mysteriously breaks on day two, we'd be able to decide in a matter of seconds who would take charge of the repair.

Of course, we had our spats, but I don't recall them ever being about who did what. In fact, people would sometimes gush about how "lucky" I was to have found a man who was an equal partner in domestic tasks, a compliment that I almost always found irritating. Was I really supposed to be grateful to my husband for doing his fair share? I couldn't imagine any other kind of relationship for myself.

But after we had one child, then two, the number of tasks we had to handle grew exponentially. Winging it was no longer an option. One person had to do the mental work of running the household, and since I was working from home, it fell to me. Without debate or even discussion, I became the memory bank for our family, the person in charge of details, big and small.

I'd notice when the car needed an oil change, the dishwasher had to be emptied, the kids needed school supplies, new clothes, haircuts or doctors' appointments, the piano teacher had to be paid, birthday gifts had to be bought . . . the mind-numbing list goes on and on. As my husband's work became more demanding, he seemed to notice less and less, and I became more frustrated and resentful. If I complained and pestered him enough, he'd finally get around to doing some of these things, but often I'd just do the chores myself. At least that's how it has seemed to me.

From his point of view, I frequently don't give him a chance. "Sometimes you ask me to do things I can't do at that moment, then you keep asking as if I have no intention of doing it," he says. He also protests that I don't give him credit for all the work he does do around the house without my prompting, such as the yard work, home repairs, and all the cooking, including making the kids' school lunches.

Plus he does all the dirty, nasty jobs. Just last week, he climbed into a damp, dark corner of the crawl space in our *Silence of the Lambs*-like basement, in order to find the source of a persistent leak. And there was the time he—wearing a bandanna around his nose—removed the carcass of a stray cat that had somehow wandered into our garage and died, unnoticed, until we were overwhelmed by the noxious fumes.

When he reminds me of all that, I am often chastened. "You

definitely deserve six months' credit for that cat!" I'll say, smiling. He laughs. And the tension melts away.

Nagging doesn't overwhelm our relationship. It's not a constant. But it's like a cold sore on an otherwise healthy relationship; it flares up occasionally, and when it does, it hurts. And we both wish it would just go away for good.

Whenever I've raised the topic of nagging with married women friends, I've discovered that each of them nags in their own way. Some admit to being loud and pushy. Others have a more quiet manner, but they're just as persistent. Their explanations for nagging, however, tend to be similar: Men drive them to it. "Men don't know how to multitask. They forget everything unless they're reminded," said one friend. "Men want to turn us into these mommies who take care of everything, people we desperately don't want to be," said another.

My sister objects to the word *nag*, saying it's an unfair term invented by men to turn the blame on us. "We're called nags when we ask a man to do something, and he doesn't do it (either because he doesn't feel like it at that moment or he doesn't think it's important). So we're put in the position of having to ask again and again. By calling us nags, they relieve themselves of the responsibility of doing something they don't want to do. It makes us the bad guy!"

Such conversations remind me of Georgetown University linguistics professor Deborah Tannen's best-seller *You Just Don't Understand* (which my husband used to jokingly refer to as *It's All Your Fault!*). Opening a worn copy from my bookshelf, I read:

> That women have been labeled "nags" may result from the interplay
> of men's and women's styles, whereby many women are inclined to
> do what is asked of them and many men are inclined to resist even
> the slightest hint that anyone, especially a woman, is telling them

what to do . . . A man who wants to avoid feeling that he is follow-ing orders may instinctively wait before doing what she asked, in order to imagine that he is doing it of his own free will. Nagging is the result, because each time she repeats the request, he again puts off fulfilling it.

Rereading the passage, I think about all the times David has com-plained that I was ordering him around "like I'm your employee," when I just wanted him to remember to empty the dishwasher and take out the garbage. My brother-in-law says, "Women act like men have to jump to it! And men don't like being told what to do."

It sounds to me as if men's masculinity is challenged by a wife's request, but I can't fathom why. My husband, brother-in-law, and most of the men I know have no problem working for and with women; they're open-minded, progressive men who admire and, in most cases, married strong women whose ambitions they encourage.

So why would they bridle at a wife asking, or even insisting, that they take out the garbage? "This is when you start thinking the men are from Mars, women are from Venus stuff has some validity," my sister says.

This is also when I start getting depressed and feel a pounding headache. I refuse to believe that despite all the years of the femi-nist movement, we nonetheless are subject to some kind of gender determinism, in which we revert to old gender roles once we get married and have kids. My husband is not one of those loafs, who thinks he should be able to lounge on a couch watching football while I pick up his dirty socks. He is deeply involved in his family and does quite a lot around the house—though, I would argue, still not nearly as much as I do.

I decide to call a friend who is a women's studies professor, hop-ing to hear a more hopeful, feminist perspective on nagging. Herself in a long-term lesbian relationship, she surprises me by saying that she nags her partner, and that she thinks nagging may be prevalent these days not because of gender but because of our demanding, overscheduled lives. "We're stressed out and don't have enough time, and so one person becomes the organizer," she says. "And the other person may simply not care as much about those details, so that's when the nagging happens." Also, she says, because there isn't the clear division of labor between couples anymore, that may lead to resentment, too, as one person is saddled with more domestic responsibilities.

A plausible and more palatable explanation to me. I think I ended up becoming the household organizer because it just made sense—I work from home and have the flexible schedule. I don't believe that my husband, by virtue of his gender, is incapable of handling these tasks; it's just that my working from home makes it easier for him to get off the hook. Besides, I know that when I've been away on business trips, he has done what needed to be done.

Still, I keep thinking of what my friend said about husbands wanting us to be mothers, and I realize that it may also be true that I am trying to make my husband my father—someone who will take care of me, so I don't have to worry. If there is one thing becoming a parent does, it makes you worry. You feel an incredible responsibility. You worry that something will be overlooked—with disastrous results. If you don't get that rash on her arm looked at by a pediatrician, it may develop into some weird flesh-eating disease. If you don't find her a good orthodontist soon, she might develop a terrible overbite that will ruin her looks forever.

When I nag, I'm saying, "*Please*, take some of this responsibility away. Please make me feel like nothing will fall through cracks." I'd love to be in the position of knowing I don't have to remember it all because someone else will take care of it. And I think my husband would, too. As we become parents and take on all these responsibilities and worries, could it be we're simply looking for a place to put them?

Slowly I walk up the stairs to find my husband on the floor of our bathroom, recaulking a section of our bathtub. He looks up at me and we both smile sheepishly at each other. We say our apologies, and they're heartfelt. We never want to have this fight again. We really do appreciate each other.

As we get up to leave the bathroom, I think about saying, "Don't forget to call the orthodontist tomorrow," but this time I stop myself. Then I hear my husband say, "Tomorrow, I'm gonna call. Really."

And the next day, he did.

how we worry

· Leah Stewart ·

"*A*re you sure you want to go by yourself?" my husband asks. "When will you be back? Will anyone you know be there? Where are you going to park? Do you have your cell phone?" I'm going to a local rock club to see the singer Neko Case, and I'm going by myself because Matt has to stay home with our toddler. Matt wants me to call him when I arrive at the club, and call him when I leave. He wants me to stay off the cell phone while I'm driving, though, and keep both hands on the wheel, and remain within the speed limit, and watch out for deer on our country road. He wants to know how much I'm planning to drink.

I stand at the door, wearing the new skirt I'm thrilled to get a chance to wear, because it's a going-out skirt and these days I almost never go out. He's making me feel something only my parents have ever made me feel. It's a potent combination of guilt, resentment, impatience, and a burgeoning worry. Part of me wants to rebel—to drive fast all the way, steering with my knees while smoking a cigarette. But another part says surely there's a reason why he's so concerned. *Should I not be going to the club myself? Where* am *I going to park? Why is he looking at me like he's afraid I won't make it home?*

Matt and I have been together since we were twenty years old, which now makes for twelve and a half years of cohabitation. This is not how he used to be. I can't dredge up even a single memory from our early years in which he seemed worried about me. Mad at me, sure. Wary of me, yes. Amused by me, definitely. In love with me, of course. But worried? When we were in college, I was the one who pushed him to finish his work on time, who woke him up before he slept through class. And then, when I was in graduate school and he worked at the library, I was the one who was concerned that he'd never write the book or record the music he wanted to, that instead he'd continue to spend all of his nonwork hours playing video baseball on the Sega Saturn I'd foolishly given him for Christmas. We're both procrastinators, both perfectionists who often can't start or finish a task because we're just not sure we can do it right. In the two years I was in graduate school, I managed, after much dawdling, to produce barely enough pages to meet the minimum length requirement for my thesis. But Matt never seemed worried. When I was supposed to be working and he came upon me watching TV, or writing e-mails, or doodling a hundred little flowers on what were supposed to be my notes, he never feared that I wouldn't finish. He always assumed I would. He never asked why I was gaining so much weight or sporting such an unattractive haircut—even though he told me later, after I'd lost the weight and grown out my hair, that for a time I seemed to be trying to turn myself into a frumpy, middle-aged woman at the age of twenty-two. When we moved to Boston, and then again to North Carolina, he never harassed me about applying for a job—the pusher was me, standing over him making sure he wrote his résumé. He's never suggested I wear sunscreen, get a physical, stop eating sugar, or go to the dentist. I'm the one who does that to him.

When I was pregnant, we went to a birthing class at Duke University Hospital. I noticed how the other men helped their wives in and out of chairs, kept a hand on the small of their backs, gazed at them in this goopy you're-having-my-baby way. Not Matt. When I was pregnant he treated me like he's always treated me—like an independent person who might enjoy his company but didn't much need his help to get through the day. When we went for walks he did what he always does—he got lost in thought and kept up his usual pace. I'd lag farther and farther behind, plodding along and panting, feet so swollen it felt like they were encased in lead boots. Then he'd notice I wasn't with him anymore and circle back to urge me onward, like a sheepdog herding a particularly recalcitrant sheep.

I've never wanted the sort of man who raced to open doors for me or pulled out my chair in a restaurant. What is chivalry, after all, besides the notion that a woman is weaker than a man and therefore in need of his protection? When I was younger I actually felt offended if I was carrying something heavy and a man offered to take it. In high school I dated a Southern Baptist who cried because I wouldn't say that if we got married he'd be the head of the household. He was an odd choice for a girl who didn't even want doors opened for her, yes, but at the same time his beliefs did provide me a constant platform for stating mine, as though I were engaged in a perpetual election campaign. By the time I met Matt in college, I was more interested in agreement than debate, and I've been perfectly happy ever since to be with a man who feels no need to be in charge of me, who never treats me like a dainty little flower. But when I was pregnant, my raging hormones and the discomfort of my huge, slow, heavy-breathing body made me clingy and vulnerable. I craved a little more solicitude.

But what I wanted wasn't solicitude of a physical kind, of the opening-doors, hand-on-my-back variety. What I wanted was emotional solicitude, and Matt wasn't used to my needing that. I've never been a crier. I don't like to talk about my feelings. When people offer sentiments like "I miss you," it makes me nervous. Matt and I are alike in this way. When I was pregnant, he assumed I was the same person I'd always been, plus a fetus and a whole lot of water weight. And while I wanted this to be true, and drove myself crazy trying to make it true, it just wasn't. The person I'd always been didn't watch episode after episode of *A Baby Story*, sobbing so hysterically that she felt dehydrated afterward. The person I'd always been didn't ask, "Where are you going?" in a forlorn voice every time Matt left the room.

I didn't like being this person, so subject to the demands of my body, so easily knocked around by what I felt. I thought all of this emotional upheaval would end when the pregnancy did.

Eliza was born by C-section, eighteen hours after my water broke. Matt showed me the baby immediately after she was born, and then I didn't see her again for three and a half hours. I was waiting for the rush of profound, intense love I'd been told to expect. Instead, through a haze of exhaustion and morphine, I felt something more along the lines of "Well, look at this. Where did this baby come from?"

Eliza was nine pounds, three ounces, and on the first day of her life she nursed well. But then her interest waned—she didn't want to work for the colostrum—and her weight began to drop. When we went to the doctor for her first posthospital appointment, she had lost eleven percent of her birth weight, putting her in the danger zone on their charts.

My milk still hadn't come in, and the doctor wanted me to supplement with formula. I sat in her office, trying to nod and act sensibly, but I couldn't stop crying. My mother was staying with us, and she and Matt were doing a fair share of the diapering and changing and rocking. My primary responsibility was to feed Eliza, and I couldn't even manage that. Late one night I gave up, handed the baby to Matt, and let him feed her. I felt both relieved, because her nourishment was at last someone else's responsibility, and guilty, because it was supposed to be mine.

Finally, my milk came in, nursing actually worked, and Eliza recovered enough of her weight to stop going to the doctor every day. During my struggle to figure out how to feed the baby, I'd continued to feel like I had no idea where she came from. Despite all evidence to the contrary, I couldn't stop feeling that I was Eliza's baby-sitter, and wondering when her parents were coming back. In the meantime I relied on my mother to make the necessary decisions—when to trim her nails, what day she should have her first bath. I was just the baby-sitter, how was I supposed to know?

Two weeks after Eliza's birth, my mother went home. I haven't been so sad to see her go since I was a very small child. Matt and I were now alone with the baby, and to my surprise, I still wasn't the person I'd always been. My tendency to cry at the drop of a hat had been joined by a tendency to let a small frustration send me into a rage. Matt and I have always teased each other. Now, when Matt teased me, I had visions of stabbing him with a fork. I told him I had these visions. He laughed. I said, "No, I really want to stab you with a fork," and he looked at me like he'd never seen me before. I knew the feeling. I'd never seen myself like this before either.

Without my usual routine to anchor my days, I began to obsess about what we should be doing with Eliza. The first focus of this obsession was the issue of the pacifier: the baby liked to suck, and what she wanted to do every fifteen minutes was suck on my breast. This was becoming exhausting. So was it okay to give her a pacifier? I wanted an instruction manual. I wanted rules. I read the baby-care books and I went online and all I discovered is that nobody agrees.

Pacifiers? Great for soothing! Terrible for teeth! A mom's best friend! A mom's worst enemy! The lack of consensus threw me into something of a panic. It meant there was nothing to rely on but my own judgment, and I needed more to go on than that.

Being certain I could look out for myself turned out to be different from being certain I could look out for someone else. Especially now since, for the first time, I wasn't convinced I *could* take care of myself. In one of our prebaby classes, we'd had a lesson on childproofing and watched a video in which a character named StarKid—a blue star topped with a red baby head—narrated a tour of all the dangers our home posed. Toppling bookshelves. Strangling blind cords. Suffocating plastic bags. Poisoning laundry detergent. "How would you feel if something in your home injured or killed your child?" StarKid asked, in a deep Darth Vader voice. "How would you feel?"

I imagined I would feel pretty bad. In the meantime what I felt was overwhelmed. The list of what had to be done to childproof our house was so long, and I was so tired. My once-beloved cats now looked to me like carriers of dirt and disease. When I was nursing the baby and my longhaired cat leaped onto the sofa, a rain of litter pellets hit the floor, and I wanted to weep. And the dangers in our home were just the tip of the iceberg. I needed to make sure she wore sunscreen. I needed to stop her from smoking. I'd have to decide how much TV she could watch and whether she could eat sugary cereal and when she could get her ears pierced.

The truth was that I just didn't want to be in charge, even of something as small as her pacifier. I tried to relieve this overwhelming sense of responsibility by bringing Matt into it with me. But he wasn't interested in the parenting books. He didn't want to listen to me outline the various arguments. About the pacifier he said, "If even the experts don't agree, let's just go with our gut and give it to her." He was right—we gave it to her, nothing bad happened, and our first decision as parents was successfully made. Still, I felt despair over his refusal to enter into the project of weighing the pros and cons of such decisions, because it meant I was alone in them. He and I were supposed to be doing this parenting thing together, but if he didn't also see the importance of reading ten different books on creating a bedtime ritual, how could we be a team? Why was he acting like I was driving him crazy? Why wasn't he worried like I was?

Ah, but he was. He just worried differently, though it took me a while to see it like that, because his way of worrying was as maddening to me as mine was to him. Before I was pregnant, back in 2000, I wrecked my car on our road, a twisting two-lane rural route with a speed limit of fifty-five and people driving pickup trucks considerably faster than that. After the wreck Matt checked Department of Transportation statistics and learned that an accident on this type of road is three times more likely to be fatal than one on a city street. He started writing letters, asking for the speed limit on our road to be lowered. He went so far as to write our congressman, who wrote back that while the speed limit on our road was outside the jurisdiction of a member of Congress, he would forward the letter to the appropriate person. Lo and behold, the speed limit was lowered to fifty, new signs posted every quarter mile.

For a while this satisfied Matt. Then I got pregnant. Suddenly the walks we used to take along the shoulder of our road were verboten. I was clumsy and a little out of it, said Matt, and I might wander into oncoming traffic. Someone swerving to avoid a deer might hit me. Someone passing a bicycle on a blind curve might hit me. I stopped walking along the road, for the most part, but I felt rebellious, and a couple of times when I was angry at Matt I went for a defiant walk. But mainly my walks were limited to repeatedly traversing our quarter-mile-long gravel drive.

It wasn't just the walks, either. He no longer liked the idea of my driving that road, and after Eliza was born his anxiety intensified. He started writing more letters, suggesting now that the speed limit on our road should actually be forty-five. When he went back to work, I was left at home with a newborn, in a neighborhood where I couldn't easily get out. Anywhere I wanted to go was a fifteen-minute drive, and Matt took to saying, before he left in the morning, "Don't go anywhere today." When he got home, he'd relate the traffic incidents he'd witnessed—the stupid moves, the near misses, the guy talking on his cell phone who'd rolled right through the stop sign. News of a traffic accident in our vicinity would ruin his mood for a week. He e-mailed me articles about drivers with repeated DUIs, about studies that show driving while on a cell phone is worse than being drunk.

My mother said his concern was sweet. Sweet? I thought. More like patronizing, controlling, and confining. He was giving me a complex, so that I'd spend the morning in a state of indecision about whether to have an outing in the afternoon. If I didn't go anywhere, whole days passed in which I didn't lay eyes on another adult besides Matt. I'd been driving since I was fourteen, and he was making me feel like I didn't know how to do it. Was I careful not to tailgate? Did I stay within the speed limit? Had I properly adjusted my mirrors? Did I keep both hands on the wheel?

Which brings me back to standing at the front door, ready to go out, with him peppering me with questions like the overprotective father of a teenage girl.

"You never used to worry about me like this," I say.

"What do you mean?" he says.

"You've never worried about me," I say. "You never bugged me to go to the doctor or finish my work or any of those things."

"Because I knew you'd do it," he says. "And turning something in late wasn't going to kill you."

"So now you only worry about what might kill me?"

He reminds me that he's worried about my health in the past. For about a year and a half I had a hand tremor that no one could diagnose, and I do, now, remember him worrying, urging me to go to the doctor, spending hours looking up possible causes on the Internet. "Things that can harm you," he says. "That's what I worry about. And things that can harm Eliza."

I say, "The world's a scarier place since she came along."

He nods. We're in agreement about that.

So maybe I've been an obsessive lunatic for fretting so much about the details of her upbringing. And maybe he at times has gone too far in his concern about our road, in his feeling that protecting Eliza also means protecting me. But it turns out I was completely wrong to think I was alone in wrestling with a level of responsibility unlike anything we'd ever confronted before. My mind runs both to tiny details and to outsized fantasies, from how to properly give a pacifier to preparing for an unlikely outbreak of the avian flu. Matt's interested in the facts of the case, the probabilities, and so he worries about driving in a car, which is, after all, the most dangerous thing we do every day. He has his worries, I have mine.

For a long time after Matt and I became a couple, it was important to me to preserve our separateness. We waited nine years to get married, even longer to get a joint bank account. But now we have a daughter who likes to chant, "Mama, Dada, Mama, Dada," and sometimes she just unites our names into "MaDa." To her we're a unit—her parents—and more and more that's how I see us, too. Together we do our best to offer her the security of believing, at least for a while, that somebody else is in charge.

anger management

· Ilene Rosenzweig ·

*M*y husband and I used to fight a lot. Big fights over nothing. Not speaking for hours over things as petty as tone of voice — a complaint so common we could simply hiss "Tone!" to egg the other person on. Some couples fight over legitimate issues: "I hate your friends!" or "You lied to me!" But when Rick and I were still single and living together, we could conjure a full screaming, temple-throbbing blowout from the smallest complaint, say, leaving a bag of garbage in the back of the car for too long before going to the dump. He says he's taking out the garbage and doesn't need to be criticized for how he does it. I ask, why is my position a criticism? It's just logic. "Garbage in the car could attract bugs. . . . You just hate being told what to do!" And onward and upward the sparks would fly.

That's not to say we'd fight over everything. We never fought about traditional things. Like when I found boxes of slides of him and his ex-girlfriend on a romantic weekend in Nova Scotia chilling in our freezer, I didn't clobber him with a frying pan. *That* I handled with cool ironic detachment, smoothly proffering the slide box and asking if that's what broke the defrost.

In general, Rick and I tend to get along well because we share a sense of humor and agree about big issues. Perceived slights and insults on minor issues are the things that get our Mr. and Mrs. Roper dynamic flaring. And we were fine with that. We accepted this about our relationship. Until I got pregnant.

The pregnancy was only partially planned. Rick goaded me into "trying" because, based on his calculations of how many months of ovulation therapy and sperm spinning our friends had undergone, it would take years for us to conceive. Then we walked into the bedroom and moments later I walked out pregnant. I don't think we even had sex.

We weren't ready.

Another reason Rick and I get along so well is that as a couple we share certain maturity handicaps—and were equally panicked about the prospect of becoming parents. Among the myriad fears— losing our identity, becoming a cliché, *being bad* at the job—most of all I was afraid of becoming like my parents and fighting in front of the kids.

My parents never should have been married, and if it weren't for me they wouldn't have been. The only things they had in common were bowling and two little girls. Oh, and passionate tempers. Their union was mined by a lethal combo of short fuses and bad behaviors. I remember when I was a kid, going to the Long Island Rail Road station with my mom to pick up Daddy, and everyone else's daddy coming off the train but mine. He was playing poker. My mom had her secret pastimes, too—guitar lessons that required afternoon shuttles to Boston. Such deceptions led to marriage-ending blowouts. By the time I was five, my mom "split," went the hippie route, got into modeling and Black Sabbath; my dad retreated to a Manhattan Upper West Side playboy pad. This was in the seventies, before enlightened divorce protocol about behaving for the kids' sake existed, and exes could be friends like in *The New Adventures of Old Christine*. This was more a *Kramer vs. Kramer*, full-throttle custody battle that dragged on for what seemed like forever. And the rancor worsened.

My parents' fights were opera, and words from their bellowed librettos still reverberate in my memory:

Cornea: My father grabbing a phone from my mother's hand and his ring scratching her cornea, and her going to the hospital.

Private detective: My mother discovering my father had hired a private detective in his quest to track her affairs and prove her an unfit parent.

Alimony: Them both screaming through the screen door after my father had made the ninety-minute drive from the city to our house and my mother refused to let us out for the visit, claiming he wasn't up-to-date with the alimony check.

Rick's white picket fence upbringing in Toronto was far tamer than the psychological safari going on in my Long Island home. But his parents bickered—over money. His superfrugal dad complained that his only-slightly-less-budget-minded mom wasted money by putting too much water in the teakettle.

We didn't want to become the Bickersons. We wanted to be trustworthy steady parents, models of decorum and cuss-free living, whose kids would grow up in a relaxed environment where they could enjoy their childhood. We vowed not to fight. And to that end, I invented "heart to heart," a concept to stave off an escalating argument. A time out for adults wherein either party could call "heart to heart," and the other person would be compelled to come in for a hug close enough to feel the other's heart beating.

It didn't work.

the communication challenge

As hormones and preparental anxiety mounted, so did the tenor of our rows. A memorable one, as usual, sprang from nowhere. This one before the day even started. It was about who had to take the early boxing session with our trainer that morning—some disagreement about who had scheduled it. And neither of us wanted to wake up for the 8:30 bout. (Clearly we were not prepared for the rigors of baby rearing ahead). But we did rally for a Rocky-level quarrel that ended with Rick, in a fit of frustration, punching a hole in our bathroom wall. A few weeks later, another beauty climaxed with Rick hurling his glasses on the floor, shattering the lenses, and me crawling on the ground to gather up the shards, sobbing at the violence, "We're going to be miserable parents!"

Enter Dr. Caroline Perla, couples therapist. We managed to commute to her office for only half a dozen visits. But in those meetings, Dr. Perla made a most notable diagnosis: We were fighting as a substitute for sex.

Certainly, six months into "our" pregnancy, as it is now politic to say, our sex life wasn't a thrill a minute, more of an accomplishment. And when you stop to think about it, fights *could* be construed as a turn-on. The adrenaline flows, you get flushed and light-headed. And they're often a sign of passion. Think of Ava and Frank, Liz and Burt, Jessica and Nick. (In fact, when I think back on some of the romantic comedies of my life, the fight scenes measure as exciting as the love scenes. Like the time my college boyfriend kicked down a street sign in a jealous fit over a lacrosse player, or the boyfriend who locked me in the bathroom just to get a word in edgewise.)

Of course, none of those famous couples ever spawned. The conflation of passion and anger loses its glamour as a parent, as we learned a few months after our son was born. The halcyon bliss subsided and we were no longer obsessing over the wobbly neck and soft spot and had the confidence to act more like ourselves. That's when we had our first fight. Somewhere between squabble and quibble—a squibble really, a mere three on our personal Richter scale. But it was carried out from the living room to the kitchen and across the little person in the high chair in between. His startled face collapsed into sad clown and started to bawl, red, panting, and spraying tears. Our son had no words yet, but he looked so nervous and sad that it broke our hearts.

We were living out exactly the scenario we had both wanted to avoid. Seeing in our son's face what had previously been abstract—how damaging parents' acrimony and bitterness can be—we had the motivation we lacked before to rein it in. We learned to exhibit control, to postpone a disagreement until we were alone. And by then, who can remember? With the built-in cooling-off period, the friction lessened. We both tended to say "I'm sorry" more. For a time, peace seemed more valuable than being right.

But then we had another one, baby that is. Just weeks after he was born we moved to Los Angeles and changed careers. This stress trifecta was aggravated by the fact that the new house—a rental we leased online—was a disaster, with broken windows, a dead lawn, a live rat. We had to reclaim it, like *Little House on the Urban Prairie.* And while we pulled together like good life partners should, the tension took its toll. One morning we were driving our two-year-old to his new school and Rick and I were cross. In his haste, he'd forgotten to strap the car seat into the car. We weren't half a block by the time the quarrel warranted a pull over. The tremors of the Richter scale were rising when I abruptly stopped it, indignantly refusing to argue in front of the baby. Self-righteously I stopped speaking, and we drove to the Sunshine Shack in muteness. But I learned that day that kids can hear a fight even when it's silent. From the backseat a little voice cracked, "Aww, nee luh." Huh? Then again, "Aw nee luh." I choked up when I realized he was singing the Beatles song he'd learned at camp that summer, "All You Need Is Love."

the communication challenge

Babies make it plain that it's not enough to not fight in front of them. Bottling up and shelving hostility wasn't the answer either— I'd end up turning our family into *Ordinary People.* An emotionally shrink-wrapped Mary Tyler Moore wasn't the mom I wanted to be.

I wanted to show my sons how to manage stress with humor. How to be forgiving. How to love someone even for their faults. And while I'd started out trying to better my behavior for the sake of the kids, it turned out to have a residual effect on my marriage, since the same skill set that you acquire to be a good mommy can be applied to being a good spouse. I learned the importance of appearing good-natured, being able to discuss irritating behavior rather than criticize character, to attempt to understand the source of brattiness—tired, hungry, out of gas?—rather than react to it. To think of your commitment to your spouse as as permanent as your commitment to your child. To take a long view of your relationship so you don't take slights personally. And of course, to schedule play dates.

After we made the LA house habitable, Rick and I planned a much-needed one. A naughty spa getaway in Laguna Niguel to get our groove back. We left the babies with my aunt and sped out of town—just the two of us. In the Pacific inlet with neo-Mediterranean views reminiscent of the Italian seaside town where we were married, Rick and I nipped around the tennis court, noodled out during double massages, nuzzled over a romantic dinner, and then afterward repaired to our ocean-view room. And with no kids around to intrude, indulged in some very naughty behavior we could never have dared with little ears in the next room—a fight. A big one. A wing chair briefly took flight. It was hot.

making time for intimacy

tour of duty

· Muffy Mead-Ferro ·

*I*s there something the matter with me? As a wife? Because here's the thing: I don't always like to do my "wifely duty."

I should elaborate on that statement, though, because I think my lack of enthusiasm truly runs more broadly than that. What I really find distasteful is the whole idea of sex that comes with any feeling of indebtedness or obligation. I mean honestly, when sex is one's job, I believe there's a name for that.

We married women will probably never be referred to in such unsavory terms just for having sex with our own husbands, but still. I can't get excited about the idea of giving my body to somebody else, even if it is my husband, for their own personal gratification and use while I lie there doing . . . what? Going over my grocery list? Mentally returning phone calls? Planning a renovation of the breakfast room?

Our breakfast room could really use an overhaul, too, ever since that upstairs shower started leaking six years ago, but I still have to wonder if picking paint and cabinets during sex would result in the kind of sex even my husband could be happy with. I was on a talk show one time with a woman who admitted to actually watching television while her husband did "his business." Although I tried not to snort or cackle or make any other strident noises in response to that unfortunate statement, I was on the side of the studio audience members who did groan audibly, and I was even more embarrassed for that woman's husband than I was for her.

I can't criticize her though, because for all I know she dislikes obligatory sex as much as I do but just doesn't know how to get out of it. I ought to e-mail her about my trick of diligently searching eBay for cowboy-boot salt-and-pepper shakers into the wee hours, or at least until I hear snoring.

I hope my husband knows that I'm totally and completely kidding right now. Cowboy-boot salt-and-pepper shakers!

All kidding aside, I do have a genuinely sexual side of my being, and I think my husband would be as sorry as I would be if it were diminished to the point where I was just "getting it over with," so I could feel like I was off the hook for a while before it was time to service him again.

And yet I do have some idea of how easily sex can go by the wayside, how sex can start to feel strictly obligatory in a marriage. I believe I know whose fault it usually is, too, when this happens.

Often, it's the children who are to be blamed, the little buggers.

When my own children were born, I never imagined they'd be romance wreckers. On the contrary, they were romance redefined! Quick as a wink I fell madly, helplessly in love with them. I knew this would happen, of course, because so many of my friends told me it would, but no amount of forewarning could have prepared me for the overwhelming feelings of devotion that the mere existence of my own little babies evoked. The moment I saw their faces I was like toast dipped into tea, soaked through and soggy with ardor. I was infatuated and enthralled with their every feature. My little girl, Belle, my firstborn, felled me with her perfect, rosebud beauty. And when my dark, round-faced little boy, Joe, came along . . . well, I just wanted to put butter and salt on him and eat him up.

The angelic nature of these darling human beings provided quite the unmitigated contrast with the person, who had been up until then, the sole object of my affections and physical desire: my husband. He actually became less attractive than I remembered him being before. First of all, the lummox was not nearly the help he should have been with the babies. And let's just say he did not think the fact that I had become a mother to his two small children, only twenty months apart, was a good enough reason to start doing laundry, grocery shopping, or the diligent picking up of stray coffee cups.

Oh, he tried. He thought he was being a good husband and father, I'm certain of it, when he said, "Here honey, let me change Belle's diaper for you." And I'm sure he was surprised when I reacted to that suggestion with appalled indignation rather than cheery gratitude, because I'm sure he didn't think there was anything wrong with his use of the phrase "for you." Naturally, my new view of my husband and the corresponding slow burn of irritation I felt didn't do anything in particular to enhance our sex life.

And then there was the fact that for a long time after my little stint in the delivery room, intercourse really didn't feel very good. I would just as soon have stuck a dinner fork up my nose again and again, to tell you the truth. Up-down, up-down, up-down. Oh, this is fun, let's do this again tomorrow night.

My preference for dinner forks lasted for a period of about six months, postdelivery. Just about the time I started to regain my libido and felt I might possibly enjoy a little hanky-panky without a topical pain reliever and a Valium, I was pregnant again and, after the usual nine months, had another baby. Didn't want sex after that either. Sex painful . . . body exhausted . . . husband inept . . . the same litany of reasons as the first go-around.

What's more, I didn't feel at all guilty because I knew I wasn't the only mom who felt that way and for those exact same reasons, too. In fact, for the first time in my life I could read articles in women's magazines and feel that they were talking in very specific detail and with intimate personal knowledge about me. I was not only just like all the other moms I knew, I was even like all the other moms on television and in magazines! Like each of them, all I wanted at the end of the day from my marriage bed was mindless rest. If every woman in America appears to feel the same way, how can it be wrong?

The demise of married sex, especially once children have entered the picture, has been women's magazine fodder almost since the beginning of women's magazines. I've certainly engaged in conversations on this topic in my own book club plenty of times, and my girlfriends all had similar stories to tell, lest you think we actually talk about the book we were supposed to have read.

But I started to hear my girlfriends (and myself) say things in book club that I realized I didn't really feel good about. Things such as "I've been pawed and sucked and groped by two little kids all day long, and the last thing I need is to have my husband all over me when I get into bed."

When I first heard that, all I wanted to say was "Amen sister!" but just before I got to the "sister" part I felt the words sort of dry up and evaporate in my throat. I had to actually turn on my brain for a moment there, and do some independent thinking. Are pawing from a husband and a child at all the same thing? Are they coming from the same place or going in the same direction?! Could the one, in any way, shape, or form, ever be any kind of a substitute for the other? Cripes, that whole idea just gives me the willies. It's true that they can each sap your energy, but so what? You still need both in your life. Vacations sap your energy, too, but it doesn't mean you give them up to do nothing but work.

That's what I started to think about, once I stopped wallowing in the support I was getting from the swell sisterhood of my sex-avoiding, nonreading book club. It started to occur to me that I was letting intimacy with my children replace intimacy with my husband, and in spite of the fact that so many other women seemed to be doing it, too, I realized it was just plain dumb. No wonder sex had begun to feel like a chore and an afterthought!

It occurred to me that perhaps Belle and Joe weren't the romance wreckers I'd thought they were, either. In fact, I take back what I stated earlier about the little buggers being to blame for the demise of romance in a marriage. Because I realized that my kids weren't actually coming between me and my husband. I myself may have been putting them there.

Who could blame me? I felt like I'd actually been encouraged to put my children before my husband in our childcentric, parenting-obsessed, and socially competitive culture. Everyone is racing to raise the best kids, but having a great marriage seems to get lost in the shuffle. And I knew just from looking around my own neighborhood that if I didn't change my thinking, I wouldn't be the first mom who had (although perhaps not deliberately) sacrificed her relationship with her husband in favor of her relationship with her kids. I realize there are many reasons why marriages head south, but I'd venture that one of them is when a woman sets out to be supposedly the most fan-damn-tastic mom in the world.

In fact, if I got it in my head to do that, I'm sure I'd have to let a lot of things besides my marriage head south. I'd have to sacrifice not only quality time with my husband, but quality time with my wonderful friends, too. I would certainly have to sacrifice the writing career that has been so very rewarding to me. And I suppose I wouldn't be able to have much in the way of hobbies or personal pursuits if I were utterly determined to be, above all else, the most devoted parent imaginable.

I guess I could always try to make myself feel better by saying, "Look how much I've given up in my life — I must be a fabulous mom!" But I don't think I'd feel better. I know myself, and I know I'd have a hard time biting off a piece of that kind of a motherhood-as-martyrdom scheme, and an even harder time choking it down. Because deep down I really don't buy the idea that sacrificing all the other things one cares about really goes hand in hand with being a great mom. I've also asked myself what I want my own kids to know about the world around them and about their own family, and one thing I want them to know is that there are four people who matter in our family, not just two. I don't want to raise them with the idea that the world revolves around them, because that will certainly set them up for failure and disappointment, not to mention that it wouldn't do my marriage any favors. I also want them to know that indeed I have a life beyond them, and I want them to see me living it.

What's more, I don't think Belle and Joe really want to take me away from the father they also adore. Yes, the little imps scrunch up their faces and say "gross" when they catch us hugging and kissing, but it's easy enough to see through that. And I can understand why they are not-so-secretly pleased, too, because the bond that I share with their father, which predates and is quite distinct from the bond we share with them, tells them our family has a strong foundation.

The bottom line is that I realized I'd fallen into a pattern that, while it seemed to be the expected norm for the average American mom, I didn't believe in. It took me a while to get my mind around that because I was getting so much encouragement from society to make my kids the center of my world, the primary object of my affections, even as my marriage started to drift into routine disconnectedness.

When my little brain finally processed all of this, I realized that despite the fact I loved my children beyond measure, it was unnecessary and illogical to let my feelings for them supersede my feelings for my husband. What's more, I noticed my husband hadn't ever let that happen. He loves our children immeasurably, too, but he didn't fall head over heels. He wasn't soaked-through-soggy-toast infatuated the same way I'd been. His intimate feelings were still, and always had been, reserved for me.

Don't get me wrong. I still don't like the idea of sex as duty one bit, and I don't think anyone should feel they have to have sex if it rates on a par with a fork up the nostril on the pleasure scale, but fortunately that hasn't been a problem for quite a while. My body has healed. It wasn't sex that I didn't like anymore, it was the idea of obligatory sex, the idea of *wifely duty*. Although I knew I was probably the one who could take most of the blame for it, I hated the way sex seemed to gradually have been positioned in our marriage during the four or five years since we'd had kids. I hated that I'd started saying to myself, "Well, it's been two weeks now . . . so . . . you'd better put out tonight."

So I sat down and told my husband in pretty frank terms that although I don't blame him, I do not like the feeling that I owe him, especially concerning something that is supposed to bring us mutual satisfaction. The feeling of obligation was turning me off. Not on.

Now before I describe his reaction, I have to tell you that my husband is quite clever, and also that he knows me very well.

First of all, he wasn't defensive, which threw me because men are always defensive. (To the men reading this: Women are not defensive. We just have comebacks for everything, which are typically prepared in advance. But back to my husband.)

"Fine," he said, placidly. "I hear what you're saying. We don't ever have to have sex again, then, if you don't want to. Let's just forget about it. I'm fine with that."

Can you imagine? He didn't even add, "But it can't stay this way for long." Or even, "But I'm here if you want me." He just dropped it . . . he left it at that. Never again! I was floored.

I was also extremely grateful. Glory hallelujah, I'd been set free from bondage! I'd had the great weight of sexual indebtedness lifted from my weary wifely shoulders! I could sleep! Oh my goodness, I was in a state of near bliss.

Well, I should clarify. I was in a state of near bliss for about two or three weeks. After that I started to feel kind of lonely, to tell you the truth. And—this was even more odd—I started to feel a little frisky. Getting ready for bed at night I'd be thinking such alien thoughts as, *I wonder if my husband would be up for a little roll in the hay? I wonder how I could get him in the mood?* I started looking at him walking around in our bedroom in his boxer shorts and thinking, *Yum.* Suddenly, somehow, he was different. He'd gone from being my oppressor to being the forbidden fruit, just beyond my reach.

You can see where this is going. Yes, my husband had played a little psychological trick on me, and it had worked precisely the way he'd planned. It worked even though I knew he was tricking me. Because I wanted to be tricked. I wanted to stop thinking of sex the way I'd been thinking of it. I wanted to get it sorted out in my mind, and separated from the issues of child rearing and chores. It seems that all I really needed was to yank my perspective around.

And of course, I needed the breathing room in which to do it. I'm grateful to my husband for giving me that.

I just wish I could get in touch with the woman who was on the talk show. The one who watched TV while her husband did his business. I wish I could tell her she doesn't owe her husband sex. That it's not *his* business, it's *hers.* And that if she really wants some cute cowboy-boot salt-and-pepper shakers, not to look on eBay because I have some I can give her a super good deal on.

dating the hubs

· Sandi Kahn Shelton ·

So, you see, we had this baby. Life changed.

I don't mean to brag, but before the baby came, we were good—really good—at going out on dates with each other. In those days, I was capable of finding my car keys and my purse at a moment's notice without even once having to look in the refrigerator or between the couch cushions. My husband could be counted on to stay awake past eight-thirty in the evening. And—this is key—we could both locate clean clothing simply by looking in our closets.

We went to movies, out to dinner, to clubs, to concerts in the park, to plays. We went to friends' houses and on late-night picnics. It was so easy for us. We were even capable of looking across the living room at each other at, say, ten o'clock on any given evening and deciding on the spur of the moment to head out for dessert, and actually *making that happen.*

"Wouldn't a napoleon taste great right about now?" my husband might ask, and within two and a half minutes, we'd have our jackets on and be pulling out of the driveway.

And then . . . well, as I said, we had the baby, and life changed.

She was a delightful baby—rosy and pink, with plump fingers and toes; bright, curious eyes; and a completely round, warm, fuzz-covered head that reminded me of peaches in the summertime. The curve of her ear was like those delicate little seashells you see on the sand when the tide is going out. She had a way of widening her eyes and looking around when you spoke to her. And when she sneezed—well, she would squinch up her face and pull her arms and legs in close to her body. Seeing these sneezes, I would have to call people on the telephone to report how incredible she was.

I don't mind telling you that this led to certain of my friends becoming alarmed. There are apparently people in this world who don't think the occasion of a baby sneezing should lead to a telephone call, no matter how startling or charming this event might be. I could sense that people were beginning to worry about me, perhaps even to band together to see if an intervention might become necessary. Once, for instance, when I had finished explaining to my friend Katie how the baby had a way of gazing fondly after her little fist as it floated past her head, Katie, who herself has three children, cleared her throat and said, "So, are you getting out much?"

Of course I was getting out. Very patiently I listed the doctors' appointments, the walks around the block with the stroller, the car rides to the store to buy more diapers, pacifiers, and the special baby detergent.

Katie said, "No. I mean are you getting *out*? Like, have you found someone to watch the baby so that you and The Hubs can go someplace . . . you know . . . together?" (Katie believes that all husbands, her own included, should go by the nickname: The Hubs.)

Others soon started asking the same question. My mother, of all people, wanted to know if we were ever alone anymore. "I know how you two like to go out!" she sang. "I was wondering if you still remember how that's done." I was stunned. We were happy at home. What was the big deal? What was this horror people seemed to feel toward the idea that we were now pleasantly attached to a baby and did not need the outside world so much?

The fact was, as I informed everyone who inquired, The Hubs and I *had* managed to get ourselves out of the house a few times since the baby arrived. But we didn't need a baby-sitter, I told everyone. We had wisely decided to have the exemplary kind of baby you could simply take along. It was better that way, in fact. We were too tired to trust ourselves to let her out of our sight. What if we got a baby-sitter, fell asleep somewhere, and forgot to come back home? No, really.

And, besides, as I told them, it was nice having her along. Her car seat made a delightful centerpiece on the tables of restaurants, and she enjoyed waving her arms and staring at the lights. And conveniently, by the time she was tired of the décor, we often discovered that we, too, were in the mood to move on. Twice, we had even gone to the movies with her. I had simply tucked her underneath my shirt, where she had nursed and dozed for the duration of the movie. I had curled my body around her and slept like a baby myself. It was the deepest sleep I'd had in weeks.

"Hmm," said our childless, dateless, and perhaps bordering-on-clueless friend Rob. "I would think you'd want to go out by yourselves sometimes, *without* having to always wear a baby underneath your shirt."

I rolled my eyes at The Hubs. Clearly Rob didn't understand the magnificence of parenthood and the dazzling notion that one human could nourish another using only objects already found on her own body.

Later that evening—okay, so it was 6:30 P.M., and yes, we were climbing into bed with the baby for what we hoped might be a family-style early evening nap—The Hubs said to me, "So what do you say? Should we go out by ourselves, just to prove we can still do it?"

"Well," I said. "Okay." I swallowed hard.

He said, "I know."

Perhaps this would be a good time to tell something about the baby that I might have forgotten to mention. She did not believe in sleeping at night. That's right: She was only two months old and yet she already had a policy against it. During the day, she took fabulous naps, but at night, if, by some careless accident, she happened to slip off into sleep, she would jerk herself awake immediately and look around, almost apologetically, as if we might think her rude for not paying closer attention.

And, oh yes, one more thing: having awakened herself that way, she insisted on being taken into our bed with us. She wouldn't even *hear* of leaving us bereft of her presence by going back to her bassinet. We therefore spent most of our nights with a baby cradled between us, or else with one of us walking her around and around the dining room table, singing songs to her. When it was his turn, The Hubs claimed her favorite go-to-sleep song was "Go, Speed Racer," from a cartoon show he'd watched as a child. I tended toward "A Hundred Bottles of Beer on the Wall" because it had so many verses and didn't require much memory power.

We were so tired that we were perhaps bordering on being mentally ill.

And so we started making plans.

Right away I could see this was not going to be so easy—nothing like the old days, that was for sure. I sat down and made a list of the obstacles that stood between us and an evening out:

making time for intimacy

1. Must find perfect baby-sitter.

2. Must figure a way of getting milk from breasts into bottles, enough to last baby for entire evening.

3. Must find evening clothing that: (a) fits rounded postpregnancy body; (b) does not have visible milk stains; (c) is not technically in the bathrobe, sweatpants, or maternity category.

4. Must summon missing organizational skills. Important to locate car keys, shoes, jacket, and purse before the moment comes to leave the house.

These are, of course, major obstacles, and solving them took a little while. Katie, hearing of obstacle number one, actually volunteered to baby-sit and promised me she'd walk the baby around the dining room table endlessly if necessary, and she would sing every bar ballad known to man. But she had conditions: I had to really try to have fun—preparenthood fun—and I had to make a rule that we wouldn't spend the whole date talking about the baby.

Not talk about the baby? Was she out of her mind? What else was there to talk about? She suggested I make a little list of possible conversational topics in advance. I thought up two things and jotted them down in a little notebook: "Best inventions of the last century" (I planned to nominate pacifiers and wind-up swings), and, on another topic altogether, "Why, on a menu, does the word *Florentine* mean you're getting spinach?"

Katie laughed at me. Okay, so I knew these weren't the most *fun* topics, but at least one was about culture and the other about cuisine, so I figured they could carry us through to dessert, and then we could go home again.

Next, to solve the breast milk dilemma, I actually went to the drugstore and bought a breast pump, the cheap kind with the glass vial attached to a little bulb thingie that looks like a squeezable bicycle horn. The woman in the store assured me that all a person had to do was to hook this up to the nipple, and breast milk would just flow like an open faucet. "Do it while you're nursing the baby on the other side," she advised. "Then the milk just *gushes*."

Ha! Other people's breasts might fall for this, but mine weren't fooled by this gambit for one second. They knew they were being asked to commit fraud here, and no bicycle horn was going to trick them into giving up their hard-earned milk. By relentlessly pumping and squeezing and cursing and sighing and finally mooing, I was able to collect two and a half ounces over the next several days.

Which I then dropped on the floor and spilled when I tripped over a box of diapers.

I called Katie to tell her that I would probably not be able to gather enough breast milk again for at least the next twenty years and that going out was an overrated enterprise anyhow. Katie said I should just nurse the baby before I left, and in case of a starvation emergency, she'd give the baby a little bit of formula. Formula, she said when I gasped, had been known to actually nourish babies. It wasn't going to be the end of the world. Reluctantly I agreed.

Second obstacle overcome. I turned my attention to finding something to wear.

Through some miracle, I managed to find, on the floor of my closet, a pair of stretchy black pants I'd forgotten about and a silk tunic top that had yet to be spit up on. If I sucked in my belly very hard, I didn't look as though I were five months pregnant. I could even button the thing, and that made me so happy I did a little victory dance with the baby.

The big night came at last.

I found my car keys at the bottom of the diaper bag, underneath a soiled diaper and a half-eaten granola bar. I was able to locate two matching shoes, one underneath the wind-up swing and the other under the plastic baby bathtub. My jacket was crammed into the bottom of a shopping bag. The Hubs managed to locate a clean shirt and some socks that very nearly matched each other, and we were off.

Leaving the house was not easy. I had to run back several times to tell Katie things she might not know: the baby sometimes squirms in your arms, and it's important not to drop her. Also, she prefers a clockwise movement around the dining room table. We never go counterclockwise. Never. And had I mentioned that, really, two and half seconds of crying was all we thought we could bear? So don't get her used to crying more. Please.

I'm not going to lie to you and say that the date was a roaring success. For starters, the restaurant lost our reservation and said we'd have to wait an hour, so we left and went to a fast-food place that fed us in five minutes.

"What shall we talk about?" I said to The Hubs, blinking in the fluorescent lights. "Katie says we have to try to think of some topic besides the baby."

"I agree," he said. "What did we used to talk about?"

We couldn't remember.

"I think when we were out, we used to talk about the food," I offered.

"Oh. I can do that. These fries are good."

I was about to initiate a discussion about my Florentine-means-spinach discovery, but then he suggested we play hangman on the placemat, which was fine with me. His first entry was the baby's name. My eyes filled with tears.

"That's it," I said. "I have to call home."

Katie said the baby was fine, and when she heard where we were, she said that we were pathetic and hopeless and we should just go somewhere else and have a good time. I looked at my watch. We had been out of the house for twenty-two minutes.

"We want to come home, because there's no place to go," I told her.

"Go to a movie, go bowling," she said. "What, are you socially impaired or something? Walk along the beach. Go make out in the woods. Just go have fun."

I hung up the phone and looked at The Hubs. "You don't want to go to a movie or bowling, do you?" I asked him.

He didn't. "Let's go grocery shopping," he said with a sigh. "That would kill some time, and at least it'd be productive."

I kissed him in the car for having such a brilliant insight. He kissed me back. He said the baby made him so tired he sometimes couldn't think straight. I said I didn't think I'd ever have enough sleep again and that my IQ points were dropping by the hour. I told him I couldn't even work a breast pump, and he laughed. I confessed that often it was four o'clock in the afternoon before I managed to get out of my bathrobe, and that I'd taken to eating vanilla frosting out of a can rather than think up something for lunch on some days.

We strolled through the grocery store, holding hands. He read me the nutritional information on the boxes of macaroni and breakfast cereal, using a crazy German accent. We sang along with the Muzak. I asked him what the finest invention of the twentieth century was, and he said it was the supermarket, hands down. I couldn't remember what I thought it was, which made me laugh.

We were laughing so hard I started to feel sorry for all the single, harried people in there, rushing past us to pick up prepared foods and then rushing back out again. When we got to the frozen food aisle, we said this had been an insane idea, thinking we could go out on a date. We weren't daters anymore.

"We're cocooners," The Hubs said. "Hopeless cocooners, and we need to go home."

I said, "Let's go," and we raced each other to the car.

It was only eight-fifteen when we got back to our house. Katie and the baby were cuddling in the living room watching a movie together. Katie smiled and shook her head at us when we brought in the groceries, and said we were the most pitiful individuals she'd ever met in her life.

The baby hadn't had to drink any formula. She hadn't cried or needed to be walked yet. It was still early. We'd have a night of "Speed Racer" yet to come. I felt a wave of crazy relief as I took her out of Katie's arms.

Of course, The Hubs and I did finally learn how to go out on dates again, just the two of us. We learned how to say good-bye to our child, find our shoes, and make a run for it. We even learned to have conversations once we were out, conversations that did not have to do with children, to turn back to ourselves as people rather than simply parents.

Standing there that night, though, next to the frozen dinners, I caught a glimpse of the truth: We were never *really* going back to the way we were before. We were forever altered by the startled awareness that the two of us had become three, and that part of our hearts were forever after going to belong with this child, no matter how many times I'd have to say good-bye to her and close the door.

Our daughter is seventeen now, a senior in high school preparing to go away to college next year. Tonight I watch her doing her homework and combing her long brown hair in front of the mirror, and I am nourished by the memory of a time when we lived with her in our own delicious, tiny universe. It was like being in love, the way the three of us shut out the world and found completeness in a string of hazy, milky, sleep-deprived days, as blurry to me now as a faded, jerky videotape. The world beckoned, but on a night of french fries and Stop & Shop, we learned to hold it at bay until we were good and ready to let it in.

do ya think i'm sexy?

· Neal Pollack ·

My son has taken control of the living room, as he usually does when something about sharks appears on TV. He's declared that he needs to be left alone in his "shark fort." This means that I can possibly sneak away for some nookie. It's late afternoon, that magic horny time of day when Regina and I are neither too tired nor too busy to mess around. I press her against the kitchen cabinets and nibble on her neck. She clamps her hand on my butt.

"I love your ass," she says.

"Oh yeah?"

"Yeah."

"Well then," I say, "maybe you should fuck it."

It's a meaningless suggestion that doesn't resemble anything that actually goes on in our bedroom. But it's fun to say anyway. People who have actual sex lives say stuff like that, right?

"Maybe I should," she says. "Naughty boy."

"I'm not a naughty boy."

"Yes you are."

"Yeah, well, you're a naughty girl."

We make out. Before we became parents, this moment would have occurred about fifteen minutes in advance of actual sex. Now, it could be days.

"Can we have some nik-nik tonight?" I ask.

Yes, I refer to it as "nik-nik."

"We'll see."

"But . . ."

"Let's just enjoy each other right now."

So we do that for a little while. It gets pretty hot. I pin Regina against the pantry. We swap tongues. There's grinding and heavy breathing and even a little moan or two. She opens her eyes.

"Um," she says.

I turn around. Elijah has poked his head around the door. He grins like he has a secret, which I guess he does.

"What are you doing, guys?" he says.

"Daddy is giving Mommy a hug," says Regina.

"And a kiss," I say.

"I want a hug!" says the boy, as he runs over and throws his arms around our legs. Nothing kills erotic momentum quite like that. Paradise has been postponed again.

Later, we get him to bed, though Elijah in bed often means an hour of mindless shrieking on his part. Also, he likes to press the snooze button on his clock radio and has a fit if it's not tuned to an urban contemporary station. He's three.

Regina checks her e-mail. I watch a TiVoed episode of *The Office*. Eventually, the child collapses, but not until 10:30 P.M. Regina often complains that by the time I make serious advances, she's already way too tired. Tonight doesn't deviate. I make pleading eyebrows.

"Why did you wait so long?"

"I waited forty-five minutes!"

"That's too long."

"But I wanted to give you a chance to do what you wanted to do. . . ."

Occasionally in these situations, I'm able to parlay guilt into something. It always turns out desultory, but I rarely end up disappointed. I've really come to enjoy the alternative.

"You have your computer," she says.

"As always."

"Let's try it again tomorrow. Maybe a little earlier this time."

"Okay."

About ten minutes later, she's all cleaned up and ready for bed. I tuck her in and give her a nice little kiss.

"Are you comfortable?" I ask.

"Yes, honey. Can you bring me the dog?"

I go into the living room, pick up our Boston terrier, walk back to the bedroom, and drop him on the bed. He immediately dives under the covers and settles in between my wife's legs, albeit about a foot lower than I would have settled. Then there's a brief pause, which I break by saying, "Can I go masturbate now?"

It took me a while to get my wife into bed. At the time Regina and I met, I had some left-wing friends who believed that monogamy was a bourgeois institution imposed upon us by our patriarchal society. In reality, these friends were just looking for a pretentious excuse to cheat on their spouses. But I was lonely and impressionable, and I imagined I'd enjoy sleeping around if given a chance. Therefore, I spent a good portion of the conversation on the first date with Regina telling her that I, too, didn't believe in monogamy.

Around the time Regina stopped kissing me at the end of our

dates, I realized that this wasn't the best approach to seducing a nice, mannered Protestant girl. So I changed my line. "Monogamy is wrong," I said, "as it's structured in our society. But I have no problem with being monogamous, particularly with you." I must have sounded sincere. Maybe I even *was* sincere. Regardless, we had sex for the first time that night, and it was great.

My sex life before Regina had been uneven at best: a few one-night stands, a few two-night stands, a long termer in high school with a girl who was terrified of getting pregnant and therefore wore a diaphragm *and* contraceptive foam in addition to making me put on a condom, and several years of dating a traumatized young woman who had good reasons, none of them printable here, that prevented her from getting in the mood very often. My wife-to-be, on the other hand, had no sexual neuroses, no hang-ups, and no bad history. She simply enjoyed sex, and wanted to share that enjoyment with me.

I listened in amazement as she related the story of how she lost her virginity. Toward the end of college, she became friends with a hot, sexually experienced guy. He agreed to initiate her, and he did it with the skill of an expert. Then, once in a while, they'd get together when it was convenient and he'd give her graduate courses. By the time it ended, she really knew what she was doing.

A few years later, I reaped the harvest of her knowledge. Regina had a hatbox full of sex toys, which she kept under her bed. Never before had I been with someone who lit candles, or used oils, or who kept handy more than one shape of dildo. She had a solid supply of plugs and tubes, and would have been willing to try ropes and blindfolds, if that's what I'd wanted.

That first night together, we lay naked under her ceiling fan, watching her Native American dreamcatcher twist in the artificial breeze.

"I'm falling asleep," I said.

"So am I," she said.

"Don't you want to put on some pajamas or a T-shirt or something?"

"I sleep naked."

"You do?"

"Of course," she said. "Everyone likes to sleep naked."

This was news for me. I'd never known anyone who slept naked before. At that moment, I pretty much decided that I was going to marry this woman. It's incredibly hard to find someone, male or female, who believes that sex is a natural part of life, for whom love-making isn't inextricably intertwined with body-image problems, difficult childhood memories, or issues of power and control. Sex with my wife would be fun, without complications.

We had sex, and plenty of it, but because of that, ours wasn't one of those relationships that simmered with passion at all times. We *could* keep our hands off each other. Some nights, we'd skip sex entirely. And then occasionally we'd skip several nights in a row. Sex, we figured, would always be available to us. As it turns out, we should have been stockpiling the experience. The drought would soon arrive.

As it does for so many couples, our sex life dried up after the birth of our first child. I understood that Regina had other priorities. Our son, Elijah, kept both her breasts occupied. She needed to recover from an unplanned C-section. When she was in bed, all she wanted to do was sleep. Plus, Elijah was sleeping next to our bed, in a Pack 'n Play. Oils, toys, and a laid-back attitude weren't going to change the situation. Hell, Barry White singing live in the next room wasn't going to lead to sex. Coitus, and related activities, was simply off the table.

So we took a break. But, unlike Regina, my biology hadn't been inexorably transformed by the rigors of childbearing. I had plenty of time to sit around, thinking about all the sex that I wasn't having. At the same time, I was enduring a nasty little career "correction" that left me very depressed. I went on pills.

Many people who've gone on antidepressants lament their neutering effect. They may no longer be sad, but they also no longer experience sexual desire. I, on the other hand, got a prescription for the only antidepressant on earth that has an aphrodisiac side effect. I felt horny all the time, summer-camp-counselor-in-training horny. Monogamy was about to take on a whole new meaning for me.

Even though I knew Regina wasn't interested, I pressed my case. Several times a day, I'd sneak up behind her, kiss her neck and rub up against her so she could feel the result of my prescription.

The response usually went something like this:

"Oh, my," she said.

"Daddy's got a boner," I said.

"I can see that."

"Can you do something about it? Now?"

She indicated our son, who was waiting in the dining room for his mashed yams.

"Maybe later," she said.

"I really can't wait until later."

"You've got to be kidding me," she said.

Later, in those early years of parenthood, rarely came. Fortunately, the decline in my sex life coincided perfectly with the rise of wireless high-speed Internet and the golden age of speedy online porn. The buffet lay before me. To paraphrase Woody Allen, I began to have frequent sex with someone I loved.

And I do mean frequent. I found myself jerking off twice, sometimes even three times per day. The erections sprang up unbidden, like back pimples. They were quite distracting, and I had to take care of them. Maybe I'd masturbated this much when I was fourteen, but it seemed unlikely. Nothing, it seemed, could sate the self-loving beast within.

As habits go, this one was pretty enjoyable. For the first time in my long career as a masturbator, I developed technique. I read websites and learned that I needed to exercise my perineum if I wanted to extend orgasm. Soon, my orgasms became double or even triple the length of before. I learned how to come twice in a row, and how to do it without ejaculating. Essentially, I became a virtual stud.

This was something I wanted to share with my partner, but the terms of our partnership had changed. Since having the kid, she'd developed body-image issues, which was normal, but I didn't care. If anything, *I* was the one who was pushing monogamy now. I was tired of being monogamous with myself, and I wanted my marriage to be about something more than fiscal commitment and bringing up baby.

"You just can't expect me to turn on a dime," she said.

"Um. It's been almost three years."

"Something went wrong with my body when I had the baby," she said. "I'm just not that into it anymore."

"Regina," I said. "I'm thirty-five years old. I'm just not ready to give up sex yet."

"But I'm ugly," she said, her newfound insecurity manifesting itself again.

"No, you're not. I think you're an extremely sexy woman."

I began to kiss her neck.

"You turn me on all the time."

But I got little response.

We had other problems. Money got tight. Our kid was a biter for a little while. We lived in a neighborhood frequented by prostitutes and speeding beer-delivery trucks. There seemed to always be another priority. And she was tired. Disparity in sexual interest wasn't going to break up our marriage. Still, I felt sad, and lonely.

making time for intimacy

○ ○ ○

Fortunately, even in the darkest hours of my relentless jerking, our sex life as a couple didn't diminish altogether. I'd occasionally catch Regina in the right mood, or our kid would miraculously fall asleep early. Still, the joy had mostly gone out of it for her.

"There must be something wrong with me," she said. I assured her there was nothing wrong with her. But I did, sometimes, think that there was something wrong with me. Suddenly, I found myself feeling needy and emotional.

"Don't you think I'm sexy anymore?" I said.

"Aw, honey. I think you're very sexy."

"Then why . . ."

"I don't know."

"You're really starting to hurt my feelings."

Sometimes, if I poured the guilt on thick, I'd get some. But what I'd loved about Regina in the first place was that she'd enjoyed sex without guilt. It had no psychological component for her. How, I wondered, could I recapture that?

By now, I've realized that those carefree days of newlywed sex are as much in my past as the days, before I had a driver's license, when I used to kiss girls whom I met at the roller rink. As our kid gets older, our opportunities for sex have become more frequent, and the sex has improved. But no one can ever be entirely carefree again once they become a parent. I don't know if I believe in monogamy any more now than I did when I met Regina. That said, my definition of monogamy has changed. I can't say for certain that I don't want to have sex with anyone else, ever again. In fact, I'd be lying if I said I didn't. But I do know that life is good with Regina, and I don't want to have a kid with anyone else.

time trials

· Andy Steiner ·

*T*he other morning, I was digging around for something in the back of my closet when I found a framed photograph I'd stashed there in one of my fits of manic tidying.

My two-year-old was in the other room, busy pulling all of the books out of her older sister's bookshelf, so I had a moment to sit on the bed and wipe the dust off the glass with my sleeve. When I was younger, I dabbled in photography, and this was a black and white I'd developed and printed myself. I was so proud of my work that I'd framed it. Every time I moved to a new apartment, I hung the picture up in my bedroom.

Later, when my husband and I bought our first house, we followed tradition and hung the picture on the wall across from our bed. It stayed there for seven years. Then, a few weeks before the birth of our first child, we decided to rearrange our bedroom to make room for the bassinet. Somehow my photo looked out of place hanging over a bassinet, so we took it down and replaced it with an old poster print that we deemed more appropriate for an infant.

My husband and I started dating in college. I'd taken that photo one sunny weekend morning. He lived in an apartment near school, and his bedroom was on the chilly converted sunporch. We'd spent the night before on his futon under a pile of quilts, and when I woke he was asleep on his stomach, his arms splayed out across the pillows. I spent several quiet minutes admiring how the late-morning sun cast shadows from the blinds across his bare shoulders, then I slipped out of bed, took out my camera, which I sometimes carried with me in those days, and snapped a few shots.

Later, when I printed the roll, I fell in love with that shadowy picture, the way the light played on his warm skin, the way it reminded me of that particular lazy sunny morning—and of the night before. Because the photo was a close-up, viewers had a hard time figuring out what the image was, but *I* knew, and I treasured that secret. At first, hanging the picture on my bedroom wall was a public declaration of my love; later, when the bedroom wall became *ours,* the photo was an important reminder of our shared intimate history.

I realize now that we should have been able to read the deeper symbolism when, in less time than it took for me to roll out of bed and grab the camera on that long-ago morning, the imagined needs of our baby-to-be supplanted our lives as lazy, sensual, childless adults and transformed us into parents.

Obviously, we knew—intellectually at least—that the long-anticipated birth of the baby swelling in my belly would officially make us *mother* and *father.* But we didn't fully realize the responsibilities those titles held. Few of our friends were parents yet, but those we knew had already frightened us (intentionally or unintentionally) with horror stories of sleepless nights, diaper rash, and colicky cries.

blindsided by a diaper

One couple, parents of a then three-year-old girl, kept saying they hadn't had a chance to see *a single movie* since their daughter was born, and the idea sent shivers up and down my still-child-free spine. Under the mistaken belief that a person could bank movie time like spare change, we spent the months leading up to the due date seeing every movie we could stomach. Even if we didn't have time to see movies right after the baby was born, we figured, we'd see a lot now so we'd have plenty to talk about with our friends later. (Little did we know that for the next several months, movies and their plotlines would suddenly feel trivial compared to the more pressing realities of sleepless nights, diaper rash, and colicky cries.)

As "countdown to baby" continued, we bought parenting books and took a childbirth class. In the evenings we'd sit in bed together and talk for hours about what we had learned, noodling about baby names and planning for the future. I worried (I'm a worrier at heart) about how introducing a child into our lives would change our relationship; my mostly easygoing husband fretted to a much lesser degree. The changes I anticipated were textbook: dried-up sex life, child-care versus career juggles, body transformation. I kept a journal during that pregnancy, and I scrawled my "worry lists" there. In what has been a typical pattern in our relationship, I showed my husband my lists, and he gently countered my worries, reminding me that a well-lived life is a series of calculated risks. That was an important reminder for me at a time of such doubt and change.

All this mental preparation took time, but that was okay. Even though our days were filled with paid employment and the distracting busywork of getting ready for a child, we actually had time to spare. Time for my worries, yes—but we also had time to touch and admire and ponder each other's bodies, especially my rapidly changing one. And time to look each other in the eye and talk until we got tired of talking.

Six years and two children later, the idea of talking until we get tired of talking seems incomprehensible to my husband and me. But there were times not that long ago when we did just that—on a regular basis.

When Time Was on Our Side

In the years immediately following college and graduate school, we were rich with friends. We had a tight bunch of buddies, most of whom we met at the small, urban liberal arts college we had both attended. Though life had scattered some of us, a strong core group remained in the city. We formed a family of sorts, supporting each other, sharing inside jokes, watching movies, going on weekend trips, laughing, debating, falling in and out of love. Often, we'd gather at a nearby coffee shop or in one of our homes, and in the winter we had a standing weekly ice-skating date.

As the lone married couple in the group, my husband and I always had each other to fall back on, but our friends—and our relationships with them—were central to our lives. Until we gave in to our breeding impulses and became parents, it seemed like our world would always be the same—comfortable and easy and satisfying. But somehow, while we were distracted by our little daily dramas, the wheels of life kept turning, and we were getting older.

Things were about to change.

Before I had children, I thought I was busy, and I was, in the singular, focused way of the childless professional. In the years leading up to the births of our children, I worked as an editor at a newspaper, and, later, at a magazine. At both jobs, I'd often assign stories to freelance writers, women whose circumstances (children, partner, busy household, ambitious professional goals) now match mine.

These writers were busy juggling everything, I realize now, but I have to confess that at the time I often had to fight the impulse to see them as dilettantes, as stay-at-home moms with a bit of extra time on their hands—empty, desperate hours they filled with writing projects. When, occasionally, the sound of these writers' children crept into our telephone conversations, I'd feel a mix of pity and frustration. I was sorry that they had to spend so much of their days trying to keep children entertained, that their overwhelming breeder impulse had sidetracked their careers, but I was also frustrated that they couldn't keep their children out of their professional relationships. If kids needed to interject themselves into *phone calls,* I thought, imagine how quickly they could screw up a marriage. (When I think back on how I felt then, I didn't *really* think of kids as marriage wreckers, being that I am the youngest child of happily married parents, a couple whose relationship remains spicy, romantic, and loving after sixty years and six children.)

In fact, for a few years in my midtwenties, I pretty much decided I didn't want to have children. Change makes me nervous, and children equal major change. I liked the life my husband and I had made for ourselves. I felt busy and happy and mostly satisfied. Children have a tendency to upset the apple cart, to mess things up and make noise when you're on an important call. I wanted our tidy little life to stay the way it was. I felt safer that way.

My husband, Mr. Change Is Good, didn't agree.

I'll never forget one particular conversation: We had been away on a weekend trip, and the drive home, like all of our prechildren drives, was filled with long, uninterrupted conversations about work, family, friends, future. Somehow the subject of children was raised. I talked (at length, I'm sure) about my freelance writers, about their marginal careers, about their intrusive children. I said I wasn't sure I ever wanted to have kids.

My husband is a kind, funny, understanding man, but he can also be passionate. I always knew he loved children, that he enjoyed being an uncle to our many nieces and nephews, but I had no idea just how deep the desire to one day be a father ran inside his heart.

"If you don't want to have children," he told me, clenching his jaw, "I want to find another way to be a father."

We had a friend whose lesbian sister and her partner had asked him to be a sperm donor; we also knew a young man in college who made extra money by making donations at a local sperm bank. On some base, embarrassing level, the idea of someone else carrying my husband's child made me feel sick to my stomach. I couldn't imagine this happening. The truth is that even in the earliest, most carelessly passionate moments of our relationship, I'd always felt a biological desire to someday conceive this man's children, a desire I'd managed to bury under other ambitions and careful plans. And so, a few years and several long conversations later, we set out to make a baby.

I remember when we finally told a group of our friends that I was pregnant. Their reaction was awkward, stunned silence. In that moment, it seemed to me that the earth's plates shifted, that my husband and I (and our unborn child) stood marooned on one island, while our single, childless friends occupied another. The water relentlessly swirled around us, pushing our islands farther and farther apart.

But the wheels of life kept turning, and eventually the tides shifted back. In a few years most of our friends started having children of their own or settling down in other ways. The pull of biology was clearly inescapable. Try as we might, our lives couldn't stay the same forever.

Love, Interrupted

Even if we chose not to have children, we'd still be different at thirty-eight than we were at twenty-eight. Our relationship is now almost twenty years old, and together we've weathered sickness, doubt, death, and in our daughters, new life.

I could keep bemoaning the fact that parents are so much busier than people without children, that a life that felt fully occupied before babies was nothing, *nothing* even close to life after birth.

But it's not that exactly. The truth is that children demand time and attention, and there's only so much time and attention to go around. Still, life with small children isn't the same as meeting deadlines and juggling meetings. It's a series of rude interruptions, surrounded by short bursts of trauma, wrapped in a blanket of overwhelming love.

This is the truth: Children are living organisms, planted into the earth of your relationship, and like plants, they need to drain the earth of nutrients in order to survive. Before children, the nutrient that our relationship was rich in was *focused time alone.* Our own little offspring need focused attention to thrive, and because there's only so much time for that attention, we have given up most of our spare focused time to our children. What's left for us are time's dregs, but we try to make the most out of them that we can — to stay up late, to talk to each other, to laugh, and to make love.

Early in our married life, we used to meet up at home in the evenings after work and talk about our days. We'd make dinner together, discuss our problems, spend hours blowing them out of proportion. These days, because we have very little uninterrupted time to talk, the minutes we grab alone are stripped down to the most important details: How was work? Is your boss still crazy? How is your writing going? How are you feeling? What was hard for you today? What do we have scheduled this weekend?

These days, our intimate moments usually don't allow time for admiring the play of sun on my husband's shoulders. But parenthood clearly illustrates that life's opportunities are brief and therefore must be seized.

At times I fantasize about guilt-free time away from our daughters, about late-night talks and long, quiet mornings in bed. I must admit that while appealing, the idea of being freed from our children's cycle of needs for any length of time is frightening.

This winter, my husband's family encouraged us to leave the children for a night and get away. We did, and in many ways the less-than-twenty-four-hour jaunt to Milwaukee felt like a one-week trip to Paris. We lolled in bed, read the newspaper, ate dinner slowly, watched a movie, talked, and laughed, returning home the next day with our relationship renewed.

A month or so later, we were out for dinner with two other couples, also parents of young children. I gushed about our amazing overnight trip, and asked if anyone else at the table had thought about going away for an extended period of time. We all agreed that we had fantasized about the ultimate child-free getaway, but one friend revealed the true parental conundrum when he admitted, "I don't know how long I could actually stand to be away from them." We parents dream about leaving, but we can't stand to tear ourselves away.

If we can't tear ourselves away *physically,* sometimes we let our imaginations take us away. Lately, I—and my husband, to a much lesser degree—have become obsessed with the details of our single friends' love lives. The other day, one of my best friends told me about a four-hour makeout session she had with a boyfriend. Four hours making out? Even when I was single, I may not have had the patience required to make out for *four hours,* but the idea of being able to attempt such an experiment sounds so freewheeling and *childless* that it had instant appeal. While I'm not jealous of my friend's quest for true love, or of her tiresome wrangles with online romance, I am intrigued by the adult-only content of her life, by her many days spent focusing on her own concerns and nothing else.

I have another good friend, a notoriously unattached child-free man in his early fifties. When I told him the story about my photograph, he just laughed. "Time marches on," he said. Whether you have children or not, eventually everyone has to get out of bed.

What I think my friend was trying to say was that free time's downside is that free time can quickly turn to overanalytical self-obsession. In many ways, having children has stripped our relationship to its bare bones, and from this less-obstructed vantage point, we've come to realize that too much reflection can sour even the freshest milk.

"You can only loll in bed so long," my friend insisted. "Nothing ruins a conversation faster for me than trying to do it in my pajamas. In the real world, you can't sit there and delve and explore each other forever. You can only go so deep before you hit the bottom."

Herding Cats

So what have my husband and I learned about time, not just mourned, from the fractured experience of raising children? We've both tested and expanded our patience, that's certain. Children's sense of time is so different from adults'. For them, time is condensed (as in "When is *Sesame Street* going to be on? In fifteen minutes? That's soooo long!") but also limitless.

On a warm winter day, the half-block walk from the bus stop to our house can take forty-five minutes. It's like herding cats, with stops everywhere: to eat the snow, to argue when told not to eat the snow, to climb the snowbank, to slide down, to take mittens off to make a snowball, to complain about having cold hands, to get a bucket to put snow in, to put snow in the bucket, to spill the snow, then get more snow and artfully sprinkle the snow on the neighbor's front stoop, to sing each verse of a song learned in school that day, to hug and topple the younger sister, to ask to play at a friend's house, to attempt (five times) to make snow sticky enough to build an igloo block.

Through all of this I have to breathe deeply, to try to move at my daughters' pace, to follow my youngest girl's circular path up the sidewalk, to pick her up when she falls and wipe her nose. All this is busywork, completely unimportant but at the same time heart-breakingly important. The chaos and noise of small children rattles our house until evening, and then a sudden quiet descends when they are both finally asleep. Then comes the rush to accomplish all the things that were not accomplished when they were awake. Then comes sleep. Then morning. And it starts all over again.

having a baby can waylay getting you way laid

· Moon Unit Zappa ·

The day after you deliver your baby your husband has the gall to ask your ob-gyn when you can have sex again, and the good doctor says, "Wait six weeks," not noticing you are behind your husband making rabbit ears, hoping she'll extend the first-time-postbaby sex window by about, um, eighteen years. See, you aren't feeling even remotely sexual, but it's been *months* since you and your mate have had any of THAT kind of intimacy (save the occasional pity blow job so he'd stick around for the birth). Six weeks to the day arrives, but actual penetration at that moment seems positively ludicrous, so you and your hot musician husband opt for some saucy foreplay, more specifically your hot musician husband opts for giving you the lady bizness "down under" while your colicky newborn daughter sleeps soundly in the bassinet beside you. Even though you have observed new-parenting sex rule number

making time for intimacy

one—cover your face with a pillow to drown out the sound of any possible pleasure—your child suddenly wakes up mid . . . yunno, and your naked husband, who is closer, picks her up. Without thinking he kisses your crying child's adorable face to soothe her, thus accidentally planting some of you onto her tiny baby-acne-ridden cheeks. Which prompts an immediate, grisly discussion about nurture versus nature and whether or not you have just engaged in a form of incest by letting your baby see your nakedness and coating baby's face with . . . yunno, and/or whether or not you just made your little princess a little lesbian in the process. Or slutty. Or creepy. Or all of the above. Surely it could be construed as child abuse to "do it" with your infant in the same room, right? Or do you simply reframe first-time-postbaby intercourse into caveman language and use lighthearted words and concepts like *primal* and *natural* to describe the heinous, spontaneous act that just transpired?

Well, the first thing you do is move the baby into her own bed in the other room at the far end of the house. It's awkward enough trying to get "back in the game" after the birth of your first bambino (especially considering your husband's visual trauma over seeing your boobs as food and your vagina as a blowhole) *without* a petite voyeur loitering nearby. Add some good old Catholic shame, and you have a powder keg of awkwardness and anxiety waiting to go off. Which is crazy because back in the good old days (last year) you would have leapt at the opportunity for some rebellious down 'n' dirty misbehaving, and if you added in the naughty thrill of getting caught by a friend, neighbor, or countryman—good times!

Back when sex wasn't under constant surveillance, you and your husband did it all the time—in your bed, the shower, kitchen counter, in the garden, a moving car, strange town, skuzzy motel, fancy hotel, in a box, with a fox. . . . The old you couldn't wait to use sex to express your emotions, relax, let off steam, get closer to your man. If you were angry you had sex; if you were happy you had sex; if you were bored or lonely or mentally foggy you had sex; be it noisy or quiet, speedy, leisurely, passionate, silly, exploratory, or fun. Back then you never hemmed and hawed, never looked for ways to avoid, postpone, or permanently prevent sex from occurring. But let's face it, when you have a baby there just isn't time for the luxury of your basic needs. Post-tot lovin' simply deteriorates to a wholly artificial, time-consuming, unnatural act. *And* it's a nap threat. I mean, if you don't even have time to shower, eat, or cry, why on earth would any-one choose recreational copulation when they could be catching up on much-needed sleep? I mean, MY GOD, wouldn't we all rather be SLEEPING?

Or is it just me?

Sorry, but I just don't feel sexual these days. Not yet anyway. I just feel like a mom. I just feel like feeling like a mom. Like a person who simply cares for another person in a pure way. It makes me feel clean, which is a tremendous relief after feeling so disgusting during my ten-month pregnancy. (Why do they even say nine months?) See, I spent most of my sand-through-the-hourglass gestational period on bed rest ballooning from 130 to 214 pounds, living in a house during a major renovation. Throw in the stress of discovering we had an unlicensed, negligent contractor at the helm; the worst storms in LA history; a cranky, out-of-work husband; and two needy-ass, previ-ously spoiled dogs, and you will start to get an idea of the state of my pregnant mind. There we were, hemorrhaging money, and I started spotting—not good—so my ob-gyn forbade any penetration to ensure a full-term pregnancy. To make things worse, due to the mas-sive blood flow to my pelvic region, I had never been so horny in my life. I wanted sex—badly—and as a result wound up making all kinds of sexy promises to my oh-so-patient mate that I am sorry to say I don't feel up to making good on at the moment. Not even the sworn oath about letting him touch my breasts, which went from a 34A to a

38DD. "In fact darling, don't even look at them or think about them in a sexual way whatsoever. . . ."

Besides being dangerously sleep deprived, I think another obvious reason sex turns ick after having a baby is that my body is now unrecognizably gelatinous. (Actually, with the addition of a little sympathy weight, my husband isn't exactly firm either.) And fuppy. I am, of course, referring to the flap of skin that now hangs above my vagina, that second tummy below my navel, my Fat Upper Pussy (codename FUP). If I can't fit into my pants, why would I want someone else trying to get into them? Plus the adorable creature we made with our bodies wants to swing from my tits and limbs morning, noon, and night, which is claustrophobic enough without having someone else (even though it is my husband) trying to plug up my holes with his ramming loneliness, unmatched desire, with the sheer heaviness and weight of his oppressive NEED.

Then there's the psychological stuff. Since sex is largely mental for me, and these days our kid is the sun we orbit around, it is rare that I actually think about sex, not to mention mentally unwind enough to let myself "go." Additionally, the things that used to turn me on, like my husband brushing past me and lightly placing his hand on the small of my back, or suddenly grabbing me by my hips and stealing a kiss in a corridor, just aren't doing it for me now. I'd far and away prefer help with the baby's laundry or keeping the kitchen sink area tidy. Unfortunately he still prefers the same old regular sexy stuff that used to do the trick. Little does he know, if he wants a nice halfhearted hand job he should rub my feet instead of my clit, since I have been on *those* bad boys all day doing the baby jiggle dance to get our motion junkie of a child soundly off to slumberland. Or better yet, make sure I have some bottled water by my nursing station and he might luck out and get spooned for a few minutes before we go to sleep on opposite sides of the bed.

It's funny: Common lore is that men have a problem being physical after their wives become moms because of the whole Madonna-whore complex thing, but I really think women have the harder time adjusting to interlocking body parts, since it's her body that's been traumatized and nothing really changes in the man's physical world. Presto, they get a new miniature roommate, and emotionally it seems the only thing husbands have to adjust to is no longer being the baby of the house themselves. Meanwhile, we get the happy burden of an uncharted, solo, often invisible inner journey back to our selves, along with a very public outer journey back to the gym—AS WELL AS a baby to care for.

I am told this nonsexual phase, though rarely discussed publicly, is perfectly normal and will naturally pass (somewhere around the time I get my stomach back, my hormones regulate, and my kid legitimately sleeps through the night). In the meantime, I could take the advice that all the therapists, self-help books, and other moms before me glibly suggest: dim the lights, drink some alcohol, and celebrate that I have morphed into a spider-veiny, love-handle-laden, stretch-mark-ridden creature that my husband still WANTS to get down with. And, by God, cheerfully force myself to get *into* the nastiness of dry-tunnel, milk-shooting, new-mom hanky-panky!

Or . . .

I could be true to myself. I could wait out this weird period, trust my instincts, and be honest with myself and my husband. In so *not* doing, my marriage will be healthier and stronger, because we'll be showing up for each other in the best possible way: with trust, honesty, integrity, and love.

As for getting back in the groove, my inner Catherine Deneuve is lurking and will surely emerge someday. I look forward to once again *wanting*—GULP—*sex* with my dear, sweet, loyal, patient, sexy, loving husband . . . as gross as that sounds to me right now.

PART FIVE

learning on the job

parents without parents

· Jacquelyn Mitchard ·

I never had a mother-in-law.

Never had a father-in-law.

My firstborn didn't have a grandmother — or a grandfather in the traditional sense.

Despite the way most of my friends bewailed how excessive and intrusive parents could be — they spoiled the kids, offered unwanted advice, criticized — I *longed* for those things, warts and all. My mother died when I was only nineteen. And I was the only "mom" my much-younger brother really knew. My father lived until I was in my thirties, but in a world so socially soaked in booze and babes that my brother and I didn't quite come first on his list of priorities; and his grandchildren didn't come close.

Only one of my kids ever spent a single night at my father's house; and during that night, my dad called me four times, enraged about the inconvenience and roaring, "Never again!" I loved my pop, but he wasn't exactly the Burl Ives of the Midwest.

My poor husband's situation was even more poignant. His parents were gone by the time he was only twenty, and he raised his three younger siblings, who ranged in age from nine to seventeen. With a legacy of so much sadness, we were doubly excited by our expectant state. Still, having been a peer parent to younger sibs didn't help us when we were faced with our very own firstborn infant son.

Now, my first husband and I weren't *children* when we had children: I was almost twenty-five and Dan was a little older. That said, I would probably have a fit if any of our own children had children at what now seems to me to be a bizarrely immature time of life. Ours was a different era, though: Girls started to worry at twenty-one if they didn't have a "sparkler" on their ring fingers. Guys' parents began to wonder about their gender preference if they weren't linked up in their early to mid twenties. We had very little in the way of life experience when we became pregnant, and no one around to serve as models, teachers, or even supportive onlookers. We didn't even have *aunts*. We didn't have *parents or grandparents*. It seemed as though our parents and extended families visited the earth long enough to have us and then took off. And, while I definitely became a better mother as time went by, to call me a novice at the beginning is to vastly understate the truth.

What we didn't know was a vast uncharted wilderness that stretched before us. Sometimes not knowing what we didn't know helped. Sometimes, it didn't.

We didn't know about exhaustion. (We thought babies slept.)

We didn't know about crying. (We thought something was wrong with them when they did it.)

We didn't know about green poop, teething, crawling backward (we called a neurologist), nightmares, the truth that our child would never wear a matching (or clean) outfit for more than two hours at a time, and that, if he did, there really *would* be something wrong with him. We didn't know about yellow snot as opposed to clear snot, or that medicating a temperature of less than 102 degrees was worthless and counterproductive.

We were batso about everything being "perfect." Rob never saw a Twinkie. (This is true; I swear on my mother's grave: He's *still* never had a Twinkie.) He never had a cookie. He never ate a piece of chicken that came from a fowl that hadn't willingly given up its life.

Dan sterilized Rob's bottles and nipples wearing what looked like a level-four biohazard-containment uniform. I wore a mask when I held him. I insisted others do so. I ran like a grizzly sow at anyone who dared light up a cigarette in our house or on our block for that matter—back then, people still smoked. Probably as a result of his bubble-boy environment, Rob had more illnesses and neuroses than any of our other children—he was sick from the day he was born. He had ear infections and allergies, injuries and intolerances. He never slept and was precocious to the point of obnoxiousness. And whenever he got hurt, I called the doctor, including when he rolled off the sofa onto a carpeted floor on Christmas Day.

What did I know? What did either of us know?

When we weren't doing things exactly as the books told us to do, we were improvising.

À la Britney Spears, Dan drove around the neighborhood with Rob on his lap, holding the steering wheel. We decorated the nursery, but Dan could only bear to leave Rob "alone in there" for one whole night. "He cried," Dan explained when I woke up to find Rob between us like a sweet-smelling little blue foothill. "He hates it in there." And so, Rob never went back to the crib. After a while, we realized we were using it as a clothes hamper and took it down. Never once did we feel inconvenienced or "put out" by the baby or that he "came between us," even when he literally did. In fact, we'd both been so lonely all our lives that the things that are supposed to drive young parents nuts with newborns didn't affect us at all. Some changes were inevitable, but we didn't go into mourning or therapy over them.

Of course, we made love less often, and not in our bed but in front of the fireplace — although we didn't have a fireplace. Dan drew one on a piece of poster board and stood it against our stereo speakers, which, in the eighties, were the size and shape of the Empire State Building. We never again took a shower together — or alone. We always had the baby.

Dr. Spock said to do what felt right to us. So, we did. A friend occasionally would express discreet horror that Rob slept in our bed — "You can't do that!" my boss, Susan, cried. "You'll . . . ruin him!" My only reply was "Ruin him for what? Sleeping alone? Who likes to sleep alone?" My theory was, and still is, that every night he spent in our bed as a baby was one less night he'd spend in someone else's as a teenager.

And if we sometimes wondered aloud to each other about whether we were doing this right — if we felt like the Lewis and Clark of parents, breaking trail alone, without signs on the trees — we reassured each other. There was no one else to reassure us. If we ever disagreed with each other it felt awful. Sure, we enjoyed our debates as newlyweds, but as parents we became almost telepathic when it came to our babies. We were one.

Despite the satisfaction of that partnership, there was no denying that we were . . . only we. Though it was fun to take our firstborn everywhere with us (he was an attention getter, the most beautiful of all our babies, a stunningly lovely, long-lashed blond with the only eyes I've ever seen that truly are gray), there also was no alternative. And though we relished what we called our nightly dinner ritual of "reverencing the baby," there also was no one with whom to share him, no one who would admire him as extravagantly as our parents would have. And little offhand comments from pals had a barb:

"The grandmas were bickering about when Nicholas would be old enough to spend the weekend," one thoughtless friend complained.

"Every holiday is like Macy's window now that there is a baby in the family," boasted another.

"First grandchild," one coworker sighed. "You know what I mean?"

We nodded, but sadly. We didn't know at all what she meant; but we assumed it was more wonderful than not.

Neither of us ever felt so keenly our orphan status.

On the morning Rob was born, although I am not particularly religious, I offered God years off my life (I thought I had plenty to spare then!) if my mother could somehow see her grandchild, the woman I had become, and see . . . how much I needed her. For my mother had not been an A-plus mommy, but I knew she'd have been a goofy, funny, extravagant grandmother, the very best kind—a sort of Auntie Mame, who'd have bought the children sailor suits and taken them to see *The Nutcracker* live at the Oriental Theater. Dan's mother was a domestic genius, an old-fashioned girl who even made his father's suits on her sewing machine, who made and canned homemade "gravy." (No Italian ever called spaghetti sauce "sauce" back then, any more than anyone ever called spaghetti "pasta.") She would have adored our children as well, and been the more cuddly of the two grandmothers. Dan's dad owned a restaurant before he died. I imagined our boys sitting at the bar at their grandpa's place, eating olives and maraschino cherries out of the bar glasses.

Why did we get so ripped off?

They were ever so *not* there on Christmas morning. They were ever so *not* there when Rob found his first Easter egg or took his first step. And then, when Rob was nearly three and our son Danny a newborn, I surprised Dan with an epic crying jag. Over and over he asked me what was the matter, until I finally hiccuped and choked out, "I want . . . my mama!!"

And oh, how I did.

I wanted her advice. I wanted her comfort. I wanted the backstop of unsolicited suggestions, the same ones that made all my girl-friends complain so bitterly. I wanted her to tell me what I'd been like as a baby (there are, that I know of, exactly two pictures of me as a baby), about what I'd done and when. I wanted to call her and crow about Rob's many achievements and Dan's extravagant jolly-pumpkin affability. I wanted her to "drop over" with little outfits and fuzzy toys, and carry a brag book in her purse.

Dan felt his loss keenly, too. He was the first in his family to have children, and his surviving siblings were . . . well, kids themselves—college students and a teenager whose object in life was to avoid pregnancy. To them, our kids weren't cunning miniatures with expressions and attitudes. They were blobs that smelled funny—cute for a few moments, boring over the long term.

Because we hadn't been handed traditions, or had time enough to really observe and adopt them, we sort of mooshed what we recalled together for our own theory of relativity. The holiday traditions we finally did concoct—driving out at night to look at light displays, making our own stockings with a little bit of felt and more glue than was probably used to repair Apollo 13—felt . . . small. They always did.

So I think that our having three boys in rapid succession was a function of our need to ensure that, somewhere down the line, there would be a gathering of grandparents, aunts, uncles, and cousins, even if we had to wait decades for that to happen.

Then, one night, when we were covering Bill Clinton's second inauguration for our respective newspapers, Dan felt poorly. I remember telling him, "Honey, one day, we'll be able to tell our boys that we danced with the president." Four months later, Dan was dead. And there was no mother to rock me and stand with me against the winds of certain impecunity and emotional devastation. My father said he was sure I'd be fine.

He was ultimately right.

But this all felt horrible — and yes, also resoundingly familiar. The last thing on earth Dan had wanted, and he'd told me this often, was to leave his children as his parents had left him. But he had no choice. Still, he hadn't left them alone. He'd left them with me. We had figured out how to be parents together. Now I would have to figure out how to go on raising our kids in small, purposeful ways. My three older sons and I recall our first Christmas after Dan died: They were nine, six, and three. We made pasta and ate together, the four of us, and then joined hands and, one by one, I led them in a Christmas carol. Afterward, we drove around and looked at the lights.

The boys remember this Christmas as particularly beautiful.

Ironically (and unexpectedly) some years later, I remarried, to a younger man who'd never had children. Together we gave birth to and adopted two more daughters and two more sons. I got a mother-in-law and a father-in-law; and for my children and myself, I was delighted.

That said, there would never come a time when I would turn to this new extended family for help or even child-rearing suggestions. There would never come a time they'd offer advice.

Dan and I charted that territory long ago, and my husband, Chris, doesn't resent it. And though the verdict's still not in, we seem to have found our way well enough. The family's huge now, with all but Rob living under our roof, and we try to make a practice of gathering for at least most of the evening meals. Marty, now seventeen, complained only the other night, "Why do we always talk about important stuff at dinner? And why do we always have to eat together?"

I could have told him that when you're an explorer in a new world, where it seems no one has gone before, you take things very, very seriously.

But instead, I cast my eyes up at the ceiling, and the sky above it, and grinned.

why my husband and
i love our son more
than each other

· Molly Jong-Fast ·

My husband and I love our son more than we love each other.
This was a conscious decision on our part. Recently the idea of
loving your children more than your spouse has fallen out of
favor. In fact, a popular author recently preached and gained much
recognition for a kind of love your spouse, tolerate your children
maxim. But as someone who was raised by people who needed "me
time," kid-free vacations, adult conversations, and beautiful child-
unfriendly homes, I needed to do something different.

From the moment we met him, we loved our son more than each
other. It was only natural. Perhaps women who claim to love their
husbands more than their children have to fight against that innate
obsession and mind-blowing love. Or perhaps it's just me. I started
to understand the reason for and importance of loving our son
more than each other from a number of my own painful childhood

memories. The one that sticks like Krazy Glue is of a Sunday night at my mom's weekend house in Weston, Connecticut. I was with my mother and her boyfriend, Chip. We were eating rotisserie chicken on my grandfather's dishes.

My grandfather gave up his dream of being a drummer so that he could be rich, and he became an importer of dishes, figurines, and dolls. Because of his dishy career we always had tons of free dishes and glasses and creepy dolls (but that's for another essay, or perhaps a therapy session). The dishes I'm thinking about today are the huge blue dishes my mother used at her house. They were thick Mexican dishes covered in white concentric circles. They were heavy dishes, and that was what my mother blamed my accident on, their weight.

It was a typical Sunday-night "family" dinner. Mother's bichon puppy peed on the pink and brown rag rug in the dining room. Chip screamed at my mother (who immediately burst into tears). Margaret (my nanny) cleaned and chattered nervously. Our house was one of those houses where it always seemed as if we were on the precipice of disaster, and on that muddy October night we were.

My husband and I never fight in front of our son. We never let him watch TV (except the rare episode of *Sesame Street*). We never let him eat candy. We are the clichéd politically correct parents who call our nanny our "caregiver," push puzzles, and only allow books that don't feature TV characters and other noncommercial toy options. Of course after two years of these parenting techniques, all our son wants is to eat lollipops and watch *Dora*.

My mom had wanted me to help clear the table. I remember picking up too many plates. Perhaps it was a hostile gesture: If they wanted me to clear the table, then clear the table I would. And then I remember fragments of what occurred next: Mom's dog barking, my mother screaming, Chip cursing, food flying everywhere, Margaret comforting. And then for a minute it all went blank, dark, like the end of the world. What felt like minutes but was probably seconds later, I was lying on the floor and feeling an enormous pain, like nothing I had ever felt or I hope to ever feel again. A few seconds after that I looked across my mother's cold brown tiles and I saw something pink and bloody on the floor. A few seconds after that I realized that the thing on the floor was in fact my pinky.

My husband and I met on the Internet. He was thirty-eight years old. I was twenty-three. He thought he was too old for me. We had our first date at a crappy un-air-conditioned Italian restaurant on Second Avenue. I had spaghetti marinara. Nine months from that day we were engaged, nine months after that we were married, and three months after that our son was born (so for those not great at math we were together for about twenty-one months before our son was born). We had always had a very even, undramatic relationship. We never fought. We hardly ever even got mad at each other. This didn't change when our son was born.

The moment he was pulled out of the giant cut in my uterus something changed. Not something, everything. January 5, 2004, was the day that our lives changed forever. We had been nothing before our child was born. We had been self-indulgent cut-out silhouettes of people. But once our son was born everything changed. We became people with a larger, more important calling, which was raising this little boy. We had been sleepwalking before that, our lives had been meaningless. That day, when we looked at our nine-pound-five-ounce son we both knew that our time of narcissistic self-indulgences was over. We now had other priorities and there wasn't going to be time to spend a day lying on the couch.

Seeing my finger on the floor was perhaps the least confusing moment of my life. I had been in so much mental pain, and now finally I could feel something real: the frantic car ride from ritzy Weston to Bridgeport Hospital, Chip screaming at the toll attendant, the police car that escorted us, the concerned doctors, the slightly hostile overworked nurses, the crying mother, and the chaotic sleep of anesthesia—these frenetic things comforted me.

I became the center of the world around me. For a slip of a second, I was the only thing anyone talked about. I went into the ER high on the knowledge that my parents (my dad and stepmom were also there) loved me more than they hated each other. The operation was blissful, and as a chronic insomniac, I found that the anesthesia gave me the best sleep I had had in months.

Under the anesthesia I dreamed of green turtles as the doctors pleaded with me to come out. I would have liked to stay under forever, with the green sea turtles. I woke with my arm in a huge cast that went to my shoulder. My father and mother sat at the end of my hospital bed worshiping me. I was "everything to them." And then I got well.

A few days later they were screaming at each other over my hospital bed. I was pretending to sleep, which was ironic, because they should have known I would not have been sleeping. As I said, I suffered from insomnia back then.

"This never would have happened if . . . ," my father screamed.

"You bastard!" my mother yelled.

"Well, I'm sure I'll be reading about all of this in your new book," my father said. And that was it, the end of my four days of quiet. It had taken about four days before my sawed-off finger was forgotten, eclipsed by the larger reality of my parents hating each other. My mother started a book tour, my father started working on a new novel, and the huge gray doctor took out my 120 tiny stitches of black medical thread. My finger felt different: it no longer had much feeling in its tip. My finger also looked very different from my other fingers: instead of having a tip it had a blob of red flesh on it. But something else had changed in me. For the first time in my life, I truly knew the score. I knew I wasn't so important, I knew I was a supporting character in my parents' life, and that's what I would always be, and that's okay.

There is something oddly liberating about being a supporting character in life. I don't feel like I have to carry the whole world. I don't feel like I have to be famous. I don't feel like I am hugely important, and in some ways that is a great thing. But I want my child to have a better life. My husband and I don't have the perfect marriage, but we get along very well. We talk a lot and don't fight much. We love each other a huge amount. That said, though, our love for our son is a totally different kind of love. The love we feel for our son is more like narcissism, more like some kind of profound and unselfish self-love. We try to make as much of our lives about our son as we can. He is our lead character.

My husband is a professor and I'm a writer. Together we have careers that are all about memory—the preservation of it, the destruction of it. If life is about memory, then nothing is more important than the memories we give our son. We try to make him our most important thing because the truth is, he is.

making the most of our very own unplanned pregnancy

· Steve Almond ·

On an unseasonably warm evening last January, I attended my weekly poker game, made what I often describe as a "short-term charitable donation" to my opponents, and headed out to my car.

I had left my cell phone on the front seat and was surprised to find two messages from my fiancée, Erin, who was at the time out in southern California, finishing up her MFA program. The first message said this:

"Hey hon, it's me. It's nothing bad, but can you give me a call as soon as you get this message? Like, tonight. I'll be up."

The second message said the same thing, at a slightly higher frequency.

Now, Erin is a calm person. She is not prone to panicky phone calls, nor, somewhat regrettably, to drunk dialing. I figured maybe she had gotten a short story accepted in a magazine, or perhaps run into someone who hates me.

I looked forward to talking with her, as it would afford me the opportunity to complain about my brilliant play at the poker table that had, once again, for the 153rd straight week, been undermined by outrageous fortune. You know the deal.

I dialed.

"Hello?" she said.

"It's me. What's up?"

"I'm pregnant," she said.

She started laughing a little.

"Pregnant," she said.

I will now attempt to represent my shock. Let each blank line represent 160 volts, as applied to some tender region of my body, such as the armpit:

"Isn't that crazy?" Erin said.

"Honey?"

To clarify the situation: I had just returned from a visit with Erin. On the morning she drove me to the airport she had reported an upset stomach and "spotting," which she took as a sign her period had arrived. I had not given any thought to pregnancy, hers or mine.

I was more preoccupied by the idea of being—after thirty-nine years of fairly disreputable male behavior—engaged. I should mention that, at the time of her phone call, we'd been engaged for a grand total of four days.

I should also mention that we'd just spent her winter break together and that, yes, we'd had unprotected sex a few times.

Then again, Erin was over thirty. I was pushing forty and had smoked, over the previous decade, the equivalent of a very large marijuana tree. Neither of us had ever been involved in a conception scenario. We were both pretty sure we were going to have the opposite problem. This is why Erin had been checking fertility websites all week. In fact, she had actually gone to the pharmacy intending to purchase an ovulation kit. She had just picked up the pregnancy test on a lark.

I don't mean to imply by this brief digression that I was anything less than tickled to hear her news.

I was tickled to a deep, delighted red.

I was especially thrilled to have knocked up Erin *before* we got married, because it seemed like such a Bohemian arrangement. I was an artist. It was my *job* to scandalize polite society. I loved the idea of being, even briefly, a baby daddy.

Erin was delighted, too. The ensuing conversation was characterized by much giggling. We were so pleased, in fact, that we sort of forgot our original plan, which had been to hold off on the pregnancy until:

1. We were married.

2. We were living on the same coast, presumably in the same house.

3. She had been granted a couple of years to work on her writing.

Instead, we had undergone a *radical paradigm shift*. In the space of a single conversation, we morphed from your typical self-absorbed-young-couple-eating-at-swank-restaurants-drinking-too-much-wine-and-fucking-to-the-best-of-our-abilities to parents in waiting.

The main thing that had to happen is that we had to make a bunch of decisions, pronto. That was fine with me. I'd spent long enough mucking about in that postadolescent haze known as the indecisive thirties. I had spent whole hours pondering which goddamn facial cleanser to purchase, whether to splurge on dessert, whether I wanted my groceries packed in paper or plastic bags.

Marriage was the first thing. We had to get married. We had to get married because we didn't want our child to be a bastard (I am already a bastard) and because we needed family health insurance.

Erin had insurance, but it would only last until she graduated. In true starving-artist fashion, I did not have health insurance at all.

There was also the matter of making sure we were in the same room during the ceremony, which, as I understood things, was standard operating procedure.

I hatched a plan I felt was ingenious—this should have been the first red flag—we would elope! Yes, we would elope over spring break, during one of those beach parties where coeds pantomime performing oral sex onstage! Or perhaps, more manageably, Erin would fly out to visit me in Somerville and we could get hitched at city hall.

There were several advantages to this plan, only one of which was that it would save me several thousand dollars, which I had no intention of handing over to the retail racketeering firm known collectively as the wedding industry.

Of even greater importance was keeping our relatives far, far away. One of the advantages of being, well, the technical term is *old*, is that you have been witness to enough weddings to recognize that they are basically driven by familial obligation. You tell yourself, at the outset, that it will be a small ceremony and before you know it, you're pricing circus tents and crab cakes by the gross.

I was able to convince Erin to go along with this plan. In fact, I was able to convince her that we should keep both the elopement *and* the baby a secret. My reasoning ran something like this:

- There was a significant risk the pregnancy would not go to term.
- We could break the good news to our friends and family together.
- I was totally freaked out.

I'm not sure I was completely forthright about this last factor.

The first sign that Erin's pregnancy was not going to be easy already had occurred: She had puked.

In those early, heady days, we were almost pleased: This was morning sickness! It meant the hormones were kicking in, that she really and truly was knocked up.

We joked! I took to calling her Pukey Pukestein. I suggested she start a band called Pukey Pukestein and the Puke Stains. Ha ha ha!

Over the next month, her morning sickness began a steady green creep across the hours. One evening Erin called me simply to moan into the phone. On another occasion, I would have greeted this turn of events as an erotic invitation. But this moaning was different: anguished, exhausted, not really all that sexy.

"Awuahuhhawawuhhh," she said.

"What's the matter?" I said

It didn't really sink in until I saw her a month later, in Santa Fe.

I'd heard all these stories about how horny women get during pregnancy, so I naturally assumed this first rendezvous would be an even more ecstatic version of our usual visits, which centered around, ahem, lovemaking.

Erin arrived at our very romantic bed and breakfast just before midnight. She looked terrifically sexy, too, her belly already swelling a little.

We hugged. I rubbed against her.

"Baby baby baby," I said.

Erin smiled queerly and slipped into the bathroom.

"Are you okay?" I said, through the door. "Is there anything I can do?"

"No," she murmured.

I stood, listening to my future wife throw up. It was unclear what I should do. A late-night quickie seemed pretty much out of the question.

"Do you want me to come in?"

"No."

Erin emerged twenty minutes later, on the verge of tears, and began apologizing.

"Why are you sorry?" I said. "Don't be sorry."

"That was disgusting. Could you hear me?"

"I couldn't hear you."

"Yes you could!"

I tried to cheer her up with a naked rendition of Pukey Pukestein's first and final hit single, "Save the Last Chunk for Me." This did not work.

Erin had made reservations for us to go the next day to this Japanese bathhouse place, where, I assumed, we would fuck in a totally hot Buddhist-porno manner. We certainly tried. We tried to fuck in a totally hot Buddhist-porno manner. But Erin still felt sick and we couldn't find a decent surface. So we settled for some light frottage and green tea instead.

And it occurred to me, as I lay next to her that night, pressing my unrequited boner into her slumbering hip region, that Erin's body was no longer exclusively available for my pleasure. It was now engaged in the vigorously disruptive process of gestation.

This was cool. I could deal with this. It was part of the broader paradigm shift. I needed to recognize that and not be one of those sexually demanding baby daddies constantly banging on the cervix door with the tip of my insatiable johnson.

Because the nausea was really just the beginning, something like a warning shot over the biological bow. I knew this because of my advanced age. I had lots of married dude friends. I had heard all the stories about the long, anguished sex sabbaticals that awaited me.

But now here's the weird thing, the thing I'm not even sure is a good thing: My own sex drive had been dampened by news of the pregnancy.

It's not that Erin was any less attractive. Pregnancy suited her, accentuated her shape, brought a pale glow to the cheeks. No, it was the idea that her body now had a greater mission, something far more essential. The ancient business of the species had taken up residence inside her. All those years of hoping and groping and sweet-talking, and what was *I* after actually? An ecstatic twinge. A bioemission. It felt kind of paltry.

There is more to sex than bioemission, of course. It is an entire language of intimacy, a central pursuit of human happiness.

Still.

Still, things felt different now. It was impossible to view Erin as the dirty girl with whom I had done such dirty things. She was greater than that now. She was growing an entire person inside her.

A bit of psychosexual whiplash was to be expected.

For most of human history, after all, bearing children wasn't a conscious decision. It was a biological consequence, and, a bit later, a matter of economic import. (It is still this way in most of the world.) Only in the superabundance of the present era has pregnancy become a discretionary matter. But as couples wait longer to get married, as breeding becomes a lifestyle decision rather than a cultural assumption, as women test the age boundaries of fertility, you wind up with more and more folks like us who figure, what the hell, why not let biology decide? Call it the half-planned pregnancy.

I'm not saying that we launched into this adventure with a devil-may-care attitude. On the contrary—as much as we enjoyed the illicit notion that this was a half-planned pregnancy, we were instantly plunged into a world of full-time anxiety. Suddenly, the most minute detail of Erin's physiology felt like a matter of life and death.

This was something neither of us expected: how entirely preoccupied women get by their own pregnancies. How much they need to feel *supported* and *validated* and other verbs that men generally don't get.

The problem was that I was the only person she could talk to—owing to my brilliant notion about not telling anyone our good news until we eloped in March—and I was three thousand miles away.

A typical phone conversation ran something like this:

Steve: How're you doing, baby?

Erin: [Unintelligible]

Steve: Did you throw up today?

Erin: Uh-huh.

Steve: How do you feel now?

Erin: I want a McDonald's cheeseburger.

Steve: You're a vegetarian.

Erin: I don't care.

Steve: Okay. If that's what you want, you should get yourself one.

Erin: That's disgusting.

Steve: Did you try the ginger ale?

Erin: I feel sick.

Steve: Remember what Dave said about the ginger ale?

Erin: Ginger ale makes me sick.

I don't mean to suggest that we didn't have our bright spots.

The sonograms, for instance.

Yes, we had pictures of our fetus! The big head, the delicate, sepia bones, the fishy appendages. Our favorite showed the child in profile, nestled in a kind of inner-uterine hammock, hands clasped behind its head, feet up. Stone cold chilling in the amniotic crib. We took to calling the kid Peanut. Peanut Almond. Sure. It had a certain ring to it.

Somewhere in there Erin flew out and we quietly, happily, eloped. All proceeded calmly for the next few weeks. Then, in the middle of April, the ob-gyn got in touch. Erin assumed the doctor was calling about the nausea, possibly with an explanation that entailed a cure more effective than ginger ale.

Instead, she told Erin that the blood work had come back with abnormally high alpha-fetoprotein levels, which indicated a one in a hundred chance of trisomy.

Erin asked for a translation.

"Trisomy 21 corresponds to Down syndrome."

I was not there for this conversation, of course. I can only imagine the dread that must have lurched through Erin, the sudden dimming of our sudden joy.

"Anytime the test profiles indicate a probability greater than one in two hundred we recommend an amniocentesis," the doctor said. "The best thing would be for you to talk to a genetic counselor." She also informed Erin that any action she might want to take—to use her oddly chilling, sanitized language—would have to occur by week twenty-four. We were at week eighteen.

Once again, we needed to decide a bunch of stuff in a hurry.

The first thing was whether Erin would have an amnio. The procedure involved plunging a big needle into her belly. Erin was understandably reluctant to have a big needle plunged into her belly. There was also a small but nagging risk of damage to the fetus.

But it was more than this: Erin felt betrayed. She had thought pregnancy would be this beautiful, glowing experience. Instead, she had retched through her first four months, mostly alone, and now, just into the magical second trimester, the sickness had (perhaps) migrated to her unborn child.

It sucked.

And it sucked in that particular way modern medicine sucks, wherein the huge, amazing advances in technology carry with them a corresponding increase in data, contingency, and anxiety.

As recently as a few decades ago, there were no triple screens, no sonograms, no genetic counselors. Most of the women of the world, in fact, still experience pregnancy as a process largely divorced from medical intervention.

I'm not so foolish as to advocate for this approach. I know too many moms who have suffered preeclampsia or given birth prematurely, whose lives and babies have been saved by modern medicine.

At the same time, the prenatal process has become so fraught, so micromanaged. From the earliest stages of pregnancy, parents can see their baby and listen to its heartbeat and all that is terrific fun.

But we also spend more and more time fretting over the baby's development and safety.

The modern fascination with the unborn child—one skillfully exploited by the antiabortion movement—proceeds from a peculiarly modern fantasy: that with sufficient precaution we can keep our children safe from all harm.

The fact remained: Amnio was the only way to know for sure if Peanut had a genetic problem.

But did we even want to know? Wasn't there something unnatural, unseemly even, about preapproving the child's genes? What did it say about the limits of our love? That we wanted a child, just so long as he or she wasn't too much of a burden? Or worse, what if we got a bad result and disagreed about what to do?

These were not discussions we wanted to be having while three thousand miles apart. We wanted to be able to touch each other. I felt sick at the idea that Erin was having to shoulder all this without me there.

At the same time—and I know this will sound pretty sucky, but it's true—being on opposite coasts probably helped us deal with the situation. It forced us to talk our way past the histrionics and self-pity, to the real issues: our fear, our sense of indignation, our guilt, and ultimately our desires as parents.

We spent a good week chewing on these issues, via phone and e-mail. We were perfectly sweet and terrified. I kept reminding Erin that the chance something was wrong was still one in a hundred, that we shouldn't worry until there was cause. Then we would both spend another hour on the phone, worrying.

There's a tendency, after all, when a possibility like this gets raised, for the couple to feel (usually subconsciously) that they've brought on, and secretly deserve, the worst-case scenario. Erin and

I had gotten pregnant too easily! We didn't deserve such happiness! There had to be a catch!

This brand of logic is total shit. But it's also oddly comforting. It grants you a measure of control over fate, which otherwise feels completely and sadistically random.

Erin decided to get the amnio. It was that or spend the rest of the pregnancy in a state of dread.

The amnio was as miserable as billed, but it also revealed—after a few tense days—that Peanut was healthy. It also revealed that Peanut was . . . a Peanutta.

This, I believe, was our reward for the big scare. From the earliest days of the pregnancy, we had been rooting for a girl. Both of us had been terrorized by older brothers. So: after the great panic, great relief. Great rejoicing.

Which was important, because, as it turned out, my landlord was just about to give me the heave-ho, meaning we had to find a place to live, a new place, together, which would have to be done, by the way, while I was on a book tour.

There is no need to dwell on the particulars, except to say that this is another charming consequence of being such late bloomers: Everything happens at once. In the next three months we: found a home, closed on a home, moved me across town, moved Erin across the country, visited fourteen states, and set perfectly ridiculous deadlines for our books. (I also quit my teaching job, but that's another story.)

We live, now, amid a hundred boxes, stunned and sweaty with the onset of August. Erin is well into her final trimester. She has reached the *cumbersome* phase. Each morning, a bit mournfully, she weighs herself. She is fast approaching what we have come to think of as the "Jack Sprat parallax," the point at which she weighs more than me. We are deep into the particulars of the final trimester: weekly sessions with the ob-gyn, prenatal yoga, birth classes. And Erin's well-intentioned friends are bombarding her with birth stories: the four-day labor, the magnesium-drip delirium labor, the emergency breach labor—she has heard them all. She is a good listener, polite to a fault, actually. My sister-in-law recently related the story of her first birth, which involved a day-long labor at home, no drugs, and hanging from a tree. Erin has no interest in such heroics. She has already announced her intention to call for Saint Epidural should the need arise.

Another friend showed us her birth video, which included a rather lengthy illustrated disquisition on the configuration and operation of the (still bloody) placenta. And yet another friend has brought it to our attention that Erin will likely poop during the birthing process.

I have promised to poop in solidarity.

As I may have hinted above, we are both quietly terrified of the actual birth of our daughter. Erin worries about the troublesome physics of the thing. She worries that she will never get her old body back. She worries about handling such a small, fragile creature. My central concern, frankly, is that I will lose the undivided adoration of my wife.

And I will. It can't be avoided.

Sometimes, I walk into our bedroom and find Erin caressing her belly with a cupped palm. There is a look on her face of such contentment that I know I am intruding on something mystical. Erin has begun the process of falling in love with our daughter before she even comes out.

I will surely go through a similar process, but let's be honest here:

learning on the job

There is nothing on earth to equal mother love. If there were, we would have ceased long ago as a species.

I can feel myself getting displaced. And I can feel myself panicking a little.

A few days ago, I picked a fight with Erin over her desire to give her cats some wet food as a treat. Hadn't we agreed to feed the cats dry food only? Was it really fair to our daughter to lavish such treats on a couple of ungrateful animals? I was disgustingly manipulative and almost comically furious. It drove me crazy to imagine Erin spending any of her attention on the cats. You don't have to be a genius to figure out the problem: I was transferring my forbidden rage toward my daughter to the cats.

What can I tell you? I am angry. And frightened. I'm frightened that I'm going to slip to number two in Erin's book.

All fathers suffer this fear. And I've seen more than one marriage brought to ruin by it. My own parents nearly came apart under the pressure of their children. So this is what we've been dealing with as we wait for Peanut to make her debut. Can I adjust to a lesser role? Will Erin be able to embrace motherhood without feeling too much anxiety? Will we resist the temptation to bicker over who is working harder? Will our hearts expand as required? Can we remain happy and calm in the face of so much love?

Near as I can figure, that's the real challenge. If the parents are happy and calm, the kid is golden.

That's what Erin and I keep telling each other, anyway. We've got to bid adieu to our lives as nervous singles, to the flashy armor of our narcissism, to the notion that we will ever be able to control the course of our lives again. We're fucked, in other words. To feel such unprecedented love runs against the monstrous self-regard of the era.

We can hardly wait.

how did we get here?

· Rob Spillman ·

*B*efore we had kids my wife and I lived in an illegal cold-water flat in East Berlin, where we heated water for bathing by running it through a Mr. Coffee; we went island hopping in Greece, where we were treated to the worst martini ever in the bar of a Santorini brothel; and wound up "settling" in the East Village, where we both contemplated a dangerous liaison with a waitress with a blue-tattooed ear.

Flash forward ten years: We're living in a brownstone in Park Slope, Brooklyn, testing bathwater for a baby on the inside of our wrists; we're going playground hopping in Prospect Park where, at a children's birthday party, we're treated to an even worse martini (but perhaps most necessary martini ever); living in such a state of sleep deprivation we contemplate a dangerous liaison with our bed.

learning on the job

To paraphrase David Byrne:

How did I get here?
This is not my beautiful house.
This is not my beautiful wife.

Neither of us ever bought in to the crazy theory that having a baby would bond us or make us stronger as a couple, but we never imagined the differences it would point up between us.

How could we have known?

You have no idea what sort of parent you are going to be until you are thrown into the ring. Reading how-to books does nothing. It's as if you've been reading about bronco riding and then are saddled up on the angriest bull in the world—only experience counts. All you can do is squeeze your knees together and try to hold on.

I had no clue what parenthood would do to me and my wife. Being the child of parents who separated when I was five years old (until my wedding day I had no memory of them ever even being in the same room together), my ideas about family, and what it meant to be a parent, were cloudy at best.

Here was where I was coming from:

When my parents split—my mom leaving Berlin, where we'd lived since I was born, to return to her family in the States—I stayed behind in Germany with my now-single gay father, a classical pianist who worked in the mostly gay opera world.

It wasn't your typical childhood. Instead of tossing around a baseball, I was an extra on the set of *Tosca*. Instead of playing with classmates after school, I headed to the opera house to meet my father and run around the giant, ornate building. I was like Eloise at the Plaza; the cat walks, orchestra pit, secret passageways leading to lighting panels, the costume rooms, and set rooms, it was all my secret domain. The only thing lacking was other kids, or even other families.

I didn't feel like I was missing anything, because my parents were divorced and living in different corners of the world, it was all I knew. Didn't all kids hone their chess games with stewardesses?

When I moved to the States at the age of ten, my nomadic existence continued: four different cities, two different countries, four different schools, and two different parents. By high school I would spend the school years with my mother, summers with my father. I adapted, but looking back I realize how hard it was to pick up and move, to constantly make and lose friends.

At the same time, in an alternate universe it seems, my wife, Elissa, was growing up in the suburbs in Delaware with two loving parents and a younger sister. To this day her mother lives in the house Elissa grew up in—a house her father helped build. Her dad worked, and while she and her sister were young their mom stayed home, then later started a catering business. Elissa's childhood was one of bike riding, school plays, and family dinners. It was clear her parents loved each other and their kids, whom they seemed to parent with equal parts support and firmness. Their daughters could wear their hair however they wanted, and wear whatever clothes they wanted, and listen to whatever music they wanted as loud as they wanted, but they had a strict curfew, weren't allowed to swear or watch TV unless it was educational. Strangest of all, they were repeatedly encouraged to *share their feelings*.

Total freakville from my point of view. Not that I had many role models, but my understanding was that kids should be invisible, neither seen nor heard, and if they were invited into adult company, they should be civil, quiet—perfect miniature adults.

Yet, prekids, Elissa and I found each other and found that our different worldviews fed each other as creative individuals. In the years before our daughter was born, we lived the life of your typical New

York City writer types—bouncing around East Village clubs, writing in cafés, dropping out to spend a summer in Colorado or Europe. We lived on eggs and peppers and potatoes, we drank bad jug wine, and had a tin-foil antenna on our black-and-white TV. We always got by. We worked as waiters, did odd jobs, and if things got really hairy we'd sell records, or books, at the secondhand bookshop; and inevitably, just when it seemed we couldn't weather it anymore, there'd be a windfall—an article, a book, a writing gig, and we'd stock the fridge, buy back some of the books we'd sold, treat ourselves to takeout, or I'd irrationally insist on a meal at a nice restaurant, wiping out our safety cushion in a single evening of excess.

This was just what being an artist was about. Lying in bed at night dreaming of being able to order in burritos, and listening to the gunfire coming from over on Avenue C.

For me, this was a logical if more extreme extension of my upbringing. I thought nothing of sleeping in the car when my dad and I traveled, because we couldn't afford a hotel, so how was crashing on the floor of a friend at the Malibu Arms flophouse any worse?

While Elissa's parents dragged her and her sister all over Europe on trips, sleeping in some pretty funky hotels, that was different. Her parents had a nice house, two cars in the garage, and savings. Where my parents were making a living on their art—my father as a pianist, my mother as a singer—Elissa's parents made art as a hobby. In addition to his straight job at a chemical company, Elissa's father welded giant sculptures out of iron; her mom is a painter. The idea that you could make your art your life was a revelation to Elissa. Her worldview shifted when I told her that writing didn't have to be something she did in secret—it could and should be her life. For her it felt like she'd finally discovered the place she was supposed to be and that everything was possible.

I knew the artistic life wasn't simple. I'd watched my own parents and I knew there would be financial and emotional sacrifice—but I told her if she wanted to be a writer and was willing to not live like ordinary clock punchers, I wanted to share this life with her.

For the most part, Elissa thrived in the seven years before our daughter was born, though she was sometimes exasperated by my inability to save money and my Pollyannaish belief that no matter how grim things got, everything would somehow work out. Where I knew how much money my parents had, or didn't have (and wasn't freaked out about it either way), her family never talked about money, though nothing was ever denied her because it was too expensive. She always assumed they were comfortable.

After a couple of very lean years, we grudgingly settled into a two-year cycle where one of us had to have a stable gig—editorial assistant, fact checker, book publicist—while the other concentrated on more creative work. The one with the more creative and thus flexible working conditions would be mostly responsible for domestic chores. At the end of the two-year cycle, we would switch.

When Elissa got pregnant, we were living in an East Village walk-up, on a block that did a brisk heroin business. We figured we'd turn the little closet-office where I worked into the baby's room. That was the plan until, over a three-month period, someone was shot outside our building and there were two different OD's who blocked the downstairs doorway. Maybe the neighborhood wasn't exactly baby proofed.

Elissa was more direct: "How the hell am I going to get a stroller over a dead, blue body with a needle in his arm?"

Okay, so maybe we couldn't stay in the East Village, but beyond that, I didn't see why anything had to change, even if we did have to move uptown or out to the wilds of Brooklyn.

We'd still discover new bands and go to shows all the time, right? My mom had taken me to plenty of concerts. They were classical, of course, but still. Babies like Sonic Youth, right? I figured that since I was adaptable and portable as a kid, my own children would be the same. They'd be independent and resilient. My mother and father had flown me back and forth across the Atlantic Ocean dozens of times. I'd known how to play dozens of card games before I could read. No big deal.

Ha. Ha. Ha.

For a few months after our daughter's birth we were fine—maybe we were in shock, or maybe it was the novelty, neither of us knew what we were doing. We didn't really feel like parents, exactly. For a while we couldn't even call our daughter by her name—we just called her "the baby."

Then reality hit us like a cartoon frying pan.

Elissa went to Rite Aid to buy diapers. First she tried to pay with her debit card, and when that was declined she tried the Master-Card, and when that was declined the Visa. When that was declined she lost it. Forced to leave the diapers in the store, she stormed home, and as soon as the door slammed shut she started crying and screaming at me. She wanted me to know that these weren't even nice diapers, these were crappy, cheap diapers, and that she couldn't stand it another minute.

Wait. Was this my fault?

A little lightbulb went off—it's one thing to have to live on Top Ramen yourself, it's another to not be able to buy diapers for your kid.

Together we scrounged up enough coin to buy the damn diapers. But she wouldn't go back, no—she was pissed, and she felt humiliated. Unless I wanted my bare-assed daughter pooping on the hardwood floor, I had to go back with my handful of nickels, dimes, and pennies.

Walking over to the store, pocket sagging with change, I thought, *Here I am the father, off to save the family honor.* I could do that.

I had a harder time embracing the clichéd role of good old Dad the breadwinner, who goes off to work in my porkpie hat while the wife stays home with the baby and eats bonbons. Surprisingly, even

in the liberal, forward-thinking world of publishing, it's still generally expected that if either the father or mother has to put their
career on hold in order to take care of children, it will be the
mother. Not surprisingly (if you know my wife), that didn't appeal to
Elissa. She knew that if she didn't write she'd be unfit to live with.
And the old-fashioned model didn't suit me either. If I didn't get
time to bond with my daughter, *I*, too, would be unfit to live with.

We wanted our children's lives to be different, more like the childhood Elissa had, but unlike the lifestyle her parents chose. So we have
had to adapt. We both had to move toward each other. This meant
that Elissa had to accept a certain amount of chaos in our lives while
I had to accept more stability. We came up with a system where one
of us does all of the domestic chores for a week—cooking, cleaning,
shopping, school lunches—and then at the end of the week we
switch. One person is always responsible for all things domestic, so
there is always a "wife," but it changes from week to week. Neither of
us have traditional desk jobs, and we're able to work from home at
least half of the time. As the two of us have moved toward each other,
the kids have greatly benefited from our compromises.

The kids like having two parents whose work is flexible enough
they can pick them up from school and spend the afternoons with
them. They like their house even though it's small for us. They like
being able to see their grandparents when they want. They have
friends they've had since birth. They have a regular school routine.
Roots. Routine. Rules.

Now we don't have as much money as Elissa would like, and we
don't have a big enough or tight enough safety net. And me, I've
had to accept that we will not be living abroad for years at a time.
Months, maybe, but not years. And I've had to face financial reality
and mostly moderate my wilder monetary impulses. My old philosophy of "spend it if you've got it" isn't exactly the best way to get
through the school year.

learning on the job

While I am comfortable with the way my children are growing up, I sometimes feel as if we are domestic bureaucrats, heads of a small struggling company, punching the family clock, efficiently ticking off the list of tasks for our nuclear project—food, check; school, check; vacation, check.

The flip side of this is that, given the stability of our life, I am having a second childhood along with my children. I've learned to ski and scooter, and I've taken up bicycle racing. I haven't given up my love of the spur-of-the-moment road trip; it's just now that instead of going to Niagara Falls, I'll throw the kids into the car and drive them out to Coney Island.

While I haven't completely converted to the power of the stable, domestic unit, Elissa hasn't completely given herself over to anarchy. Children entered our lives like an anarchist bomb, and if we hadn't been able to move closer to each other's ideals, we would have been blown apart. With two kids there is always chaos and anxiety, but together we've figured out how to handle our own particular crazy family.

the torah for the trees

· William Squier ·

*T*here used to be a Christmas tree lot just down the street from where my family and I live. Actually, it was a vacant lot for most of the year. But, shortly after my wife, Beth, son, Levi, and I moved into the neighborhood a tractor-trailer truck pulled up in front of it and dumped a load of fir trees onto the sidewalk. They were organized into tidy rows, strings of bare lightbulbs were hung overhead, and Christmas carols began to trickle out of a couple of tinny speakers. And for the next few months, we found ourselves living near a forest of evergreens.

Levi, who was about a year old at the time, paid the trees very little attention. He was still at an age where he found his toes much more interesting. But Beth and I regarded the trees, and then each other, uneasily. One of the great unresolved conflicts of our marriage had not only been dumped onto the sidewalk, but into our laps: whether or not to celebrate Christmas in our home.

Of course, we should have seen it coming: Beth is Jewish and I'm a Christian. But, what caught me off guard in particular was the fact that I thought we'd settled the issue long before Levi was born. Seems I had another think coming.

Back when we were first engaged, our friends took Beth and me aside and suggested the only responsible thing for an interfaith couple to do was to hash out their religious differences before marriage. So, off we trudged to the 92nd Street Y to work through the big issues with a bunch of other interfaith pairs.

At the top of everyone's list was the question of how to raise the kids. For the three or four other couples in our circle of folding chairs, this was a major sore point. They talked of being threatened by their parents with being disinherited, disowned, or reclassified as "dead to the family" if they sired progeny outside of their respective faith. These people had real problems. On the other hand, Beth and I took all of about a minute to settle the kid question. "Wanna go with Jewish?" "Sounds good. Can we stop for ice cream on the way home?" It was just that easy.

It's not that I was a lapsed Christian or anything. It's just that Beth and I wore our respective faiths lightly. We could be sidetracked by services that started a little too early, weather that was a little too icky, or temple dues that grew a little too pricey. But, living and working in New York City, first in high finance and then in live theater, I had, in effect, become Jewish by association. So, it seemed like the spiritual path of least resistance.

All the same, I began to wonder if Beth and I shouldn't be taking this discussion a bit more seriously. Then, someone mentioned Christmas—more specifically, the idea of having a Christmas tree in an interfaith family's home—and I suddenly thought that I saw Beth bristle.

"Is that going to be a problem?" I asked her, out of the corner of my mouth. She didn't answer right away. Uh-oh. Was it possible that I wasn't going to be allowed to share a Christmas tree with my child?

The reason this caught me by surprise was that we had already lived together for several years, and Beth hadn't objected to having a Christmas tree in our apartment. Though I had to admit that she was wary of it at first. But, I attributed her initial skittishness to early childhood trauma.

Beth's family had "experimented" with Christmas when she was small—they baked a few cookies, sang a carol here and there. However, their one and only attempt at celebrating the holiday full-out nearly ended in disaster. Beth's father threw all of their wrapping paper into the hearth on Christmas morning and lit it on fire without first opening the flue. After practically burning the house down, he announced that "Jews don't do Christmas" and that was the end of that.

To make Beth feel more relaxed around the tree, I suggested that we keep it nondenominational, with lovely blown-glass pickles and "Crabby" the Christmas crustacean dangling from its limbs. She met me halfway when it came to the points on which I was inflexible, such as proper tinsel distribution. She respected my rule that tinsel be hung strand by strand and not heaved all over the tree in clumpy handfuls. My parents even pitched in with a yearly gift of a sterling silver ornament, which Beth accepted gracefully.

Now, here I was, proposing that our yet-to-be-conceived offspring make the same compromises. And I could sense that she was resistant to the idea. Yet, to my surprise, she agreed! I could have "my" tree! Now we could live happily interfaithfully ever after, so long as I ignored the nagging feeling that something wasn't quite right.

Levi's first Christmas was a cinch. He was only two months old. The tree was a tiny sapling so loaded down with our collection of silver ornaments that it looked like a Miami matron after a trip to Fortunoff. We took snapshots. We sang "Jingle Bells." And as our son lay beneath the tree like one of the gifts, gazing up at its branches, all felt right with the world. It brought me back to my earliest memories of Christmas—of sprawling on my back under our tree in a circle of dappled light. I'd stare up into a heaven of glass ornaments and see my face reflected—an army of multicolored Jiminy Crickets, grinning back at me—while all around me swirled the sounds and smells of Christmas.

Growing up in a house where the guy to gal ratio was four to one, my family wasn't a huggy-kissy clan. But, Christmas was the one time of year when we found millions of ways to express our affection for one another. And it all centered on the tree. And now, here I was passing the joy that I felt at Christmastime on to a child of my own. I was going to be somebody's goofy ol' dad—the guy he'd hear laughing downstairs as I tried to assemble a tricycle at 3:00 A.M., on December 25th. And it felt good.

The next year, thanks to that handy lot down the street from our house, the tree got a lot taller. I added lights and brand new ornaments. I justified the extravagance by making sure that Hanukkah got equal time. For every sprig of holly, we bought a bag of gelt. There were blue-and-silver ribbons for every red-and-green bow. I polished my accent for the saying of the *brachot*—the blessing over the candles—by listening to Jackie Mason routines. We even made up our own Hanukkah songs with lyrics like "We're feeling too fat 'cause / Of too many latkes."

But, the taller the tree grew, the more the boy beneath it became a person. And everything that involved Levi gained added significance.

Beth's attitude about the situation began to change when our son was three. In keeping with our "decision" to raise him Jewish,

Levi was enrolled at the temple nursery school. Despite the fact that a third of the congregants in our little interfaith haven were Fitzgeralds and Carusos, more and more of Levi's "homework" centered around the rituals of Judaism. And my nonpracticing wife began to rediscover her roots.

It's not that Beth bought a second set of dishes or covered her head with a sheitl. But, a copy of *Yiddish for Dummies* did find its way into the bathroom reading matter. And she began to wonder aloud if maybe, just maybe, we weren't sending Levi confusing messages with this Christmas *and* Hanukkah thing.

I have to admit that it really started to bug me, this change in my wife. This was not the marriage that I signed up for beneath a *chuppah* held aloft by an equal number of Jews and Protestants. I couldn't understand how she could possibly see anything as harmless as Christmas as a threat to Levi's Jewish upbringing.

But, like the proverbial salmon swimming upstream, Beth began to feel determined, desperate almost, to provide Levi with a total Jewish identity. When Levi told people he was "half-Christian, half-Jewish," she was quick to correct him. "Religion isn't a nationality," she'd explain, adopting a schoolmarm's tone of voice. "It's a belief system. And you can only be one thing." I'm not so sure that Levi understood what she was saying, but I certainly did. I heard her loud and clear.

As Beth became more and more enamored of our temple, its rituals, and her heritage, I began to feel like something of an outsider. If we could "only be one thing," where was I in all of this? Every time I heard Beth tell someone that I had "a Jewish soul," I felt apologized for, tolerated. "Well, I thought he *was* Jewish when I first met him!" she'd exclaim, with a laugh. Granted, I wasn't the most devout Christian on the planet—my memories of church having mostly to do with spaghetti suppers and rummage sales—but I was *something*. And my soul was my own.

Things came to a head when Beth and I attended an evening for interfaith couples at our temple. But this time, when we entered that circle of folding chairs, we were the pair with a real problem. As if he could sense what was on our minds, our rabbi used the occasion to stress the need for interfaith parents to choose one religion for their children. If, as a family, we tried to be both, he warned, our son was likely to end up as neither.

Our son.

Though much of what the rabbi was saying was simply an echo of what I'd been hearing from my wife, the addition of those two words—*our son*—pulled me up short. This wasn't about Beth. I wasn't about me. It was about what was best for our son.

Digging in my heels over something as silly a Christmas tree suddenly seemed incredibly dumb. Beth was clearly getting a lot out of reconnecting with Judaism—I couldn't deny that. And all she wanted to do was share what she was experiencing with Levi. It was the same impulse that had moved her to make compromises that she felt would bring me joy—such as welcoming a towering *tannenbaum* into the middle of her living room.

I began to realize that my summoning up of Christmases past had mostly to do with reliving the handful of celebrations a year that provided my family with an excuse for togetherness. That's what I was really after: that feeling of connection. The rituals, the stories, the traditions of Judaism—these had mainly to do with daily life, not special occasions. Yet, they provided the same excuse for closeness. And they did it a lot more often.

I decided then and there to give up my tree. It was debatable whether or not having it in our home was truly confusing Levi. But, it was definitely muddying the issue for his parents. And we needed to present a united front. So, I wrapped the ornaments that I'd collected over the years into tissue paper and packed them into empty cookie tins. The scent of pine was relegated to an aerosol can kept in the bathroom. And I recycled our strings of twinkle bulbs into my annual Halloween display.

I hadn't counted on the reaction that my decision would get from my wife's side of the family. One of Beth's sisters insisted, "Bill has to have his tree!" My mother-in-law, on seeing the single, tiny ornament that we'd hung from the mantelpiece as a token, frowned and declared it the saddest thing she'd ever seen. But, I stood firm.

That's because once Beth and I decided, for real this time—with thought and feeling and commitment—to make a Jewish home, we stopped struggling. Beth loosened up. She became comfortable with us as an interfaith couple and no longer felt the need to make such a show of her religious identity. She lost any inner conflict she might have felt over joining in my parents' Christmas and Easter holiday celebrations, and even nibbled the occasional slice of Easter ham.

And I felt like I had become a part of my own home. Levi, Beth, and I were finally creating our own unit by building memories around the rituals and traditions of Judaism. Memories that are now every bit as precious to me as those I held of Christmas. But, they were our memories—those of my new family.

Levi's excitement over attending his first toddler Sabbath service at the temple, where he had so much fun that he asked if we could go to another temple the same night.

When he was first aware of the lighting of the menorah, how Levi expected it to come with a cake and sang "Happy Birthday."

The sound of his six-year-old giggle mingled with those of his cousins as they hunted for the *afikoman* during the Passover Seder.

The way his hoarse adolescent chuckle joined with the adults' at his Uncle Jon's exclamations (repeated verbatim at every holiday meal) about Grandma Carol's brisket.

His mastery of both Hebrew and a terrific Yiddish accent, used for delivering the punch lines in his bar mitzvah speech.

Yeah, there used to be a Christmas tree lot just down the street from where my family and I live. But, a couple of years ago someone bought the lot and in its place they built a home. A beautiful new home.

not what we were expecting

welcome to the babyhouse

· Michael Finkel ·

So this is what it's come to: the middle of the night, a need to pee. I'm thirty-seven years old. I've been peeing in the night, without concern, since the Nixon administration.

But now I have a baby. A newborn. She's sleeping in the room with my wife and me. The baby is a sound-sensitive sleeper; if I get up, I'll likely disturb her. A bedspring, a floorboard, a door hinge—something will bleat or squeak or groan. A disturbed baby is a crying baby. A crying baby means a wakened wife. It's difficult for the baby to return to sleep, and even harder for my wife. When my wife has a tough night, she's cranky in the morning. Which means we'll bicker even more. The calculus is unappealing.

I decide, therefore, to simply lie in bed. I lie for a while. Needing to pee. I'm hoping that the baby will soon wake herself, so I can escape to the bathroom without triggering a marital earthquake. I wait.

A little more. Soon, I grow angry. *How did I tangle myself in such a trap where using the toilet is no longer a simple matter? This,* I conclude, *is asinine. I'm getting up.*

Carefully, gradually, I shift to a standing position. I move across the floor in a slow-motion hopscotch, avoiding the loose planks. Wife and child are still motionless—a minor miracle. I open the bathroom door as if I'm disarming a land mine. I reach the commode.

I'd made it this far once before. Then I blew it. Our house is old, our walls thin. The sound I'd made, the splash into the bowl, was enough to unbalance the baby. This time, consequently, I sit. Yes. I sit and pee. A grown man. This is what it's come to.

I relieve myself. The house remains silent. But just as I'm starting the return trip, I perform a motion that's been subconsciously ingrained in me over the past three and a half decades. I reach behind and flush. It's too late to take it back. A small tsunami passes though the house. The roar swiftly fades, but in its place is the unmistakable shriek of a wailing baby.

The baby did not come as a surprise. How could it? My wife was pregnant for nine months, which was more than enough time for us to read the books—the *Sears and Sears,* the *What to Expect*—and to figure out how to install an infant car seat, and to interrogate all our baby-stocked friends. We were braced for the sleeplessness, prepared for the upended home life, attuned to the sad electronic squawks the baby-toy company has the audacity to label "Mozart."

What did come as a shock was that these changes were not obviously for the better. My friends with babies had gushed to me. Every one. "It's the greatest thing ever." "My soul is enriched." "I never knew such love." Stuff like that. No one told me that my life with a baby might not add up, that the sacrifices perhaps wouldn't compensate for the gains, the joys may be trumped by the frustrations. No one told my wife, either.

What I'm trying to say—what is apparently taboo to say, judging from those I've spoken with—is that this whole baby thing may have been a mistake. Perhaps I haven't been able to hypnotize myself the way my friends have. Maybe it's even illegal to admit this. Who knows these days? But I'll say it anyway: I was happier when I didn't have a child.

It took all of twelve hours for my daughter to begin ruining my life. The little bug was born, via C-section, early on a December morning. The grandparents gushed, I snapped a press conference's worth of photos, and my wife lay in her hospital bed with a blissful, morphine-laced grin. I liked being a father. The whole day I liked it. Then it was time for my hockey game.

Yes, okay, possibly you're right: It's not necessary for a guy to play a city-league hockey game a dozen hours after his child is born. But I'd developed a theory over the course of my wife's pregnancy. The theory was that having a child should in no way mark the passing of my own innate childishness. In fact, I believed that the *more* I fostered my deeply rooted immaturity, the better I'd connect with my own offspring. I thought it was a good theory. I honestly did.

I did not discuss this philosophy with my wife, and, quite frankly, I'm fairly certain that she would've preferred me not to play ice hockey at that instant. But as I mentioned, due to the C-section she was on a morphine drip. So I waited until she pressed the morphine button and lapsed into a semicoma. Then I gently and lovingly asked her, "Honey, do you mind if I escape from the hospital for a second to do a bit of skating?"

She said something like "Huuuh-yuuuh-uuuuh," which I took to mean, "Of course, dear, you've been a model father for hours now, go enjoy yourself—and while you're at it, drink a few beers with the boys after the game. I'll be fine right here."

Now, I'd like to report that I skated with the guys, had a fine time, and crept back to the hospital, kissed my tiny child on her forehead, curled up next to my wife, and continued my ideal fathering. I'd really like to report that.

But what actually occurred was something that had never before happened to me in a dozen winters of playing city-league hockey. Maybe I was overtired, or overwhelmed, or otherwise preoccupied, but what happened was that I entangled myself in my own skates and crashed shoulder first into the boards. I heard a disconcerting pop. Then the pain struck.

A teammate drove me to the emergency room of the same hospital where my wife was ensconced one floor above. I was soon given my own shot of morphine and sent upstairs. So it was that on the day my daughter was born—the very moment that my wife desperately needed me to have two hands—my right arm, my good arm, was in a sling and I was of little use at all.

The squabbling began the next morning. Though the pain in my shoulder swiftly—albeit incompletely—subsided, the fighting did not. It isn't like my wife and I never argued before we had a baby. We did, some doozies. But these postbaby fights were different. Very different. How so? Well, for one thing, I wasn't winning any of them.

We fought about how warmly to dress the baby. We bickered over the appropriate temperature of her formula, the optimal-sized feeding nipple to put on her bottle, the rate of diaper changes. We fought about how loudly I walk on the stairs. How noisily I close doors. How annoyingly I snore. (We fought about snoring nearly every night.) We quarreled over when I could take a shower. We fought about the buzz of my electric toothbrush.

We argued over whether to rush the baby to the doctor because of diarrhea. We disagreed over rushing the baby to the doctor due to constipation. And jaundice. And hiccups.

When you're chronically sleep deprived, you tend to argue like a drunk—wild verbal roundhouses, ill-considered sarcasm. That's another discrepancy between our prebaby and postbaby fights: All of a sudden, it seemed, both of us had hair-trigger tempers, and the swiftness with which our fights escalated was unprecedented. Our conflicts, over the most frivolous details, could intensify from slightly irritable to downright nuclear in a matter of moments.

One night, my wife accused me of not being properly concerned that the baby had been screaming nonstop for an hour. I said the cries didn't sound unusual, and it was obvious the baby wasn't sick. She said there was no way I could tell. I replied that she was being a ridiculous worrywart. She called me utterly heartless. I said it'd be best if we ignored the cries and went to sleep. She said I was the most selfish man on planet Earth, and that I was really only concerned with myself and my precious sleep. I said I needed some rest because my job was more important than hers (a lie—she's a university professor, I'm a journalist). She countered my lie. I ended up on the sofa.

We fought about whether to sleep with a night-light on. We had a dispute about the proper application of baby sunscreen, and another about breast-pumping frequency. We argued about the baby's nap time, bedtime, feeding time, bath time, and stroll time. We fought over whether to clean up baby vomit with a burp cloth or a paper towel.

A couple of times, in the heat of battle, one of us dropped a D-bomb. That's right: We used the word *divorce*. My wife says she once even researched local attorneys online. There have been times, to be honest, that I wondered—if we didn't have a baby, would we still be together? Then I realized that if we didn't have a baby, we probably wouldn't be fighting this severely. I'm still not entirely sure our marriage will survive the strain. But at the same time, paradoxically, both of us agree that we should have more than one child.

We battled about grandparents' visits. About the length of my exercise sessions. About the best method of making rice cereal; about how often to run the dishwasher; about which way I faced when I slept. And, naturally, we fought about whether or not it was appropriate for me to get up to pee in the middle of the night.

The thing is, I always wanted a baby. I wanted one at least as much as my wife, maybe more. I just always wanted one next year. First, I needed to squeeze every millisecond out of that sacred space I call "postcollege prelife." It wasn't until my mid-thirties—after more than a decade of blissful PCPL—that I began facing the awful truth: I was starting to suffer from oldest-man-in-the-bar syndrome. And there's little in life more shameful than a protracted case of oldest-man syndrome.

Marriage cured the condition, but then I knew it wouldn't be long before next year became this year. As my wife's belly inflated, soon enough this year became right now. I thought I'd timed everything perfectly. But I was wrong. I may, in fact, have delayed parenthood *too* long, as I'd shed oldest-man-in-the-bar syndrome only to find myself abruptly thrust into an old-dog-new-tricks situation. I was the old dog. Diaper changing, baby burping, formula preparing, you name it—these were the new tricks. Yet dealing with an infant, as I learned, isn't simply a matter of mastering a few fresh tricks. It's a whole new circus.

I'd spent the fifteen years since graduating from college working as a freelance magazine writer—traveling the world, sleeping late, answering only to virtual bosses a phone call away. In other words, I was something of a spoiled brat. Or, as my wife likes to put it, I was a baby before we had a baby.

My existence now seems a Sisyphean cycle of housekeeping—cleaning bottles, cleaning vomit, cleaning poop. Then back to bottles. Our baby is not a great sleeper; therefore, no longer are my wife and I. My time at home has become more exhausting than my hours at work. My writing output, due to fatigue, has sharply declined, which means that my income has also plummeted. At the same time, my expenses are greater than ever.

I've sacrificed my creative life, my traveling life, my mountain-climbing life, my book-reading life, my road-tripping life, my movie-viewing life, my dining-out-with-my-wife life, my backpack-ing life, my bar-hopping life, my waste-the-whole-morning-doing-the-crossword life, and my sex life. All has been eclipsed by my dealing-with-a-newborn life. That's quite a balance sheet. And a baby, it turns out, is more permanent that a tattoo. You really can't undo having a baby. There are times when I gaze at my daughter, at her chubby dimpled cheeks, and I wonder: How long are you going to be staying here?

My wife, of course, is coping with a similar set of issues. She was once an accomplished triathlete. Now her bike sits in a corner of the garage, the tires airless. She, too, was a bold traveler. Twice she jour-neyed to southern Africa to teach at the University of Zambia. Now a big trip is heading across town to the Kmart. The recovery from her C-section took twice as long as expected. She's been struggling to drop the baby weight; she's been doing much more than her share of the baby tending; and of course the burden of breast-feeding is entirely hers. She hasn't gone so far as to say that her life was more fulfilling prebaby—she's dealing with the birth with far less angst than I, and a great deal more joy—but she'll be the first to acknowl-edge that the baby balance sheet is disturbingly unbalanced.

She's also pointed out that, despite the fact we're spending more time at home than ever before, it doesn't feel as though we're spending much time *together*. It's true. Our attention is focused so completely on our newborn that we rarely have a chance to make eye contact. Sometimes it seems as if we've become little more than workmates.

We've never eaten so frequently in our kitchen—both of us were devoted restaurant goers in our prebaby life—yet I can scarcely recall the last time we sat at the same table. Instead, we've been busy perfecting the new-parent juggle: One of us sits and eats, the other entertains the infant. Then we switch. As soon as Baby falls asleep, we seem to automatically retreat to separate corners, like boxers between rounds. My wife sprawls on the upstairs couch, remote control in hand; I descend to my basement office, where I usually sit in my desk chair, slowly swiveling in a sort of shell-shocked trance.

My daughter is now eight months old. She can crawl, with ferocious intent, in a straight line, until she rams her head against a wall. A couple of teeth are poking out of her lower gums like tiny snow-capped peaks. She's started communicating a bit—this week, she's been yelling "Ha-ja!" over and over, as if her life depended on it. She's already on her fourth size of diapers.

I'm not a completely insensitive man—I feel the heart clutch when she laughs in her jiggly baby way at my silliness; I'm incapable of stifling a grin when I stare at her, asleep in her crib, legs and arms thrown in improbable directions. Do I love her? Absolutely. Has she enhanced my life? She has. My child has accomplished the one thing no one else could: She's forced me to grow up.

My wife and I still battle over the inane minutiae of baby life, though not so severely. I'm still not winning any of our fights. And I'm still peeing in the night sitting down—without flushing.

When my friends—my friends without kids—ask me about the pros and cons of starting a family, I tell them how I really feel. I say that, in the debate about whether or not to have a child, it isn't a bad decision to conclude not. The planet isn't in dire need of more human beings. We're not pandas; we're not exactly an endangered species. The landfills aren't crying out for additional dirty diapers. The work of raising a child may, for some people, not be worth the rewards.

The shock and depression I felt after my daughter's birth has dissipated—not entirely, but mostly. I see my childless friends going off on camping trips, on jaunts to Europe, on evenings of careless debauchery, and I'm jealous. Two of my least favorite notions are *compromise* and *responsibility*, and these are pretty much what my days are now about. I know that I've lost some freedoms. My wife and I can't abruptly leave the house, can't go on a last-minute weekend river float, can't pass a rainy day playing backgammon. All our activities, it seems, need to be scheduled and preplanned and specifically timed. My spontaneity muscle has atrophied to the point of uselessness. From the day we graduated high school until the day we had a child, my wife and I both felt as though our horizons were continuously expanding. Now we recognize that they've abruptly narrowed.

I'm hoping that, as our daughter grows, we'll both become more attuned to the roles of parents, and rediscover our natural rhythms. My wife is well on her way to finding that essential balance—between caring for our child and caring for herself, between the onus of parenthood and the rejuvenative effect of a big glass of wine. But for the first time in both our lives, there are days when we really feel old, or at least middle-aged. And as much as I'd like to revisit my youth, the truth is that my desire to explore, to travel the world, has been supplanted by a profound sense of protectiveness, of needing to stay close to home. I think I'm struggling with the realization that I don't *want* to impulsively fly off to Paris at least as much as the fact that I no longer can.

My only goal is to make the best of my new circumstances. It's not always easy. Nearly every time I pick up my daughter, my right shoulder emits a small, discomforting pop, and I'm reminded of all I have in my arms, and everything my wife and I have given up, and it's a difficult summation. I think about our prebaby life all the time. I miss it every day. I really do.

our life in vermont

· Dan Elish ·

When I was single I was one of those guys who got set up on a lot of dates—as I got older it was probably because numbers were on my side. I hit my late thirties still looking for the proverbial right girl, while other semipresentable men were already taken. So twice a month or so I soldiered off to meet the woman of my dreams. Needless to say, more often than not the actual dates would not equal my expectations. I would return home, slightly disappointed and vaguely lonely, to another night of reruns.

But sometimes—when the stars were aligned or if I was just plain lucky—I would walk into a restaurant and find myself taking a seat across from someone with potential. Someone I liked. A lot. Smitten, my mind would begin to wander. Perhaps the woman was telling me about her favorite book. Maybe she was discussing the tragic early demise of her pet cat. It didn't really matter. While making sure to nod appropriately, even speak actual words ("Gee, that's tough. The death of a family pet can certainly be traumatic. . . ."), I would take a diving leap months, even years, into the future. Just like that, I would be transported to an idealized state of matrimony. Life would be perfect, save one minor detail: The woman across the table usually didn't want to come along for the ride.

Then I got lucky. My friend Maureen threw a birthday party where she introduced me to Andrea, one of her writing students. She was everything a guy like me wanted. Pretty and smart. Creative but not insane. Everything seemed to click. When I made a joke, Andrea laughed. When I went to use the bathroom, she was waiting to pick up the conversation where we had left off when I got back. We even danced. Best of all, she never once uttered the dreaded word *boyfriend*. After a month of increasingly avid and humorous e-mailing, Andrea and I began to date. A month later, we were in love. Then came an evening that will remain forever etched in my memory.

The setting: a New York City street. The time: early one evening. Andrea and I were strolling arm in arm toward her apartment, when she turned to me with a slightly embarrassed smile. The following dialogue ensued:

Me: What? (referring to her embarrassed smile)

Andrea: Oh, nothing . . .

Me: No, what?

Andrea: (squirming) Well, sometimes I've actually imagined living in Vermont.

Me: (gripping a lamppost with two hands in order to remain upright) No? Really?!?

Andrea: In a house with a yellow door.

not what we were expecting

Me: With three kids?

Andrea: And a Labrador named Pete.

The medics arrived quickly. With a whiff or two of smelling salts, I was back on my feet in no time. If you are wondering why the intensity of my reaction, let me explain. From ages eight to eighteen, I had gone to camp near Rutland, Vermont. After that, I attended Middlebury College and then spent several summers at the Bread Loaf writers' conference. I grew to love the Green Mountain State, where the air was always fresh and the rolling pastureland was dotted with farms. It was to one of those farms that I had imagined moving with my future wife and raising a family. (Though I was raised in New York City, camp had turned me into a good horseback rider and general barn hand.) Now it appeared that I had found the ideal woman with whom to share it. And she wanted kids, too! Okay, so maybe I hadn't envisioned the actual paint colors of my house, but if Andrea really shared my fantasy of wedded bliss, I'd paint our front door with lime green polka dots.

Reeling from our discovery, Andrea and I began to jokingly riff on our mutual fantasies. Of course, our vision of life in Vermont did not focus on the practical chores of farm life. We didn't consider the logistics of how we would manage to milk one hundred cows by ourselves each morning. We didn't consider the price of oats. No, the farm would simply be the setting—a place where we would live a life of solitude; a place where daily activities might include long romantic walks through our one-hundred-acre pasture, felling mighty oaks with handmade hatchets, and Friday night square dances.

And then there were our children—three of them, always out of diapers, plenty old enough to bound across our spacious front yard and jump into our arms with a hearty "I love you, Mommy! I love you, Daddy!" We would be a family that enjoyed life to the fullest, and was always together. In the winter we would negotiate the black diamonds at Killington. In the summer, we would go tubing down Otter Creek. Autumn would bring running family leaps into giant piles of leaves. And the spring? After tapping our property's maple trees, we would market our best-selling brand of homemade syrup. Of course, our children would be extraordinary. At the school assembly hall, Andrea and I would watch our oldest daughter rip through Beethoven's *Pathétique* Sonata at her first piano recital. Our son's star turn as Tony in the sixth-grade production of *West Side Story* would make Leonard Bernstein himself rise from the grave, weeping tears of gratitude. And who could forget our youngest? She would recite the final paragraphs of *The Great Gatsby* from memory to her kindergarten class.

Needless to say, Andrea and I didn't bother imagining the typical minor tensions that go hand and hand with any long-term relationship. Rather, we focused on the idea that when we weren't taking care of the kids, we would be preparing lavish romantic feasts or simply sitting on our front porch, enjoying the calm of a starlit evening.

Not bad.

Our soon-to-be-lived life seemed perfect. So perfect that we were soon taking our relationship seriously enough to talk about marriage. Still, aware that we were miles ahead of where we should be, we vowed not to let the *M* word make us feel any undue pressure.

We failed. A short three months into our relationship, Andrea and I realized that we were in serious danger of derailing. Instead of having fun, we were tense. One morning, I received an e-mail from my future wife suggesting that we take a week off. Although I worried that her "time off" was simply shorthand for "Drop dead, loser," I was secretly relieved. The short break did us good. When Andrea came over to my apartment a week later, we went to the park and played catch. While tossing the ball back and forth, I did it again. It wasn't long before the small field in Central Park transformed to the Vermont countryside, complete with horses, bales of hay, and a friendly Labrador. I saw two or three children running through the pasture, screaming happily, as the sun set on another glorious country day. What a good mother Andrea would make! One who can catch and throw! Why, a woman like that could raise Olympic athletes! When Andrea and I went out to dinner later that night, I felt sure of it: Here was the girl I would marry.

Nine months after we met, Andrea moved in. Two months later, we got engaged. Less than a year after Maureen's birthday party, we were married.

The day we got back from our honeymoon, we packed our things into a U-Haul, threw a good-bye party for our friends, and set out for our Vermont farm to live a dream.

Well, uh . . . actually not.

We stayed in New York after all. The culprit was my father's small country house in upstate New York. During our engagement, we had taken a series of weekend visits there, even bought a used car. But as it turned out, our weekend experiments in country living were a bust. We never cuddled in the hay barn. We didn't attend a single square dance or fell a single tree. If we passed a herd of cows, I certainly never pulled over to milk them. Yes, it was beautiful there. But after two peaceful days, we were usually eager to get back to our friends, work, and the many advantages of city life. If we were to have a family, it would be in the city. Like it or not, we were New Yorkers.

So Andrea and I settled into my smallish two-bedroom apartment. When we decided it was time to start a family, my home office was the first to go. Out went the old plywood desk. As we remodeled, we wondered what it would actually be like to have a child. Factoring out the inevitable irritations that go hand and hand with cohabitation, Andrea and I had always gotten along easily. Would our child arrive only to demolish our laid-back rapport? Would he (or she) be a brat? One of those kids you saw on the subway screaming at the top of his lungs because his mother or father wouldn't let him swing from the railings and look out the window? Yes, we had always wanted kids—badly. But faced with the reality, we were as worried as we were excited. In short, would this child ruin our lives?

At the twenty-week sonogram we found out we were having a girl. Though hoping for the best, Andrea and I, more than a little paranoid, prepared for the worst: our daughter would be one of the difficult ones, a bad seed, a she-wolf, capable of shattering glass and sending otherwise even-keeled patrons sprinting out of restaurants with a single tantrum. Even worse, she would look like me. As the second trimester became the third, we began to wonder if having a child would really be worth the stress. The financial pressure. Not to mention, for Andrea, the pain. Worry mixed with eager anticipation until, all of a sudden, it was time. On a routine visit to the doctor two weeks before the due date, our rather hip ob-gyn, who sported a purple streak in her hair, announced, "Hey, Andrea, you're ninety percent effaced!" before adding, cheerfully, "I can feel your baby's head!"

That night Andrea went into labor. The next afternoon at 3:30, Cassie was born, to our surprise and relief with all the early hallmarks of a patient, easygoing child. She also had the good fortune to look like Andrea. We were stunned, astonished, and wildly in love. A day later, we proudly brought her home.

Every parent soon discovers what we did. A newborn doesn't bound across a lawn to express his undying love. A newborn doesn't "bound" anywhere. While we were dating, still basking in the fantasy of a life in Vermont, Andrea and I had imagined our children arriving fully formed. A day with Cassie and we realized that we were in for something far more difficult, but also more rewarding. On her very first evening home, Cassie was up all night, crying. The next morning, exhausted, I tried to put her crib together. When

I failed, I left it to my father-in-law and wrestled with the stroller. I couldn't put that together either. Then it was out to the store to buy more diapers, then back home to try to put Cassie down for a nap. Andrea, of course, was busy with her own chores, largely relating to the vitally necessary but surprisingly difficult challenge of breast-feeding.

Needless to say, this wasn't how babies were reared in Vermont. Not *our* Vermont, anyway. Clearly, Andrea and I didn't have time for long, romantic walks or even a quick roll in the hay. Our main lust was for sleep. Once the initial high of parenthood had worn off, once relatives had left town, we had no other choice but to roll up our sleeves and prepare ourselves for a lifetime of hard work. As weeks stretched into the first months, Andrea and I learned a lot about functioning while exhausted, about giving ourselves completely to someone we loved with no hope for immediate return. We discovered that the day-to-day work of raising a child is often about pure repetition: changing the diaper, warming up the bottle, chopping food into bite-sized portions, putting on the shoes and socks, pushing the swing, reading the same story again and again and again. Those with idealized visions about parenthood need not apply.

It also didn't take us long to realize the multitude of ways in which reality outstripped fantasy. How can anyone possibly comprehend how much they are going to love their child before the fact? A love that makes every push of a swing, every bath, and every reread story worth it? As single people, Andrea and I envisioned married life in broad strokes, through rose-tinted glasses—but while we certainly never fantasized about changing a diaper, we discovered that it is just those nitty-gritty details that make child rearing so rewarding. It is those details that gave Andrea and me even more to share, something uniquely ours: the joy of watching our child grow up. Rather than push us apart, upsetting the delicate give-and-take of our natural rapport, to our surprise, Cassie drew us closer. Who else but proud parents could appreciate such mundane acts as watching their child take her first step? Or deciphering her first real word? Who else would possibly care? With the possible exception of grandparents, no one.

So where does all of this leave our dream life?

Yes, we would still love to own a farm in Vermont one day and enjoy all the carefree outdoor activities we envisioned with our kids. But at this point Andrea and I wouldn't trade it for our two-bedroom apartment in New York. That's where we are drawn closer by the day-in-and-day-out, sometimes menial joys of raising our daughter. Speaking for myself, if I had known when I was single how rewarding it would be, I might have fantasized about that.

the tie that binds

· Nancy Wartik ·

I'm huddled in a phone booth in Talkeetna, Alaska, calling the friend who just a few short days ago was the maid of honor at my wedding. We've stopped in this place, a hippie-esque little wilderness town on which the old TV show *Northern Exposure* was supposedly modeled, for a couple of nights of our honeymoon. Outside the booth it's rainy and gray, the weather a fine fit for my mood. I've told my brand-new husband I have a quick errand to run, and abandoned him in a small-town restaurant, swigging his beer, munching his mooseburger.

Now I'm on the phone, dialing Kansas where my friend lives, to admit that I've made a little mistake. Just a small one. I've married the wrong man. Not in the sense that anyone else was beating down my door, God knows, but in the sense that it simply . . . won't . . . work. I married in an instant of delusion. We'll have to return the wedding presents, call the divorce lawyer, and go our separate ways. In fact, it seems next to impossible that I can even get through the rest of the honeymoon, possessed as I am by a dread feeling that I've signed away the rest of my life on the wrong dotted line.

My friend answers the phone and I begin pouring my litany of worries into the receiver.

It's a little less than two years later and I'm huddled again, with the same husband I never quite got around to divorcing. We're lying in bed, talking in low voices. Next door in her crib is our eleven-month-old daughter, Mira, whom we adopted from Kazakhstan and brought home to New York the day before. Dennis was up half the night, walking the floor with her, trying to get her to doze off. He tells me that at one point, in a state of jet-lagged delirium, he imagined she was rasping at him, *Exorcist*-style, saying something on the lines of "Thaaat's right, do your best, sucker. I'm calling the shots now."

After years spent yearning for this day, the day when I'd become someone's mother, the reality of it all has been kind of . . . well . . . kind of a bitch. Mired in confusion, blithering ignorance about parenthood, and sleep deprivation, I'm beginning to suspect that I'm not a baby person after all. Moreover, I've taken this on in my forties, my husband in his fifties: silly us. We're too old and tired to be anyone's new parents.

Too bad this whole thing was my idea to begin with. Too bad I'm only realizing the truth now that the papers are signed. Because at the moment, I'm absolutely sure the decision to bring a baby into our lives will turn out to be the worst mistake we've ever made.

One chilly night earlier this year, almost three years since the morning I'd woken in despair, sure that I'd ruined everything, Dennis and I got a baby-sitter and went out for a movie and dinner. During those three years, our outward circumstances had altered in a variety of ways. We'd moved uptown, into a new, larger apartment, forgoing Starbucks and taxicabs in order to be able to afford our new, larger mortgage. There is no more sleeping late, no more leisurely, unstructured weekends; instead, there are trips to the playground, forays to the zoo. No more keeping the fridge stocked with only leftover Chinese and a few bottles of beer. And as for me, once vocally scornful of "traditional" marriages, I now spend much of my day cooking, cleaning, and caring for Mira, while Dennis goes out and wins the bread.

But really, it's the change in our inner worlds that's been most astounding. Late in the game, parental love has walloped us both over the head with a two-by-four; our hearts have been pried wide-open, made painfully, miraculously vulnerable by our merry-eyed, tousle-haired, long-limbed, brilliant, remarkable child. My initial fears about whether I was meant to be a mother have melted away like grimy snow in the spring sun. Dennis and I both dote on our child in a way that just a few years ago, neither of us could ever have imagined possible.

Over dinner, I begin complaining to Dennis about an essay I've been assigned to write, describing how parenthood has transformed our relationship.

"What am I going to do?" I whine, in the fetching manner he's come to know so well. "You've got to help me. I accepted the assignment, but now I can't think of anything to write about. I can't even figure out if our relationship *has* changed. I'm still bitchy. You're still quiet. We were so old when we became parents; maybe we were too set in our ways for things between us to change at a basic level?"

My husband is renowned among those who know him for never responding to anything until he's reviewed it from all angles, meaning there's a pause of at least thirty seconds between a question asked and answered. It's a pause that's frustrated many a fast-talking New Yorker, but it does tend to give what comes out of his mouth the ring of profundity.

I drink some wine while I watch him consider. Dennis isn't a second-guesser, like I am. His decisions are final. Long ago, when I first brought up the idea of adoption to him, he stared at me in horrified bemusement—I might as well have been suggesting he go for a tongue piercing. In the end he said yes, and he fell in love with Mira the day we met her in Kazakhstan, and from then on, he never looked back. Often, it's been his certainty that's carried me along on the journey to where we are today.

"When we adopted Mira, we made a decision to go down a new path together," Dennis finally says: "It was an irrevocable step for us, a one-way passage. It means our lives are bound together inextricably, no matter what we do."

"Not really," I protest. "Lots of people have kids and get divorced."

"Doesn't matter," he says. "Even if we got divorced, we'd still be Mira's parents. It's like one of the Beatles once said: Even if they split up, they'd still be the only four people in the world who knew what it was like being part of the Beatles."

Then he drinks more of his wine or perhaps I drink it for him. We finish our dinner, pay the bill, and hop the subway home, to our sleeping daughter.

Inextricably bound together?

In August, we splurge wildly and the three of us fly to the island of Kauai, in Hawaii, to rent a house with friends.

Dennis and I need this vacation. Lately we've been snapping at each other a lot over small things. I think it's his turn to put Mira to bed, he thinks it's mine. He heads out with her in the morning without stopping to brush her hair, and I chastise him in the aggrieved, self-righteous tone I know he hates. The traditional roles we've shouldered feel like a trap, rather than a choice. He accuses me of being too critical; I complain he doesn't talk to me enough. Evenings, we're tired and cranky. Often, it seems, we save the best of ourselves for Mira and have nothing left over for each other. In the midst of a squabble, we turn to say something to her and our voices soften. Then we turn back to speak to each other. Our voices harden again.

It's been said before—by me, at least—that marriage is a roller coaster. If so, I'm not always sure who's in control at the switches. What's sent us into this precipitous dip? I could blame the usual suspects: the unrelenting demands of parenting, the feeling of never having enough time, the loss of freedom. Or perhaps our personalities are simply fated to grapple now and then, caught in some cycle beyond our understanding.

What if I had it right that evening in the phone booth in Talkeetna? Maybe when our trip is over, I won't get on the plane going back to New York. Maybe I'll take our rental car and drive it to the quaint nearby village, where latter-day hippies play Grateful Dead and rasta music on the green. I'll change my name, find a waitress job, and rent a cheap room. On my days off, I'll go the beach with bags of novels. I'll sit and read to my heart's content, with no one else to answer to. I entertain myself, spinning out my fantasy in detail (never mind that I'd make an incredibly lousy waitress).

The days on Kauai flow past. Dennis and Mira and I bob in the waves together. Mira chases geckos, picks fragrant flowers, and is alternately solicitous and intolerant of our friends' two-year-old. We four grown-ups drink margaritas and piña coladas, grill fish in the backyard, and let the sun burn our twenty-first-century tensions away.

One afternoon, Dennis and I find our one chance to slip off by ourselves and take a hike down a beautiful, wild trail on the island's north shore. The ocean rolls out beyond the cliffs, off to the far horizon, winking in the sun.

At one point, a tiny tragedy confronts us. On the path, we come upon a man who's slipped and fractured his leg; when we reach the next beach, we wade into the water and flag a passing boat, asking the crew to radio for help. It's a cruel axiom that one person's ruined vacation is another's novel adventure; thus we're drawn together by our rescuers role and watch excitedly to see the helicopter descending from the sky.

Years ago, in Italy, we guided a panicking skier down a steep alpine slope after she'd gotten stuck there. We laugh and reminisce about that other rescue as we carefully pick our way home. I watch Dennis swinging along in his familiar, ratty old T-shirt and fluorescent green running shorts, the man who was willing to embark with me on the greatest adventure I've ever taken. I remember that when everything goes smoothly between us, and our minds are in sync, there's simply no one else with whom I'd rather spend my time.

The reality is, I'm a doubter and questioner by nature: It's a trait woven into the very synapses of my neurons. I've gone through fits of anguished soul-searching on the heels of every crucial decision I've made. And when stress builds in our marriage, I go into a panic mode (as in, "Oh God! Two roads diverged in a yellow wood—why, oh why, didn't I choose the *other* one?").

But what Dennis said a few months ago at dinner is true: Something is irrevocably different now that we're Mira's parents. Here on this path above the ocean, with things feeling right between us again, it strikes me clearly. Two have become three; three have become one. We're a unit. A family. I contemplate the relief and responsibility of accepting that we made our real choice a long time ago. Our love for Mira is the strongest certainty either of us has known. Everything else flows from that.

One of these days, I'm sure, the roller-coaster car will head into a downward slide again, and I'll plunge along with it, waving my hands and shouting, knowing all the while in some deep corner of my brain that this too will pass and everything will be all right. Eventually, the car will bottom out and begin its uphill climb. I've bought my ticket and I'm happy to take the ride to the end.

Everything has changed.

Nothing has changed.

Everything has changed.

enemy at the baby gate

· Lisa Unger ·

Like generals heading into battle, my husband, Jeffrey, and I prepared for every possible condition in readying ourselves for the arrival of our daughter. Overwhelmed by the horror stories of those who'd headed into the fray before us, there was no attack—from colic to breast-feeding issues, from sleep deprivation to sexual starvation—for which we did not develop a counterattack. We were heavily armed with baby books and wipes warmers, breast pumps and travel systems. Little did we know how woefully we'd underestimated our opponent or that in the end we'd fall desperately, head over heels in love with the enemy at the gate.

If the women of my mother's generation were less than honest about the difficulties of raising a child and the effect it can have on a marriage, my generation appears to have abandoned any such stoicism. The newly pregnant couple is barraged with messages about how miserable they are about to become. Friends and strangers issue the ominous warning over and over: "Get ready for your whole life to change." They then expound with their stories of colicky babies who cry for six weeks straight, sleep deprivation so extreme it classifies as a personality disorder, nipple confusion, sexual starvation, and breast pumps that draw blood. Of course, let's not forget the baby blues, not to be confused with postpartum depression, not to be confused with postpartum psychosis. It would be enough to give a thinking woman pause—if she weren't already pregnant.

But Jeffrey and I *did* pause before becoming parents. It wasn't something that we entered into lightly or accidentally. It wasn't an idea we had romanticized. It wasn't anything we needed to feel whole as a couple. When we decided it was time, it was because we felt we had a lot to offer a little person, that we would take great joy in sharing what we loved about the world with a child. We'd both learned hard lessons well and felt we had a lot to teach. And we shared a great love for each other that we knew would create a solid foundation for a happy childhood. It was an intellectual decision, made by two smart and loving people.

We met on a humid November night in Key West. Jeffrey was vacationing from Michigan. I, living in New York City at the time, was visiting a close friend who'd relocated to Florida just a few months earlier. In the sweating, drunken mess that was a bar called Sloppy Joe's, I found Jeffrey. It was truly a *shazam!* moment, a point on which my whole life pivoted. We had a white-hot long-distance love affair that involved one or the other of us on a plane every weekend. Within four months, he had proposed. Within six, we'd both quit our jobs, sold our homes, and moved to Florida. We were married in Key West, a year to the day after we met. Quite naturally, our reception ended up at Sloppy Joe's.

We had an extraordinarily romantic beginning. After a slew of terrible relationships (the parade of losers and weirdos in *my* past alone is *staggering*), we'd both learned what we *didn't* want. We each knew a good thing when we saw it. As soon as we started talking that first night, I thought: *Oh, there you are! I've been looking all over for you!* And I've never stopped feeling that way.

I won't say we have a perfect marriage, because what does that even mean? I will say we're perfect for each other, that our individual sets of neuroses are wonderfully compatible. I'm married to the best friend I've ever had. Sure, we argue over the little things—what we're going to have for dinner or who has the more annoying family, if *one* (or both) of us has control issues, or if *one* of us is compulsively organized (he is), and the other is not (I *am* organized . . . in my own way)—but the really big stuff has never been an issue. We skirmish, but have never fought in that awful way that damages your marriage and your spirit.

When it came to children, we both felt that we wanted a family but that if kids didn't come, we'd have a wonderful life regardless. There would be no fertility acrobatics. We'd consider adoption, if there came a time when we were desperate for children and couldn't have them in the traditional way. And when it was time to stop "not trying," we were both equally ready—meaning *sort of* ready. Frankly, at thirty-five (me) and thirty-seven (him), we were starting to feel as if the time was now or that the time would pass. It only took a few months for us to conceive.

We were so thrilled, so unexpectedly excited, that we told everyone right away—family, friends, acquaintances, people in the grocery store. Wait three months? We couldn't even keep the news to ourselves for three hours. Our friends and family were happy for us—and a little surprised, I think, too. Our ambivalence toward parenthood was well known. In the five years since our marriage, we'd been asked about our plans for children. We'd always said, "Not yet. We're having too much fun." And I guess in some ways, we'd thought of parenthood as the end of fun. I was famous for saying things like "Once you've decided to have children, you've basically decided not to do anything else."

Maybe this reputation for ambivalence made us easy targets. Or maybe our newfound enthusiasm for parenthood made us seem green, and the veterans were just trying to toughen us up before we headed into the fray. But for whatever reason, the fact that I was planning to have a natural childbirth and to breast-feed seemed to encourage people to bring out the big guns of discouragement. Everyone, it seemed, lined up to talk about their delivery-room nightmares and lactation traumas.

"Oh, you can forget about that right now," said one cousin, refer-ring to natural childbirth. "There's *no* way to do it without drugs. You're crazy. And, by the way, if you wait too long and then change your mind, you *can't* get any drugs. You don't want to be there." Was that true? I didn't know.

"I couldn't breast-feed," said another friend. "I have inverted nipples. When I tried to pump one night, I pumped an ounce of pure blood." I looked at her in dismay; she just smiled gravely and nodded.

But I was determined, if not all that confident. And Jeffrey was totally onboard with these decisions. So we signed up for twelve weeks of natural childbirth classes, where we learned everything we needed to know about labor, delivery, and breast-feeding in unflinching detail—complete with unedited videos of women in the throes of natural childbirth. Even here, the messages weren't exactly encouraging.

In the darkened living room of our instructor, surrounded by fif-teen other couples in various stages of pregnancy, we watched as an especially vocal woman in one video screamed in agony during her labor, "Get it out of me! GET. IT. OUT!" I glanced at Jeff, who patted my leg and offered me a brave smile. I looked around at the other couples and saw their stricken faces; one woman covered her eyes.

Jeffrey offered empathetic shoulder rubs and comforting words. More than once he said, with a nervous laugh, "It's a good thing men don't have to do this. There'd *never* be any babies." Indeed.

Then, of course, there were the books. In them, I learned that I would soon come to hate Jeffrey, that he would reveal himself as a buffoon about as capable of helping me raise a child as he was of bearing one. There would be no sex, of course (either because I secretly resented my husband and what he had done to me, or because he was secretly repulsed by my postpartum body—or that he was traumatized by what he witnessed in the delivery room). And there would be no sleep—ever. That the combination of those things would turn us into a pair of Japanese fighting fish dropped into the same bowl. Maybe no one would get out alive. "Get ready to know rage in a way you've never experienced before," said one particularly awful book, given to me (unwittingly, I think) by my mother.

As my pregnancy progressed, I was assailed by the idea that independent, intelligent women who had delayed children to pursue a career are set up for failure when motherhood comes. That they *hate* it. That it's a slow, unhappy trek toward a total loss of self. In fact, I can't recall even once hearing an intellectual female voice that said: "I love being a mom. I love my husband. My husband is a wonderful father and partner in parenthood." The message was clear: I was entering into a modern-day slavery and my happy marriage was about to reveal itself as a pseudoegalitarian sham.

Even my grandmother chimed in (PS—she's not one of the stoic, uncomplaining women of earlier generations previously mentioned). I told her with enthusiasm how wonderful Jeffrey is around the house and how much he planned to work at home, our strategies for making sure I had time to work. "He's going to be such a great dad," I gushed. "He'll help a lot." She snorted, "You think so, huh?"

All these conversations and experiences began to feel like a conspiracy to rob us of our joy. I came to dread talking about my pregnancy and our impending parenthood. I found myself bracing for dire premonitions, whispered tales of misery, graphic confessions I'd rather have been spared.

I started to wonder: Has it actually become chic to be miserable in parenthood? If earlier generations are guilty of whitewashing the truths about parenthood, of staying silent about the toll it can take on a relationship, is mine guilty of painting too grim a picture? Women seem so quick to cast ourselves as harried, shrewish malcontents, beleaguered by motherhood. (Can't you see us—unshowered, clothes covered with spit up, hair wild and uncombed? Our laptops gather dust. Our Victoria's Secret catalogs are in tatters, possibly lining the litter box.) And we readily typecast our husbands as slouches, zoning out on the couch while the baby screams and we disappear behind a mountain of laundry. Maybe it's just a postmodern way of saying, "Hey, this is hard! What we're doing is important and it's a struggle and we should be lauded for our sacrifices!"

Suddenly I was looking at Jeffrey, wondering how fatherhood would change him, if he would still be my lover and best friend. I wondered if we'd still have dates, if he'd still be my "boyfriend." Moreover, I started looking in the mirror and wondering how motherhood was going to change *me*, if it would turn me into a resentful basket case, so overwhelmed by my new role that I would no longer be the wife I was before. Who would we be when our daughter arrived? How would we fare during labor and in the stressful weeks and months that followed? Could a profound experience change us both so deeply that we would no longer be compatible as a couple? I guess the truth was that we just didn't know. But a current of fear began to run beneath our excitement.

So we did what any intellectual, overachieving couple would do. Jeffrey, a computer engineer with a logical mind that had the speed and accuracy of a Pentium processor, engineered "the problem." I, a fiction writer with a wild imagination, got creative. Together we prepared for everything. There was no video we didn't watch, no book we didn't read. We developed a strategy for colic. We gathered names of lactation consultants in case there were problems with breast-feeding. By twenty weeks, the nursery was done; by twenty-five weeks we had a pediatrician who was in-line with our thinking about vaccines; by thirty weeks the car seats were installed. We spent our evenings doing pregnancy exercises and relaxation techniques for labor. I obsessed about nutrition and exercised vigorously until my third trimester, then switched to yoga. We got *seriously* into it.

Of course, what we were doing was trying to manage our anxiety. There was no real way to prepare for how we might change as people, as a couple. That was uncharted territory. But we could prepare for everything else. We could be as strong, as healthy, as organized as possible, thereby giving ourselves a better foundation from which to handle the inevitable stresses of childbirth and the famously grueling challenges of new parenthood. We were developing counterstrategies for all the difficulties we were told awaited us. The dreaded phrase "Get ready for your whole life to change" sounded to us, a happy couple with a really fantastic life, like "Get ready for your whole life to suck." But we turned it into our call to arms. We weren't going down like the rest of them; we were going to fight.

Meanwhile, in spite of all of this preparation and solution engineering, we just couldn't get our heads around the idea that there was a real baby *in there.* Our daughter was an abstract concept in spite of the sonograms and the kung-fu kicks to my ribs. It was impossible for us to imagine that a little person, someone of us but separate from us, would be living in our house for a really long time. I knew she was coming. I knew I would love her. I couldn't imagine what she would look like, who she would be. It just didn't seem real.

When my water broke on Christmas Day, three weeks early, I still wasn't getting it. I had been racing our little girl to complete my next novel. I *thought* we had an arrangement: She would stay put until her due date so that I could finish. And that's what I was thinking about when I awoke at 5 A.M. to an audible "pop!" from my abdomen. I lay there for a minute saying to myself, "That *can't* be good." Still in denial, I ran to the bathroom. A flood of pink liquid soaked through my pajamas.

"Ohmigod. I think my water broke," I said in an absurd statement of the obvious.

"What?" said Jeffrey, with terror in his voice. "Are you sure?"

When I called my mother to tell her we were heading to the hospital, I said, "Mom, I didn't finish my book." She said, "Well, don't worry about that now!"

But I was worried—about that and everything else. Actually, in retrospect, terrified might be closer to the truth in some moments. Not about labor and delivery, so much. That, to me, seemed like the least of it. I was terrified that I wouldn't be the person I was, the wife I was, the writer I was before motherhood. I feared for my relationship with my husband and for the life we shared together. I had a lot to lose, and didn't have any real sense of what we were about to gain. And all our overly intellectual planning hadn't prepared me for the tidal wave of emotion I felt on the ride to the hospital on that stormy Christmas morning.

We arrived calmly, despite our fear. After all, the bags had been packed for weeks, complete with sound dock for our iPod to play relaxing music during labor. I looked at Jeff. He seemed truly Zen. What I didn't realize at the time was that he had a miserable jackhammer of a hangover. We'd had a party on Christmas Eve, and he had some drinks for the first time during my pregnancy. (To his credit, he never mentioned his hangover until much later: "What was I going to say?" he told me later. "Sorry you're in labor, honey, but *I* feel like *crap*. Can we do this tomorrow?") I wondered if I'd hate him soon. If I'd be mean to him in the delivery room. I wondered what our baby would look like. I wondered who we'd be when the *three* of us got home.

"Our baby's coming," said Jeff, with a wide smile and wider eyes. I know he'd been told to say this by our birthing instructor to allay my fears, to remind me that all the pain to come would result in the birth of our child. Unfortunately, this statement did no such thing. Joy, anxiety, excitement, dread—it was all there on his face. I still couldn't imagine her. I was alternately thrilled and frightened by the idea of our daughter. In abstraction, she was worshipped and feared like a volatile god.

And when she arrived, this five pound, ten ounce titan, we were truly awed by her raw power. I had wanted a natural childbirth so badly, not because I had some lofty idea about it (and PS, an hour or so into active labor, drugs started to look *pretty* good). It was because I didn't want my mind to be separated from my body when our daughter arrived. I wanted to feel her pass *through* me. I wanted to be present for her arrival, not floating on a narcotic cloud. And I *was* present, more so than I have been for any other moment in my life. I'm so grateful. The pain of labor and delivery and her arrival were defining experiences. I'm not sure I'd be who I am now without the clarity of those moments, without having been introduced to my own power and strength, and to the strength of my husband, who was with me every second. He was exactly who I needed him to be—strong, funny, respectful, comforting, and encouraging. Amazing.

I remember every second. She blew our minds. There's a picture Jeffrey managed to snap as the midwife handed our baby to me, which captures an expression of pure awe on my face. All I could think as I reached for her was "*She's here. She's mine.*" I was overcome by a mighty rush of love. We were prepared for everything except that. In spite of all our busy planning and scheming, we'd never imagined the brute force of our opponent. In the end, our defenses were shattered by a blue-eyed strawberry blond cherub we'd named Ocean Rae.

No one warned us about the laser beam we'd get zapped with when our baby arrived. Or maybe we just couldn't hear it through the humming machinery of our anxiety. After Ocean's birth, I suddenly remembered other voices that hadn't resonated as deeply during my pregnancy. An author I know told me, "There's going to be a whole new level of love in your life." At the time, I acknowledged that he was probably right. Intellectually, I knew I would love my daughter; that was never a question. I just never realized that this love would color everything else, that the word itself would be redefined.

The weeks that followed were grueling and wonderful in equal measure. The fact is, we didn't sleep. Of course not. But we were so enamored of our daughter that we found we just didn't care about sleep that much. There was no sex for weeks. Of course there wasn't. Okay, that was bad—but I'd never felt closer to my husband, never felt more deeply bonded to anyone. There were awful times where we were snappish and impatient with each other. Beyond stressed, exhausted, overwhelmed—just maxed out. But for each of those dark moments, there were a hundred more where we were overcome by pure bliss. There was a baby, our daughter! This tiny, everyday miracle; each movement she made, each sigh she issued, mesmerized us. Every time I looked at her, my heart felt bigger. Why didn't anyone tell us about that?

A lot of the things we'd feared and planned for just never hap-pened. Breast-feeding was easy for Ocean and for me. She wasn't colicky. She was, in fact, mostly peaceful from the day she arrived. Maybe we'd feel differently about parenthood if we'd had those challenges. And maybe all the obsessive planning, research, and organizing we did to combat our fears actually helped us to enjoy coming home from the hospital more than we would have. Maybe having enough diapers for weeks, having meals frozen and waiting to be heated, having the nursery done and the phone off allowed us to focus on the bliss rather than the tiring logistics of day-to-day living. Maybe all those people with their horror stories and bad advice were just . . . disorganized? Or maybe we just got lucky. Regardless of the reasons, we were so awed by what we had gained that it never occurred to us to focus on what we had lost.

But of course, in their way, the veterans were right. It was immediately obvious, even through the fog of our fatigue, that nothing would ever be as it was. When Ocean Rae entered our world, she changed it not in the superficial ways we feared—or not just in those ways. She changed us from the inside out. We found that we wanted different things—from ourselves, from life, and from each other. Suddenly, I didn't want a date for dinner and a movie; I needed someone to bring me a glass of water, to sit with me at Ocean's 3 A.M. feeding and assure me that everything in this strange new world of ours was all right. This was the new romance. We wanted to celebrate New Year's Eve not in a throng of people somewhere, but by curling up on the couch and falling asleep in the glow of the Christmas tree lights. This was the new nightlife. Late evenings out were replaced with friends and family stopping by with food and tiny clothes, tiptoeing excitedly into the nursery to see our sleeping baby. This was our new social life. And it was all okay . . . even perfect.

We'd heard the horror stories of those first sleepless weeks filled with endless crying and the chaos of meddling family members. But I remember those bleary days as so quiet—lights dim, phone off, both of us totally focused on Ocean and each other, our new family. I cried constantly, was buffeted by swift and changing tides of emotion. But it wasn't depression or baby blues; I wasn't sad. I just felt plugged in to an awareness of life—the miracle of a child, the cataclysmic changes in myself, my husband, and our marriage—and how unspeakably awesome and beautiful it all seemed. In this mingling of intense pain, profound happiness, abject terror, and the deepest contentment I'd ever known, I was in a place I'd never been. And Jeffrey was right there with me.

He worked from home for almost eight weeks while I recovered and we all adjusted—he did the laundry, he made our meals, he took care of me so that I could breast-feed our baby and recover from childbirth. He hadn't morphed into a couch potato or a helpless buffoon. On the other hand, he definitely wasn't my boyfriend anymore. He was my loving husband, the doting father of our child, and my partner in every sense of the word.

And in spite of the huge shifts within me and without, motherhood has not changed me so much that I am unrecognizable from the person I was before. I am now different, but not less. I discovered a fuller, more enriched version of myself. In labor, I was introduced to a woman who was stronger and more determined than the girl I knew. In motherhood, I found more patience, more compassion, more intuitive power than I knew I had. In marriage, my love for Jeffrey is even deeper than it was; we are fiercely connected by parenthood and our shared devotion for the tiny life our love created. I discovered I am still a writer, still a wife who madly loves and ardently desires her husband. But now I'm a mother, too. I'm not saying it isn't a challenge to be all those things. Actually, some days, it's pure madness. But it's a blessing to have a life so full . . . isn't it?

So, at the moment, we can't spontaneously stroll out for a drink . . . but, hey, maybe we were drinking too much anyway.

Between my work and the baby, I'm so exhausted at the end of the day that I haven't seen the end of a DVD in months . . . but most of them have been really awful anyway. I did, however, manage to conduct a ten-city book tour (husband, breast-feeding baby, and occasionally my mother in tow). And in the weeks after Ocean was born, I finished my novel with this little bundle snoozing beside me in her bed. As different as things are, I find that the important things are the same. Parenthood, like any intense experience, is a crucible. It changes you, certainly, but it also shows you what you were made from in the first place.

In addition to entering parenthood from a good place, I think there's something else that contributes to our contentment in our new life. Instead of trying to claw our way back to a "couplehood" that no longer existed, we totally surrendered to our new existence. We adapted. Perhaps this and this alone is the key to survival—not to mention happiness—in marriage and in life: to embrace the change inevitably wrought by dramatic events, to recognize that looking back is not only pointless but destructive. What doesn't bend breaks.

Right now, Ocean Rae *is* our life. We still take trips, still head out for the day on the boat. Except now there's a whole lot more to carry—lots of gear for our little pal, travel systems, life jackets, diaper bags, Pack 'n Play, toys, teethers, sippy cups. We do have some baby-sitters now and have ventured out on our own a couple of times for dinner or parties; and it's wonderful to have a date with my husband. But we're always ready to go home to our baby.

So who are we now? Am I the blissed-out mom gazing lovingly down at the angel in my arms? Are Jeffrey and I more in love than ever? Do we still have sex? Am I more at home in motherhood than I ever imagined possible? Or . . . am I a harried, exhausted stress case struggling to find my way as a mother, a writer, and a wife? Are

not what we were expecting

Jeffrey and I squabbling in the fatigue and stress of fresh parenthood? The answer to all of these questions is, of course: yes. Because parenthood is a kaleidoscope; the picture shifts with each turn of your wrist, with each change of light. What you see depends on how long you linger on any given moment.

the dropped ball

· Susan Cheever ·

For years before giving birth to my son, I daydreamed about the blessed event. Finally fulfilled, the mother of a perfect girl and an adorable baby boy, I would be serene and seraphic. I would breast-feed our son while my husband looked on adoringly, admiring the way my body, which had given him so much pleasure, was now nur-turing and providing for his beloved son. A shelf of my books would shimmer in the soft light of the background. A friend had once told me that each time she had a child, her husband bought her an important piece of jewelry. I thought pearls would be nice.

Reality was not at all like the world of my rosy dreams once my son came along. After a while I began to notice that, at feeding time, my husband was never around. He avoided the bedroom. If he happened to come in, instead of watching admiringly as I nursed his heir and namesake, he left precipitously. He didn't seem to know about the jewelry thing. Instead he came home one day with a black lace teddy. As I took it out of the layers of pink tissue paper, I tried to be polite, but my heart sank. It was my old size—way too small now—and it looked skimpy and strange, like an artifact from another life. My husband and I made love sometimes in the bed next to the bassinet when the baby slept, but I was distracted. My body was very busy already. Slowly, with a great deal of disappointment, I realized that my husband did not want to be the admiring father watching me nurse in my daydream threesome.

Still, I kept urging him to join us at nursing time. I didn't understand his reluctance until one day when his feelings overwhelmed him. "Those are my breasts," he yelled at me. "They're for sex! Not for feeding!"

The room went silent except for the contented sounds of the feeding baby. I couldn't tell my husband what I was thinking. I was thinking that actually, they were *my* breasts. It was true, the thing that all husbands fear had actually happened. I was in love with someone else, and my husband seemed to have guessed my secret. I was in love with my son, who seemed to have a lovely connection to my body, and who never said hurtful things or bought the wrong size. The fact that the "someone else" was our son didn't seem to make it any less a betrayal.

My love for my baby boy had a blinding intensity, as if everything I had called love before was a shadow of the real thing. My flesh seemed to find its true purpose in feeding and cuddling him. The fact that my body, about which I often had mixed feelings, could actually have created this spectacular little creature seemed like a miracle. In the light of this new passion, my love for my husband seemed like old news. The baby was smooth and sweet smelling and filled with promise; my husband suddenly looked old, hairy, and very, very cranky. Because of my husband's jealousy, I weaned my son sooner than I wanted to. We were all unhappy.

A similar thing had happened when my daughter was born a few years earlier. Within four years her father and I had divorced. I regretted that keenly, but I seemed powerless to stop up my own ecstatic feelings toward her and the resulting lack of feelings toward her father and anyone else. And now it was happening again, with a different child and a different man.

As my son grew, the problem grew right along with him. My husband and I had been bicoastal, working apart during the week and spending weekends together in San Francisco and New York. I had loved flying west and driving down the coast to Big Sur or up to Innisfree to be with him. I was a big fan of long-distance marriage. Our weekends were vivid adventures, glistening with the kind of laughing conversation that had made us fall in love in the first place. I thought of what we had as a great love, one of those soul-deep bondings that many people never get to feel. Our love affair had survived years of living apart; who knew that trying to be together with a baby would be much harder?

Now I just wanted to stay home with the baby. I couldn't imagine leaving him, even for a few days. I took him to California with me once, but watching his face crumple in pain as the air pressure changed in the airplane cabin was excruciating. Nor was he a fan of long car trips that ended with barbecued oysters on the rocks above the Pacific. After the baby was weaned, my husband tried to get me to go back to San Francisco with him for short stays. We would have a weekend in Carmel, he said. We would stay in one of those cabins on the beach where we had spent some great weekends in years past. I had zero enthusiasm for this idea; my baby needed me and I needed him. More and more, my husband went to California alone.

I ran into Nora Ephron at a party on Park Avenue around then, and she told me that she thought a man will always leave the woman who bears him a son—the agony of watching someone else get the mothering he always wanted is just too great. She and the father of her sons had split up soon after they were born. I remembered Sylvia Plath's fury at Ted Hughes when she had to be writer, mother, and wife all at the same time. I recalled that Leonard and Virginia Woolf had decided not to have children. I knew that I couldn't be a serious writer, an attentive wife, and a loving mother all at once. I told myself that my husband would have to understand that.

A lot has been written about the difficulty of juggling children and jobs. It has been pointed out again and again that women, expected to perform at work like anyone else, are usually doing two jobs simultaneously—their professional job and their domestic job. Not only is this juggling act difficult in terms of time and attention, but it stretches the heartstrings to the breaking point. Nothing is more painful than leaving a baby or a toddler (enchanting, adorable, exhausting) for the office (demanding, glamorous, exhausting).

In all this examination of the balance between life and work, one thing has been oddly left out—the role of the husband and the marriage as a woman juggles her professional and maternal commitments. The husband is the ball that all too often gets dropped. How do husbands feel as their wives—once fans of sexy lingerie—shop for office clothes that will accommodate nursing and pregnancy? What is their role in the helter-skelter world of the working mother, a world in which sex and sexual desire have been abruptly abandoned because of the physical needs of a baby? Not all, but many husbands are distressed to find that they are no longer center of the wifely universe. It's no wonder that divorce rates spike in the third and fourth years of marriage, in all countries in all cultures.

In taking care of a baby, women often get a heady feeling of mastery, and this can lead them to exclude their husbands even from the children's lives. Power corrupts, and the power of motherhood is no different from other kinds of power. The mother is the expert; the mother is the boss. At last, here is something that a woman is good at and that only she can do. At last she has found the job that she was born for. In wielding power, mothers are often less than generous with their underlings—even when those underlings are the babies' fathers. In the love trance of mother and child, the father is out of place. Mother love is greedy, and it's hard to let anyone else take part in what seems like a once-in-a-lifetime miracle. Even when husbands try to help, they are often treated with contempt by their baby-intoxicated wives.

What makes this situation even worse is that having a child is also often a woman's first experience of complete social acceptance. The woman who married the baby's father was sexy and alluring, qualities that attract husbands, but which make many enemies among women. The mother is almost automatically a saint, and not just because she's lost her lithe body. It's hard not to take the opportunity to play the one role sanctified for women. The cliché wife in American culture is the ball and chain, the distaff side, the little woman; the cliché mistress is the home wrecker; the cliché grandmother is a cranky, overindulgent old lady. But the cliché mother, the mother with a capital *M*, is a young woman suffused with love and tender nurturing. Who wouldn't choose that?

By the time my baby boy was walking, I felt as if I were running all the time: diapers, nursing, formula, mobiles, high chair, Bouncinette, spit up, crying, applesauce. The running, however, was sweetened by the pure sensual pleasure of the way he smelled, moved, and snuggled against me. My husband wasn't always glad to see me anymore. My baby wiggled with joy and broke into a huge gummy grin when he saw me looming, exhausted but happy, above the bars of his crib. With him nursing, or falling asleep as I stroked his soft head, I felt whole. Many days I never got to work at all. Often I started work at three in the afternoon and worked again after the baby was asleep. Sometimes I got to work and collapsed on the floor and slept as only the sleep deprived know how. Mornings were brutal. I used to joke that the most erotic thing a man could say to me then was: "Honey, why don't you just go back to sleep for a while." My husband didn't laugh at this joke. In trying to meet my baby's needs and my professional needs, I didn't think much about my husband's needs. Who had time?

There were a thousand reasons to put my children first, before my marriage. My children needed me more. My love for them was uncomplicated and approved of. When I told people that I was putting my children first, they tended to smile and nod with loving admiration. As my son grew up and I continued to put him first, my marriage to his father began to disintegrate. I had loved my son's father for a long time, but now he just seemed like too much to deal with. For years he had been the true love of my life; now my son and his sister were the true loves of my life. There was a time when I couldn't keep my hands off my husband. Now I couldn't keep my hands off the baby. It got easier to love my son, and harder to love his father. For me, children and sexual passion just don't mix.

Looking back, I think I was blind. How could I have forgotten that the best thing I could do for my son—better than anything—was to stay married to his father? How could I have inflicted a second divorce on my sweet daughter? Looking back, I see that I should have put my son into the crib and slithered into the teddy. It may be an oversimplification to say that if I had gone to California with my husband in the days when our son was young, my husband and I might still be married. But I can tell you this: Every time my ex-husband comes to New York to stay in his own apartment, I get to see my son's life torn in half; every time my ex-husband goes to California, I get to watch my son's heart break. From where I sit now, more than ten years later, the tacky teddy looks pretty good.

about the
contributors

Steve Almond is the author of two story collections, *My Life in Heavy Metal* and *The Evil B.B. Chow*, the nonfiction book *Candyfreak*, and the novel (with Julianna Baggott) *Which Brings Me to You*. His next book will be a collection of essays titled *Not That You Asked*, to be published by Random House in fall 2007. On October 1, 2006, his wife, Erin, gave birth to a daughter, Josephine Colette Almond. They reserve the right to name their second child Peanut.

Susan Cheever is the author of numerous memoirs and novels, some of which include: *As Good As I Could Be: A Memoir of Raising Wonderful Children in Difficult Times*; *Home Before Dark: A Biographical Memoir of John Cheever by His Daughter*; and *A Woman's Life: The Story of an Ordinary American and Her Extraordinary Generation*.

about the contributors

David Elliot Cohen is the cocreator of the *Day in the Life* and *America 24/7* photography book series. He has created four *New York Times* best-sellers, including the number-one best-seller *A Day in the Life of America*. Cohen also wrote the best-selling travelogue *One Year Off*. He lives in Marin County, California, with his wife, their five children, and an enormous white Labrador.

Elisha Cooper is a writer and illustrator of both adult and children's books. His most-recent adult book is *Crawling: A Father's First Year*, and some of his most-recognized children's books include: *Beach, A Good Night Walk, Ice Cream, Dance!,* and *Magic Thinks Big*. He lives in Chicago with his wife and two young daughters.

Andrew Corsello, a writer for *GQ* magazine since 1995, has been nominated three times for the National Magazine Award and anthologized twice in *The Best American Magazine Writing*. He and his wife, Dana, an Episcopal priest, live in Virginia with their sons Quincy (age four) and Casper (age two), both of whom are rock 'n' roll incarnate.

Hope Edelman is the author of four nonfiction books, including the international best-sellers *Motherless Daughters* (1994) and *Motherless Mothers* (2006). Her articles, essays, and reviews have appeared in numerous publications, including the *New York Times,* the *Chicago Tribune,* the *San Francisco Chronicle,* the *Washington Post, Glamour, Child, Seventeen,* and *Self,* and her work has appeared in several anthologies, including *The Bitch in the House: 26 Women Tell the Truth About Sex, Solitude, Work, Motherhood and Marriage*. She is the recipient of a *New York Times* notable book of the year designation and a Pushcart Prize for creative nonfiction, and is an associate faculty member in the MFA program at Antioch University LA. She lives outside Los Angeles with her husband and two daughters.

Dan Elish is the author of the novel *Nine Wives,* as well as several novels and nonfiction books for younger readers. Dan has also written scripts for kids' TV shows (most recently *Cyberchase* on PBS) and funny corporate videos, music and lyrics for musicals, and played piano for various Off Broadway productions. Dan lives in New York City with his wife and two young children.

Michael Finkel is the author of *True Story: Murder, Memoir, Mea Culpa,* about his unusual friendship with a man accused of murder. He lives with his family in western Montana. His magazine articles have been anthologized in *The Best American Sports Writing, The Best American Travel Writing,* and *The Best American Nonrequired Reading.* His wife once referred to him as the Best American Husband, but the next day she took it back.

Ariel Gore is the editor and publisher of the award-winning parenting zine *Hip Mama.* Her books include *The Hip Mama Survival Guide; The Mother Trip; Whatever, Mom; Atlas of the Human Heart;* and *The Traveling Death and Resurrection Show.* Her daughter, Maia, is sixteen.

Molly Jong-Fast is the twenty-eight-year-old author of *Normal Girl* and *Girl [Maladjusted].* Her essays and articles have appeared in the *New York Times, W* magazine, *Cosmopolitan, Mademoiselle, Marie Claire,* the *Times* (London), British *Elle,* and *Forward.* Her mother, Erica Jong, wrote *Fear of Flying,* and her late grandpa, Howard Fast, wrote *Spartacus.*

Pamela Kruger is a writer, editor, and editorial consultant. Her work has appeared in the *New York Times, Good Housekeeping, Fast Company,* Lifetime Television Online, and *Child,* where she is currently a contributing editor. She is the coeditor of and a contributor to the anthology *A Love Like No Other: Stories from Adoptive Parents* (2005). She is also a contributor to the anthology *Searching for Mary Poppins: Women Write About the Intense Relationship Between Mothers and Nannies* (2006). To learn more about Pamela, visit her website at www.pamelakruger.com.

Elizabeth Larsen is a freelance magazine writer and editor. She is a founding editor of *Sassy* magazine and was a senior editor at *Utne Reader.* She has written extensively on cultural and women's issues for publications such as *Ms., Utne Reader,* and *Child.*

Beth Levine is a veteran freelance writer specializing in health, marriage, parenting, and personal essays. Her work has appeared in twenty-nine magazines, some of which include: *Child, Family Circle, Good Housekeeping, Parenting, Parents, Reader's Digest, Redbook,* and *Self.* She is also the author of two books: *Divorce: Young People Caught in the Middle* and *Playgroups: A Complete Guide for Parents.* You can visit Beth at her website, www.bethlevine.net.

Rick Marin is the best-selling author of the highly praised and much-talked-about memoir *Cad: Confessions of a Toxic Bachelor.* He has been a reporter and columnist for the Sunday Styles section of the *New York Times,* a senior writer at *Newsweek,* and a pseudony-mous advice columnist for a major women's magazine. He and his wife, Ilene Rosenzweig, are now collaborating on television come-dies, screenplays, and two sons, Diego and Kingsley.

Susan Maushart (Ph.D.) is a columnist, author, and mother of three, who still finds time to be a control freak. She is the author of *The Mask of Motherhood* and *Wifework,* and her latest book, *What Women Want Next,* is about guilt and happiness. She lives in Freman-tle, Western Australia.

Lisa Earle McLeod is a syndicated columnist, speaker, and author of *Forget Perfect: Love the Life You Already Have and the You You Already Are* and *Finding Grace When You Can't Even Find Clean Underwear.*

Called an "inspirational humorist" by the *New York Times*, she has appeared on *Good Morning America* and has been featured in *Glamour*, *Guideposts*, *Real Simple*, and *Time* magazine.

Muffy Mead-Ferro is the author of *Confessions of a Slacker Mom* and *Confessions of a Slacker Wife*; she has also contributed to the anthology *The Imperfect Mom* and writes a monthly column for the website TodaysMama.com. She has appeared on the *Today* show, *Oprah*, the *CBS Evening News*, and *Fox News*, and she and her books have been covered by the *New York Times*, *USA Today*, *Newsweek*, and the *Atlantic Monthly*, along with NPR's *Talk of the Nation* and PRT's *To the Best of Our Knowledge*.

Jacquelyn Mitchard is the author of the *New York Times* best-selling novel *The Deep End of the Ocean* and seven other novels, including *Still Summer*, to be released summer 2007. Her essays have been widely anthologized, and she is a syndicated columnist for Tribune Media Services and a contributing editor to *Wondertime*. She and her husband live with their seven children near Madison, Wisconsin.

Ann Pleshette Murphy has been *Good Morning America*'s on-air parenting expert since 1998. A highly sought-after speaker, she was for ten years the editor in chief of *Parents* magazine. The author of *The 7 Stages of Motherhood: Loving Your Life Without Losing Your Mind*, she writes a parenting column for *USA Weekend* magazine and serves on the board of Zero to Three, the leading national organization dedicated to the well-being of infants and toddlers. Ms. Pleshette Murphy resides in New York City with her husband and two children.

Kermit Pattison has written for the *New York Times*, *GQ*, and *Inc*. He and his wife, Maja, have three children: Eli, seven; Alistair, four; and

Siri, one. He lives in St. Paul, Minnesota, where he spends his spare time . . . never mind, he doesn't have any.

Neal Pollack is the author of *Alternadad,* a parenting memoir that may or may not be a best-seller by the time you read this. He's also written three books of satirical fiction, including the cult classic *The Neal Pollack Anthology of American Literature* and the rock 'n' roll novel *Never Mind the Pollacks.* You can read an informal account of his life as a dad at his website, www.nealpollack.com. He lives with his wife, Regina, their son, Elijah, and several strange animals in Los Angeles, where he masturbates often.

Ilene Rosenzweig is a writer living in Los Angeles. A former *New York Times* Style editor and author of the *Swell* book series, she now writes for television and film with her husband, Rick Marin.

Sandi Kahn Shelton is the author of two novels, *A Piece of Normal* and *What Comes After Crazy,* as well as three humorous nonfiction parenting books: *Sleeping Through the Night and Other Lies, You Might As Well Laugh . . . Because Crying Will Only Smear Your Mascara,* and *Preschool Confidential.* She was the Wits' End columnist for *Working Mother* for ten years, is a feature reporter for the *New Haven Register,* and her work has appeared in *Woman's Day, Family Circle, Salon, Redbook,* and *Reader's Digest.* You can visit Sandi on her website at www.sandishelton.com.

Amy Sohn is the author of the novels *My Old Man* and *Run Catch Kiss.* She is a contributing editor at *New York* magazine and has also written for *The Nation, Harper's Bazaar, Premiere, Men's Journal,* the *New York Times Book Review,* and *Playboy.* She has written television pilots for HBO, Fox, and ABC, and cocreated the Oxygen television series *Avenue Amy,* which was based on her life. Amy grew up in Brooklyn, where she and her family live today.

about the contributors

Rob Spillman is the editor of the literary magazine *Tin House*. He is a veteran magazine editor, and his essays and reviews have appeared in *Bookforum*, *GQ*, the *New York Times Book Review*, *Rolling Stone*, *Salon*, *Spin*, and *Vogue*, among other magazines, newspapers, and anthologies.

William Squier, an Emmy Award winner, has written for radio, film, television, magazines, and the theater. His television and film work includes projects for Nickelodeon, the Disney Channel, ABC Late Night, and Buena Vista Pictures. Magazine pieces include *Newsweek's* "My Turn" column. His plays and musicals have been performed regionally, in New York City, and overseas. He is also the recipient of a Connecticut Artist Fellowship, a Meet the Composer grant, the Coleman A. Jennings Award, the Jackie White Memorial Award, and the 11th Annual National Children's Festival's new-script award.

Andy Steiner is the author of *Spilled Milk: Breastfeeding Adventures and Advice from Less-Than-Perfect Moms*. She is a former senior editor at *Utne Reader*, and an award-winning writer whose work has appeared in many national publications including *Ms.*, *Mademoiselle*, *Self*, *Glamour*, *Modern Maturity*, and *Bitch: Feminist Response to Pop Culture*.

Leah Stewart is the author of the novels *Body of a Girl* and *The Myth of You and Me*. She is currently the Watkins Endowed Visiting Professor of Creative Writing at Murray State University.

Lisa Unger is the author of the *New York Times* best-selling novel *Beautiful Lies* and the sequel, *Sliver of Truth*. *Beautiful Lies* was chosen for the International Book-of-the-Month Club and is published in nineteen countries around the world. A graduate of The New School for Social Research, she lives in Florida with her husband and daughter. She is at work on her next novel. Visit her website at www.lisaunger.com.

about the contributors

Nancy Wartik has contributed features, reviews, and other stories to a wide range of publications, some of which include: the *New York Times*, *Self*, *Psychology Today*, *Glamour*, and the *Los Angeles Times*. She has been anthologized in essay collections, including *The Bitch in the House* and *Roar Softly and Carry a Great Lipstick*. A former staffer at *Ms.* magazine, she's also taught journalism at a number of New York City colleges. She lives on the Upper West Side of Manhattan with her husband, Dennis Overbye, and four-year-old daughter, Mira.

Adam Wasson is an author, teacher, satirist, and dad. His first two books, *The Self-Destruction Handbook* and *Eats, Poops & Leaves*, have been reviewed and recommended by a variety of publications, including the *New York Times*, *Entertainment Weekly*, *Elle*, *Glamour*, the *Chicago Tribune*, and the *Chicago Sun-Times*. His first two children, Ava (age four) and Dashiell (six months), have been reviewed and recommended by a variety of relatives and kindly houseguests.

Nicholas Weinstock is the author of the nonfiction book *The Secret Love of Sons*, the novel *As Long As She Needs Me*, and most recently, the novel *The Golden Hour*. His writing has been featured on National Public Radio and in the *New York Times Magazine*, *The Nation*, *Vogue*, *Glamour*, *Out*, *Ladies' Home Journal*, *Poets & Writers*, and many other publications. In addition to his writing, he works as vice president of comedy development for 20th Century Fox Television and serves on the executive council of the Authors Guild. He lives in Los Angeles with his wife, the writer Amanda Beesley, and their three children.

Moon Zappa is an author who lives in Los Angeles with her unbelievably patient, loyal, hot musician husband and their mind-blowingly awesome daughter. Unit is Moon's middle name.

acknowledgments

If it weren't for the wonderful writers who gave of themselves, this book would not have come to be. I am humbled by your talent, moved by your words, and grateful for your willingness to share so intimately of yourself. Thank you. I am also especially grateful to my agent, Cathy Fowler, who agreed to represent this project in the very early stages, when it was nothing more than a vision and a promise. And Carrie Thornton, you've been a wonderful champion of this book and it has been a pleasure to work with such a smart and savvy editor. I'm happy that you, too, will soon enjoy being blindsided by a diaper.

On the more personal side, I am grateful for the ongoing support of my family and to my girlfriends for listening, sharing, inspiring, and listening some more. Line, you have been an especially wonderful inspiration. Also, thank you for your gift, Lucy, and thanks to Katie for loving my kids while I work. I cherish our new friendship.

acknowledgments

Last, but certainly not least, thank you Dave. For choosing to take this journey with me . . . for your love, support, and your willingness to, at times, be "blindsided by a book." I could never have done this without you.

And Mom, I wish you were here to see the book, too. I love you.

essay credits

essay credits

essay credits